Evangelism in the Twenty-First Century

The Critical Issues

Thom S. Rainer, editor

Twenty-one contributors
writing in honor of
Lewis A. Drummond

Harold Shaw Publishers
Wheaton, Illinois

Unless otherwise noted, all Scripture quotations are from the King James Version of the Bible.

Chapter 15 is adapted with permission from *Witnessing without Fear* by Dr. Bill Bright, Copyright Here's Life Publishers, 1987.

Chapter 6 was originally published in the *Review and Expositor,* volume 85 (Spring 1988).

Chapter 10 was adapted from *Understanding Biblical Inerrancy* (Fort Worth: Columbia Publications, 1988), and is used here with permission.

ISBN 0-87788-238-X

Library of Congress Cataloging-in-Publication Data
Evangelism in the 21st century : the critical issues / edited by
   Thom S. Rainer.
      p.   cm.
   Bibliography: p.
   Includes index.
   ISBN 0-87788-238-X : $12.95
   1. Evangelistic work. I. Rainer, Thom S. II. Title:
   Evangelism in the twenty first century.
   BV3795.E895   1989
   269'.2—dc20   89-6149
                                              CIP

98 97 96 95 94 93 92 91 90 89

10 9 8 7 6 5 4 3 2 1

Essays in Honor of Lewis A. Drummond

CONTENTS

FOREWORD

Lewis A. Drummond has touched many lives through his personal witness, his preaching, and his writings. Perhaps, however, his influence has been greatest in his teaching ministry. Literally thousands of men and women have sat in Dr. Drummond's classes at the Southern Baptist Theological Seminary in Louisville, Kentucky. There they have not only learned the academic aspects of evangelism, but they have left with a heartfelt desire to share the good news of our Savior with others. These men and women are now serving in churches, mission fields, denominational agencies, institutions, and evangelistic teams, to name but a few of the ministries in which they are involved. Their influence has spread to thousands of people and, humanly speaking, the chain of influence began with one man devoted to God.

A book that honors Lewis Drummond is both appropriate and exciting. It is appropriate because Dr. Drummond should be recognized for his untiring efforts for our Lord. It is exciting because the issues discussed are at the forefront of evangelism.

Thom Rainer, a Ph.D. graduate of Dr. Drummond, has brought together some of Dr. Drummond's students and peers in the field of evangelism to discuss some of the critical issues in evangelism today. You will recognize many of the names of persons contributing to the book. Some of the writers are well known as denominational leaders, influential teachers, organizational leaders, and prolific authors. Other names will not be easily recognized. These contributors include past and present students of Dr. Drummond, individuals who are just beginning to make an impact in the exciting field of evangelism.

I commend this book to you because of its virtues, its timeliness, and its subject matter. But, above all, I commend the book with prayer that it will draw men and women closer to our Lord Jesus Christ, and bring glory to our God.

Billy Graham
Montreat, North Carolina

ACKNOWLEDGMENTS

This book is a labor of love for many people. Each of the twenty-two contributors, including Dr. Billy Graham, invested more than a chapter or foreword to a book. They demonstrated their love and respect for Lewis A. Drummond by their contributions. I am very grateful to each of them for their patience with me as we worked together through deadlines and changes.

Five wonderful women gave their time in typing the volumes of correspondence and changes that accompany a book such as this. To Verna Cash, Rosemary Hardin, Margie Hoover, and Linda Ross of Louisville, and Bobbi St. Michel of St. Petersburg, thank you for putting up with my constant demands.

I have learned, sometimes rather stubbornly, that everything I do must be bathed in prayer. I am firmly convinced that this book would not be a reality without the prayer support of my "prayer warriors." Thank you, Ruth Emfinger, John Emfinger, Jess Keller, Arthur Clyde King, Nell King, and my mother, Nan Rainer, for loving me enough to pray for me in all that I do.

It has been a joy to work with Harold Shaw Publishers. The Christian spirit of the organization has always permeated everything they do. I have been honored to work with Stephen Board, a man of great ability and warm spirit.

My love for evangelism has been enhanced by the three greatest churches a pastor could possibly ever lead. Hopewell Baptist Church in Madison, Indiana, and Hopewell Baptist Church in Jeffersontown, Kentucky, have made an indelible mark on my life that is reflected in this project. My present pastorate, Azalea Baptist Church of St. Petersburg, Florida, is a church experiencing real revival. The love and support of the beautiful people of Azalea played a vital role in bringing this book to fruition.

Finally, and most importantly, I must praise God for my family. What a joy it has been to hear my three young sons pray for "Daddy's book." Thank you, Sam, Art, and Jess. You are such precious gifts from God. You make an imperfect father feel so loved. And Jo, my wife, partner, and joy, deserves so much more recognition than this space could reflect. Her time, accurate proofreading, prayers, encouragement, patience, and love have been my earthly inspiration for this book and for my ministry. Thank you, Jo. In you I have learned the deepest meaning of love.

INTRODUCTION

Dr. Lewis A. Drummond, in whose honor this book has been written, always urged his students at the Southern Baptist Theological Seminary to be prepared to meet the future with the most diligent spiritual and academic preparation. Now the President of Southeastern Baptist Theological Seminary, Dr. Drummond brings to this school the same enthusiastic leadership: "Be the best you can be both spiritually and academically."

This book is written in that same spirit. Each of the contributors addresses the question: "How can Christians meet the evangelistic challenges as we move into the twenty-first century?" Some of the writers prepare us with basic information to aid the evangelistic task. Others discuss specific concerns of evangelism that are unique to our day. But each writer makes a contribution that demonstrates a heart for leading people to a saving knowledge of our Lord and Savior Jesus Christ.

Will the evangelistic task for the twenty-first century be significantly different from that of the first two thousand years of Christianity? The answer is both "yes" and "no." Some constants in evangelism are evident. People are still lost and condemned if they do not embrace in faith Jesus Christ (John 3:18). The message of the gospel never changes: Jesus Christ is, and always will be, the only way, truth, and life (John 14:6). And the Savior to whom we give our lives remains the same yesterday and today and forever (Heb. 13:8).

Yet while the need for Jesus, the message of the gospel, and the person of Christ never change, the means and methodology of communicating the gospel must change to meet the needs of every generation. And every new era will have unique problems and opportunities that must be addressed by the same generation of Christians.

This book reflects that need to be ever knowledgeable of the constants of the Christian faith necessary to communicate the gospel, but to be ever aware of the unique opportunities for evangelism in each generation. After a tribute to Dr. Drummond and a chapter dealing with the historical background of evangelism, this book immediately addresses some of the unique aspects of evangelism as we head toward the twenty-first century.

The next section of the book provides basic theological information foundational to the evangelistic task, followed by three chapters which address the issue of what it truly means to be a follower of Christ. Part five of the book looks at four different ways we are attempting to reach people with the gospel today. The final section provides three chapters dealing with evangelism in the local church.

As you read the pages of this book, you will meet many different persons from diverse backgrounds, each with a unique concern for evangelism. But you will also meet a group of people whose passion for evangelism and love for Christ bring them together in a very special bond. It is my prayer that you will not only learn about evangelism from each of these men, but that you will be encouraged to do evangelism by their writings. Perhaps more than at any point in history, the opportunities for evangelism are greatest today. May the material in this book give you greater knowledge, greater skills, and a greater desire to become a fisher of men and women in this generation and into the twenty-first century.

Thom S. Rainer
St. Petersburg, Florida
1989

PART ONE:
An Overview

In this section Thom S. Rainer presents a tribute to Lewis A. Drummond, now President of Southeastern Baptist Theological Seminary in Wake Forest, North Carolina. Dr. Drummond's ministerial, academic, administrative, and personal ministry are all shown to be filled with a zeal for evangelism. Timothy George, a former colleague of Drummond, provides historical insight into evangelism from the New Testament period forward.

1

A TRIBUTE TO LEWIS A. DRUMMOND
Thom S. Rainer

Thom S. Rainer is the pastor of Azalea Baptist Church in St. Petersburg, Florida. Dr. Rainer studied under Lewis Drummond for six years, earning two degrees, the most recent of which was a Ph.D. in evangelism. He has contributed to theological journals and denominational publications as well as serving as editor of this book.

My story is not unique. Among the students, peers, friends, and untold thousands of lives touched by Lewis Drummond, an avalanche of testimonies could be printed. But I have been given the honor of writing this tribute, so I will tell my story.

The task of writing this chapter has proved to be one of the most humbling experiences of my life. As I have prepared the notes for the final draft, I realized that I would be writing about one giant of a man. His accomplishments for the Lord have been equaled by few. But even more than his impressive resume, his heart for evangelism and for our Lord has been my earthly example for following the Savior.

I make no apologies for the sentimentality of this tribute. This book contains sufficient scholarship elsewhere to please the most critical of eyes. When I speak of my mentor and friend, however, the emotions that stir within are deep and joyous. I will make no attempt to conceal the love that I and thousands of others have for Lewis Drummond.

The Introduction

My acquaintance with "Dr. D.," his name to many students, has been over a relatively short period. I was a second year Master of Divinity student at Southern Baptist Theological Seminary in Louisville, Kentucky, in 1984. I had just begun the grieving process over the loss of my father, my role model and best friend. In addition, my relationship with the Lord seemed dry and distant. The excitement and joy of the Christian life had waned considerably. The Bible had become more of a textbook than a guidebook from God.

Though my call to the ministry was certain, I began to have thoughts about leaving. How could I lead others spiritually when I felt so empty myself? The compelling call of God, however, moved me to stay in seminary for the next semester, the two summer "mini-terms."

The course for which I registered was Personal Evangelism, taught by Dr. Drummond. I was not particularly attracted to the course or to its professor. It simply satisfied a group of electives required for graduation.

I will never forget the first day of class. The students who had taken other classes under Dr. Drummond were chattering in excited anticipation about this course. How could this be? Was not this class just another step toward graduation day?

Dr. Drummond walked into class with the announcement: "Brothers and sisters, before you leave this class, you will not only learn personal evangelism, you will do personal evangelism."

I was dumbfounded. The professor not only required the reading of textbooks, taking notes during lectures, and passing the exams, he expected us to prepare a written report weekly about a personal witnessing experience that had transpired during the previous week!

I stayed with the class, however, and a transformation took place in my life. The more I shared my faith, the more my own faith grew. I have no idea how many people I have led to Christ since that time, but, earthly speaking, Lewis Drummond is responsible for bringing the fires of evangelism back into my life.

Dr. D. is not only a man of evangelism, he is a man of prayer. Many wearied and troubled seminary students sat in his classes that were literally filled with prayer. Their lives too have been renewed by the power of prayer—in a classroom setting!

I remember one particular class that ultimately was devoted entirely to prayer. After hearing a number of prayer requests, one student was asked to begin praying. In the midst of his prayer, the Holy Spirit came in awesome power, and many of us began weeping in both repentance and joy. Real revival for many students began that moment. Several students began prayer groups at different locations around the campus. Dr. D. continued to exhort us toward more fervent prayer for revival on our campus, in our denomination, and in our nation.

A Brief Biography

Lewis A. Drummond was born in 1926 in Dixon, Illinois, the birthplace of former President Ronald Reagan. Prior to his induction into the Air Force, he enrolled in a Lutheran college to take a few courses. Through the witness of college students on campus, Lewis Drummond met the Lord he would so faithfully serve in the years ahead.

After his time of service in the Air Force, he would begin a journey of education for ministry that would earn him four degrees in three schools. His final degree, the Ph.D. in Philosophy, was earned at King's College at the University of London. This time in England would be one of many encounters Dr. Drummond would have with his "second home."

Lewis Drummond would be the pastor of five churches over a twenty-year period before accepting his first teaching position. In 1968 he accepted the Chair of Evangelism and Practical Theology at Spurgeon's Theological College in London. This position was the first full professorship of evangelism in Europe. After five exciting years in England, he returned to the United States to become Billy Graham Professor of Evangelism at the Southern Baptist Theological Seminary in Louisville, Kentucky.

For fifteen years Dr. Drummond led hundreds and hundreds of students to a greater respect for God's Word, and a new level of excitement for sharing the good news.

The courses in evangelism were numerous: Introduction to Evangelism, Building an Evangelistic Church, Evangelism and Spiritual Formation, Personal Evangelism, Evangelistic Preaching, Theology of Evangelism (Dr. D.'s personal favorite), and Principles of Spiritual Awakenings. Though the contents of the courses were different, Dr. Drummond focused on three primary themes in all of his classes: the primacy of prayer, the authority of Scripture, and the mandate to evangelize.

Lewis Drummond became the first professor ever to supervise Doctor of Philosophy students in the field of evangelism. Southern Seminary, under Dr. Drummond's leadership, was the first school in the world to offer the Ph.D. in evangelism. Only one other school, Southwestern Baptist Theological Seminary, offers this advanced degree today. Of the handful of men holding a Ph.D. in evangelism today, the majority studied under Dr. Drummond.

Lewis Drummond has preached in virtually every area of the world. He has lectured in seminaries and colleges around the United States and in eight countries. He has held countless administrative positions of honor, including the Administrative Directorship of the Billy Graham Center in Louisville and the Presidency of the Academy for Evangelism in Theological Education. He has written extensively for theological journals, Christian periodicals, denominational newspapers, and other evangelistic literature. In 1989 his fourteenth book was published, an average of almost one book per year since his first book was written in 1972.

In 1988 Dr. Drummond's ministry took a new direction when he was elected as the President of Southeastern Baptist Theological Seminary in Wake Forest, North Carolina. Most of the Christian world knows that the Southern Baptist Convention is in the midst of an internal struggle that has persisted for over a decade. When the Southeastern position became vacant, all eyes were on the school to see who would become the first seminary president chosen since the more conservative element in the denomination took control of its powerful appointive process. I observed Lewis Drummond when it became apparent that he would be the choice of the school's trustees. I prayed with him as he sought God's guidance and strength in confronting this opportunity. I witnessed his resolve when he realized that such a move was indeed God's will.

In many ways, the denominational spotlight is on Dr. Drummond. He has accepted a pressure-packed position that will remain so in the near future. But I know the source of Dr. D.'s strength, and I know his conciliatory heart. In time God will bring forth showers of blessing on Southeastern.

The Personal Life of Lewis Drummond

Lewis Drummond is blessed to be a part of a large, loving family. He and his wife, Betty, form the nucleus of the family. Though they have no children of their own, they truly have a large family of friends and students whose friendships and love can be found in most all points of the world. Hardly a day goes by that the Drummonds have not heard from some good friend in another part of the globe. Betty Drummond, the ever-faithful partner and wife, has always been the gracious hostess for the countless individuals who have visited or stayed in their home.

Dr. Drummond's outside interests include two noteworthy hobbies. One favorite activity is flying. He holds both commercial and instructor pilot's licenses. With a friend or flying solo, he is often found skyward when the demands of the day dictate a need to get away from the office.

While the task of preaching the gospel certainly should be classified as more than an "outside interest," it is undoubtedly one of the greatest joys of Dr. Drummond outside the academic environment. He still feels that same excitement and joy of witnessing people accept Jesus Christ as their Lord and Savior as he did when he began preaching over thirty years ago. It is thus not unusual to hear of Lewis Drummond leading a revival today in some small town in Alabama or in a major crusade in Europe. Preaching the gospel and witnessing to the lost will always be his first love.

I have alluded earlier to the prayer life of Dr. D. His is a life saturated with that child-like dependency upon God. I remember one morning, when I was serving as his Garrett Fellow (graduate assistant), I walked into Dr. D.'s office without knocking. I immediately realized that I had intruded on a very precious moment: a child of God in prayer with his Heavenly Father. That scene had a profound effect on my own prayer life. Lewis A. Drummond—seminary professor, world-known preacher of the gospel, author of many books, and denominational leader—took time to pray. Though a giant in the eyes of many men and women, he was but a dependent child to the Lord he serves so faithfully.

Such is the portrait I wish to paint of my mentor and friend. Of all the accolades he so richly deserves, one that is certainly appropriate is "man of prayer." On another occasion, in my Master of Divinity studies, I was attempting to take notes to the rapid lecture Dr. D. was giving in a class on spiritual awakenings. In the midst of the lecture, the professor paused. It was an awkward silence compared to the rapid-fire verbiage moments earlier. He stepped away from the podium and notes and took a deep breath. We in the class wondered why the sudden change had taken place.

"Men and women," he said softly, "it is important that you learn these facts, dates, and events I am attempting to communicate to you." He paused for another brief moment. "But," he said, "I hope you realize that, in your seminary experience and beyond, there is but one criterion of life by which you should measure yourselves. Ask our Lord and yourselves, 'Have I been obedient this day to the Lord Jesus Christ to whom I have pledged my life?' " Another pause. "That is the bottom line—obedience . . . and nothing else really matters." The bell rang, and we dismissed quietly.

Such is the man to whom this book is dedicated. Describe him in various ways: administrator, president, teacher, preacher, writer, husband, or friend. But the most telling description of Lewis Drummond, I believe, was revealed in that small class on spiritual awakenings: obedient child of God. And the ultimate reward for him will come on that grand and glorious day when he meets his Lord face to face.

The hearts of literally thousands of people around the globe acclaim in one voice our love for you, Dr. Drummond, in this tribute. And thank you, my friend and mentor, for all that you mean to me. I love you, Dr. D. . . . I really do love you.

2

THE CHALLENGE OF
EVANGELISM IN THE HISTORY
OF THE CHURCH
Timothy George

Timothy George is the founding dean of the Beeson Divinity School at Samford University in Birmingham, Alabama. Dr. George, who holds the Th.D. from Harvard University, served with Dr. Drummond for several years at the Southern Baptist Theological Seminary as Associate Professor of Church History and Historical Theology. He has written numerous books, articles, and reviews.

Evangelism is the work of the Holy Spirit in bringing lost men and women to faith in Jesus Christ in accordance with the will of God the Father. The technical New Testament term for this process is *klesis*, "calling" (2 Pet. 1:10), and it is clear that it is God himself who calls us out of darkness into his wonderful light. At the same time, it is equally clear that it has pleased God to use human instruments to announce his great good news, on his behalf and for his sake, to all persons everywhere who have yet to come into this light. Jesus commissioned the church to proclaim the gospel to all segments of human society and to disciple believers from among *panta ta ethne*, "all peoples" (Matt. 28:19).

The purpose of this article is to examine the way the church has responded to this challenge at several critical junctures in its history. We shall look briefly at the early church, the Reformation, and the post-Enlightenment period. In each of these epochs Christians were faced with unique pressures and obstacles as well as new opportunities in their efforts to bear a faithful and enthusiastic witness to their risen Lord.

Early Church Evangelism: Confronting the Culture

"They that were scattered abroad went everywhere preaching the Word" (Acts 8:4). Luke's description of the earliest Christians, dispersed by persecution from their base in Jerusalem, is an apt characterization of the evangelistic impulse throughout the entire church during the first three centuries of its existence. They went everywhere—into the arena, the academies of learning, the marketplace, to faraway lands such as India and Ethiopia, into every nook and cranny of the Roman Empire. But they targeted especially the great urban centers of the Mediterranean world. Indeed, our word "pagan" comes from the Latin *pagani*, "those who dwell in the countryside," recalling the fact that rural residents were among the last to hear and receive the Christian gospel. By the year 200 there were flourishing Christian communities in Antioch and Alexandria, Ephesus and Corinth, Carthage and Caesarea, and, of course, in Rome itself.

When, in the early fourth century, Eusebius of Caesarea set out to chronicle the course of Christian history from the days of the apostles up to his own time, he described the activity of those heralds of faith through whom the spread of the gospel was first carried out:

> Leaving their homes, they set out to fulfill the work of an evangelist, making it their ambition to preach the word of the faith to those who as yet had heard nothing of it, and to commit to them the books of the divine gospels. They were content simply to lay the foundations of the faith among these foreign peoples: they then appointed other pastors, and committed to them the responsibility for building up those whom they had merely brought to the faith. Then they passed on to other countries and nations with the grace and help of God.[1]

In this portrayal of early missionary activity, we find a threefold strategy which recurs throughout the history of evangelism: proclamation to the unsaved, indoctrination of new believers (i.e., their grounding in Holy Scripture), and the planting of local congregations led by a committed ministry.

The penetration of the Christians into the cities of the Roman Empire brought them into dramatic and often violent conflict with the ruling authorities. Seen at first as merely a heretical offshoot of traditional Judaism, Christianity soon became a threat to the imperial system itself, at whose head stood a man who claimed to be a god. Had the Christians been willing to compromise the exclusive claims of their gospel, they would have fared much better in the Roman world. Indeed, the imperial authorities were quite tolerant of all kinds of bizarre mystery religions and local cults so long as their adherents were willing to give at least a token allegiance to the imperial deity. This the Christians could not do! For them there was only one *Dominus et Zeus*—not Caesar in Rome, but the Lord Christ in heaven.

To become a Christian in the early church was not a flippant decision, nor a commitment made lightly or unadvisedly. For this reason the early church placed tremendous emphasis on *catechesis,* rigorous instruction in Christian faith and life to be undergone by every new convert prior to the decisive event of baptism. According to the *Apostolic Tradition of Hippolytus,* a teacher in the church of Rome in the early third century, this period of intense preparation could last up to three years! During this time the young believer, called neophyte, would be taught the rudiments of Christian theology as embodied in the Apostles' Creed and initiated into the disciplines of the Christian life such as prayer, fasting, visitation of the sick and elderly, and the ability to lead others to faith in Christ. As newly born Christians, catechumen were among the most convinced and convincing of the church's witnesses, and many of them were numbered among the martyrs of the faith.

It is not coincidental that the word "martyr" derives from the Greek *marturia* meaning "witness." In the twentieth century Dietrich Bonhoeffer declared that when Christ calls one to follow him, he bids him to take up his cross and die. This was literally true for many who followed Christ during the centuries of persecution. We do not know the exact number of martyrs in the early church, but Eusebius refers to "an alarming number" and records the destruction of one entire village. In the year 177 there were forty-eight Christians put to death at Lyons, including a blind slave girl called Blandida and a ninety-year-old bishop named Potheinos.

The martyrs faced their cruel deaths with a serenity and joy which amazed the masses who looked on. Just as the stoning of Stephen, the first Christian martyr, must have made a lasting impression on Saul of Tarsus who supervised it, so the death agonies of other martyrs led many other standers-by to embrace the Lord for whom these brave men and women had joyfully died. The "acts" of the martyrs— their wrestling with wild beasts, being boiled in oil, or beheaded by the sword— were recorded in lurid detail and circulated widely in the Christian communities. The martyrs were revered, and the date of their executions remembered as their "birthdays." In seeking to stamp out Christianity, the Roman authorities provided it with an effective means of evangelism! Or, as Tertullian put it, the blood of the martyrs became the seed of the church.[2]

From the beginning the early Christians practiced a holistic evangelism, confronting their culture not only with the exclusive claims of Christ but also with a lifestyle which challenged the greed and self-interest of their neighbors. In his *Apology* Tertullian described the reputation of the Christians of Carthage in his day.

> It is our care for the helpless, our practice of lovingkindness, that brands us in the eyes of many of our opponents. "Only look," they say, "look how they love one another!" (they themselves being given to mutual hatred). "Look how they are prepared to die for one another!" (they themselves being readier to kill each other).[3]

Adolf von Harnack, in his classic study, *The Mission and Expansion of Christianity*, lists no less than ten charitable activities which were practiced regularly by the early church including the feeding of the hungry, the care of poor people needing burial, the care of slaves, orphans, widows, prisoners, the sick and infirm, aid extended to travelers, and special help to churches in poverty or peril.[4] Doubtless such solicitous concern for the down and out drew many of the common people into contact with the Christians. This prompted Celsus, a cultured despiser of Christianity in second-century Alexandria, to complain that the Christians were attracting "only worthless and contemptible people, idiots, slaves, poor women and children . . . If they see a group of young people or slaves or rough folk, there they push themselves in and seek to win the admiration of the crowd . . . If they get children alone, or women as senseless as themselves, then they set to work to put forth their wondrous tales."[5]

In these words, intended as a put-down, Celsus has no doubt given us an accurate picture of early Christian evangelism. He was wrong, however, in assuming that the Christian message appealed only to the outcasts and riff raff of society. Through the writings of apologists such as Justin Martyr, Lactantius, and Tertullian, the gospel was presented in the language and conceptual framework of the leading philosophical systems of the day. Not a few from the nobility and intellectual elite in the Roman world were won to faith in Jesus Christ, finding in him not only the Way, the Truth, and the Life but also the Good, the Beautiful, and the ultimately Real.

A major shift in Christian consciousness occurred in the fourth century when the emperor Constantine embraced Christianity and endorsed it as the legal, official religion of the empire. This was the beginning of what is called the *corpus Christianum*, the conflation of church and society, religion and civil government, which has persisted in one form or another into the modern world. Doubtless the church benefited in many ways from this altered situation. Christians who formerly worshiped in catacombs and house churches were now free to erect magnificent basilicas. Christians were no longer persecuted. Indeed, eventually all non-Christian religions were themselves outlawed. But this reversal also carried with it great dangers. As Stephen Neill has put it, "With a new freedom, the church was able to go out into the world; at the same time, in a new and dangerous fashion, the world entered into the church."[6]

Now that martyrdom was no longer a possibility, many zealous Christians retreated to the desert to embrace the "white martyrdom" of the monastic life. As successors to the martyrs, the monks registered a vigorous protest against the laxity and lukewarmness of "mainline" Christianity. In time they also became the agents of a new evangelistic movement in the church. The monks, and later the mendicant friars, were the great evangelists of the Middle Ages. The missions of Augustine to England, Patrick to Ireland, Columba to Scotland, Boniface to Europe, and Cyril and Methodius to the Slavs are among the greatest chapters in the history of world evangelization. All too often, however, the kind of Christianity which emerged from the so-called "conversion of the barbarians" was conditioned more by the pagan values of the environing culture than by the biblical and evangelical norms of the apostolic faith. By the sixteenth century a reformation of the church "in head and members" was long overdue.

Evangelism and Reformation: Recovering the Gospel

The Protestant Reformation was far more than a mere protest against the corruption and abuses in the church. Essentially it was a rediscovery of the fundamental Christian doctrine of salvation. The last thing in the world the reformers wanted to do was to start a new church. Their effort was to reform the one, holy, catholic and apostolic church by returning to the sources—*ad fontes!*—of its true life, namely the Holy Scriptures and the doctrine of the free grace of God in Jesus Christ. Thus the reformers laid the foundation for the evangelism explosion experienced in the Great Awakenings of the eighteenth century and the modern missionary movement of the nineteenth century.

When Cyril and Methodius had preached the gospel to the Slavs in the ninth century, they translated the Bible into their native Slavic tongue. By contrast, the medieval Roman Church insisted that both the Bible and the liturgy (the mass) be available only in the official ecclesiastical language of Latin. Here and there were dissenting groups such as the Collards in England who violated this sanction and passed around bits and pieces of the Bible which had been translated into the vernacular. The reformers, however, building on the work of Christian scholars like Erasmus, broke down this barrier completely. Luther's Bible in German, Calvin's in French, and Tyndale's in English made the Word of God available, as Luther put it, to the "farm boy at his plough and the milk maid at her pail," as well as to learned clerics and theologians. The newly invented printing press gave a great impetus to the dissemination of the Bible among the common people. Evangelical preachers and colporteurs carried with them Bibles, gospels, New Testaments, as well as catechisms and tracts and treatises by the reformers, as they went from place to place planting churches, founding schools, and organizing the work of the new church.

The expository preaching of the Bible was a major homiletic innovation which the reformers introduced. On January 1, 1519, Ulrich Zwingli entered the pulpit of the Great Minister of Zurich and began preaching, chapter by chapter, through the Gospel of Matthew. He followed this by similar series on nearly every book of the Bible. Calvin, too, adopted this pattern of preaching. In fact, when he returned to Geneva after a forced exile of three years, he walked to the pulpit of St. Pierre, opened his Bible to the text he had been preaching on before his departure, and calmly continued the sermon! "The preaching of the Word of God is the Word of God," declared Heinrich Bullinger. The reformers knew that God alone could effect the conversion of sinners and that he had chosen "the foolishness of preaching to save those who believe."

Reformation preaching centered on the doctrine of justification by faith alone, "the article by which the church either stands or falls," as Luther put it.[7] The emphasis on the unmerited grace of God was a conscious protest against the sacramentalism and works-righteousness of medieval Catholicism and, indeed, the basic presuppositions of humanism, mysticism, popular piety, and every other religious system which led human beings to believe that they could in any measure save themselves. Justification is by faith alone, but faith is not a human possibility, much less an achievement or good work. Luther insisted, especially in his Commentary on Galatians, that faith is always, and only, a radical gift, dispersed freely in accordance with the good pleasure of God. Zwingli and Calvin agreed entirely with Luther on this point, although they stressed more strongly than he the concomitant responsibilities of the Christian life.[8]

It is frequently assumed that the reformers with their strong doctrine of election could not have been very much interested in the actual work of evangelism. If God has predestined from eternity certain persons to be saved, why should we pray or preach or witness since nothing we do makes any ultimate difference? While there is a certain simplistic logic to this train of thought, the facts of history do not prove it to be convincing. On the contrary, all of the reformers were concerned with confronting individuals with the claims of Christ and with calling them to repent and believe the gospel.

An example of the depth of this concern is the way in which the church in Geneva became a base for an aggressive evangelistic mission to France. Between 1555 and 1562 the Genevan Company of Pastors commissioned eighty-eight men who were sent forth as bearers of the gospel into nearly every corner of Calvin's native country. Also, in 1556 Calvin and his colleagues in Geneva sponsored an ill-fated attempt to plant an evangelical church in Brazil, this some fifty years before the English World.[9] This mission strategy was in keeping with Calvin's interpretation of the Great Commission. In commenting on the word "go" in Matthew 28:19, Calvin wrote:

> This is the point of the word go (*exeundi*): the boundaries of Judea were prescribed to the prophets under the law, but now the wall is pulled down and the Lord orders the ministers of the gospel to go far out to scatter the teaching of salvation throughout all the regions of the earth.[10]

Only later in the history of Protestant biblical interpretation was this missionary mandate understood as restricted to the original apostles only. This was the view, for example, of Johann Gerhard in the seventeenth century who believed that since the world had already heard the gospel in the apostolic age there was no need to offer it to them again. This idea trickled down to the level of popular piety and was reflected in an anti-missionary hymn which made the rounds in the eighteenth century:

> Go into all the world,
>   the Lord of old did say,
> But now where He has planted thee,
>   there thou shouldst stay.

The echoes of this controversy can be heard in the later debates between supporters of the missionary societies and their detractors who saw such activities as an infringement on the sovereignty of God. This latter view, however, was a perversion of the theology of the reformers who believed not only that God had elected certain individuals to salvation but also that he had determined the means whereby their calling and election would be made known to them. For this reason consistent Calvinists are numbered among the most ardent evangelists in the history of the church.

While the magisterial reformers fully supported the propagation of the gospel, it was the radicals of the sixteenth century, notably the Anabaptists, who were most active in evangelizing the far corners of Europe. As Franklin Littell has pointed out, the Anabaptists desired not merely to reform the church but rather to restore it to its primitive, New Testament condition.[11] This goal set them at odds both with the Church of Rome and the established Protestant reformers. They preached a gospel of regeneration and stressed the importance of what Menno Simons called *ware penitencie*, true repentance. It will not "help a fig," he averred, to be called Christians or boast of the Lord's blood, death, merits, grace, and gospel, as long as we are not converted from our wicked, sinful lives.[12] The outward sign of this repentance was baptism understood as the public initiation of the believer into a life of radical discipleship. It should be recalled that this was an illegal act which often meant the loss of livelihood, the forfeiture of home, land, and family. In 1554 Menno described in graphic language the consequences of such a baptism for so many of his followers:

> They must take to their heels and flee away with their wives and little children, from one country to another, from one city to another . . . Their names are read from pulpits and town halls; they are kept from their livelihood, driven out into the cold winter, bereft of bread [and] pointed at with fingers.[13]

Like the early Christians, the Anabaptists were frequently hunted down and put to death for their faith. But, just as before, their public witness on the rack and scaffold and at the stake called forth new disciples who were willing to forsake the world and follow the "bitter Christ." By insisting on the necessity of preaching the gospel outside the boundaries imposed by the political authorities, the Anabaptists recovered an important dimension of the evangelistic witness of the early Christians, even as the mainline reformers re-established the foundational doctrines of biblical faith. Though they were often at odds with each other in their own times, both traditions have something crucial to contribute to a proper theology of evangelism: the gospel of free grace proclaimed by a free church in the power of the Spirit.

Evangelism and the Modern Mind: Advancing the Faith

We have examined the two most pivotal epochs in the history of Christianity, the Constantinian revolution of the fourth century and the Protestant Reformation of the sixteenth. The third great turning point is the post-Enlightenment era which, in terms of its impact, extends unto the present time. The Enlightenment was marked by the conviction that by the light of reason human beings could find true happiness quite apart from the "props" of revealed religion. Since the eighteenth century the church has been grappling with major new challenges which stem from such a secular worldview cut loose from the traditional theological moorings of Patristic and Reformation Christianity. Destructive biblical criticism, a naturalistic understanding of the human, historical relativism, and theological modernism have all taken their toll on how the church understands its mission and how it practices evangelism.

Out of this ferment many have come to question the most basic presupposition of Christian evangelism, namely that "there is salvation in no one else than Jesus, for there is no other name under heaven given among men, whereby we must be saved" (Acts 4:12). A potent expression of this perspective appeared in 1932 in a report published by a committee representing seven American Protestant denominations. It declared that the task of the evangelist and missionary

> is to see the best in other religions, to help the adherents of those religions to discover, or to rediscover, all that is best in their own traditions. . . . The aim should not be conversion. The ultimate aim . . . is the emergence of the various religions out of their isolation into a world fellowship in which each will find its appropriate place.[14]

It is not surprising that the sending of missionaries from the mainline denominations has dwindled to a trickle and that evangelism has become for many a dirty word, a topic not to be spoken about in polite company.

While Christianity has not been without able apologists who have defended it from the inroads of rationalism and unbelief, the church's major response to the Enlightenment came in the form of two movements of profound spiritual depth:

the evangelical awakenings and the modern missionary enterprise. Both resulted in a renewed emphasis on personal regeneration, social concern, and a desire to share the gospel throughout the world.

Evangelistic renewal in the eighteenth century stemmed form three interconnected movements: Pietism on the Continent, Methodism in Great Britain, and the First Great Awakening in America. Guided by the writings of Philipp Jakob Spener, whose *Pia Desideria* (1675) was a manifesto of the movement, the Pietists sought to recover the evangelical values of the Reformation which they believed had been eclipsed by the intervening patterns of dogmatics, liturgicism, and ecclesiastical rigidity. Lewis Drummond has listed eight characteristics of this powerful impulse which he described as "a new Lutheran bolt of lightning" flashing on the darkened skies of a dead orthodoxy: the new birth, religious enthusiasm, felicity, i.e., a joyous feeling of fellowship with Christ, sanctification, biblicism, theological education, missionary-evangelism, and social concern.[15] These themes were given potent expression especially through the Moravians, who gathered around the lordly estate of Count Ludwig von Zinzendorf at Herrnhut in 1722 and from there fanned out across the globe in fervent benevolent and evangelistic activities.

Perhaps the most notable "convert" of the Pietist mission was the young Anglican priest whose heart was "strangely warmed" at Aldersgate in 1736 as he listened to a Moravian preacher read from Luther's Commentary on Galatians. John Benjamin Wesley immediately began exhorting other sinners to turn to Christ and be saved. Excluded from the parish churches in England, he was persuaded by his friend George Whitefield to turn to open air preaching. Soon the whole world had become his parish! A veritable army of lay preachers and Methodist exhorters supported the evangelistic efforts of Wesley, Whitefield, Howell Harris, and others. Whitefield was the first "trans-Atlantic" evangelist. He ignited the fires of revival, already stirred by the preaching of Jonathan Edwards, and inspired awakenings among all of the major denominations throughout the American colonies.

John Wesley died in 1791. In the following year the British cobbler William Carey preached a powerful sermon before a gathering of London ministers, urging them to "expect great things from God, and attempt great things for God." In that same year the Baptist Missionary Society was launched. Carey's pioneering ministry in India paved the way for thousands of missionaries who spread the evangel to the far corners of the earth during the next 100 years. So successful was this effort that it seemed that the whole world might be evangelized within the foreseeable future. In 1900 when a religious journal was begun in America its optimistic founders named it "The Christian Century." As we look back from the other end of that century, however, we have reason to be less sanguine about the Christian character of our times. Despite renewed efforts to achieve "the evangelization of the world in our generation," as the great missionary statesman John

Mott put it, and notwithstanding the impact of God-blessed evangelists such as
D.L. Moody, Billy Sunday, and Billy Graham, the influences of skepticism and
religious relativism continue unabated while the percentage of professing Christians shrinks with every turn of the calendar. Of the almost six billion human
beings on the planet, four billion do not claim any Christian identity. Many others
who are only nominally Christian have no vital relationship with the church or its
ministry.

Conclusion

What can the church of Jesus Christ learn from the history of evangelism as it
prepares to bear witness to its Lord in the twenty-first century?

1. The purposes of the Sovereign God cannot be frustrated. In the opening
sentence of this essay we observed that evangelism is the work of the triune God.
It is God who calls, sends, and saves. He will accomplish what he has determined
from all eternity to do. The question is whether we will be faithful in the soul-winning task he has given us to do. If we are not, God will surely find some other way
of fulfilling his divine purpose, as he has so often done throughout the history of
the church. Far from being an excuse for inaction and unconcern, this perspective
frees us to become "co-laborers with God" in his ministry of evangelism.

2. There is an intrinsic connection between sound theology and biblical evangelism. The evangelical awakenings of the eighteenth and nineteenth centuries
would not have occurred apart from the doctrinal foundation established by the
reformers in the sixteenth century. Much of the "quick fix" evangelism of our
times ignores the great biblical themes of human depravity, repentance, justification by faith, and the work of the Holy Spirit in regeneration. The total truthfulness
of God's Word in Holy Scripture must not be compromised in the interest of new
techniques or a more palatable message. In this regard it is encouraging to read the
confession of one of the church's leading strategists for world evangelization:
"The Church Growth Movement has always been rooted in conservative evangelical theology, including a high view of biblical inerrancy, and it intends to remain
there."[16] May this same fidelity to the gospel characterize every expression of the
church's life and witness.

3. True evangelism implies a genuine social concern. This principle stems from
the ministry of Jesus himself who fed the hungry and then declared himself to be
the "Bread of Life come down from heaven." We have seen how the early
Christians followed this pattern of holistic evangelism. Charles Grandison Finney,
the leading revivalist of his age, was also perhaps the leading social reformer of
his time.[17] It is not coincidental that one of the most creative prison ministries of
our day is headed by "born again" evangelist Charles Colson, while evangelical
Christians are in the forefront of those protesting the genocidal slaughter of the
innocent unborn. Of course, we must guard against the perversion of Christian

social concern into crass political ideology—whether of the liberal left, the raucous right, or the mushy middle. The Kingdom of Christ does not belong to this aeon and never will. At the same time, we must never forget the warning implied in the words of E. Stanley Jones: "The social gospel divorced from personal salvation is like a body without a soul; the message of personal salvation without a social dimension is like a soul without a body. The former is a corpse, the latter is a ghost."

4. In the face of secularism and unbelief, the church must bear a positive witness to the overcoming grace of God in Jesus Christ. When confronted with the unbelieving theology and irreverent rationalism of the Enlightenment, the church did not retreat into a cloistered conclave. Instead it burst through the barriers of nationalism, denominationalism, and parochialism to spread the good news of its Risen Lord to every continent on the earth. This remains the supreme challenge of the church today. Perhaps no one has said it better than Karl Barth: "A church which is not as such an evangelizing church is either not yet or no longer the church, or only a dead church, itself standing in supreme need of renewal by evangelization."[18]

Endnotes

1. Eusebius of Caesarea, *Ecclesiastical History* III, 37, 2-3.

2. Cf. E.R. Hardy, *Faithful Witnesses* (World Christian Books, 1960). See also the classic study by W.H.C. Freund, *Martyrdom and Persecution in the Early Church* (Oxford: Basil Blackwell, 1965).

3. Tertullian, *Apologeticum,* 39.

4. Adolf von Harnack, *The Mission and Expansion of Christianity in the First Three Centuries* (New York: Harper and Row, 1961), pp. 153-54.

5. Origen, *Contra Celsum* III, 49-55.

6. Stephen Neill, *A History of Christian Missions* (Grand Rapids: Eerdmans, 1964), p. 47.

7. In the Smalcald Articles of 1537 Luther wrote: "Nothing in this article can be given up or compromised, even if heaven and earth and things temporal should be destroyed." WA 50, p. 119. See also WA 25, p. 375.

8. For a comparative study of the nuanced differences in soteriology among the major reformers, see Timothy George, *Theology of the Reformers* (Nashville: Broadman Press, 1988).

9. Cf. R. Pierce Beaver, "The Genevan Mission to Brazil" in John H. Bratt, ed., *The Heritage of John Calvin* (Grand Rapids: Eerdmans, 1973), pp. 55-73.

10. Calvin's *New Testament Commentaries,* eds. D.W. Torrance and T.F. Torrance (Grand Rapids: Eerdmans, 1972), p. 251.

11. Franklin H. Littell, *The Origins of Sectarian Protestantism* (New York: Macmillan, 1964).

12. The Complete Writings of Menno Simons, ed. John C. Wenger (Scottsdale, PA: Herald Press, 1956), p. 111.

13. Ibid., pp. 599-600.

14. This is Stephen Neill's paraphrase of the report, quoted in Jaroslav Pelikan, *Jesus Through the Centuries* (New York: Harper and Row, 1985), p. 299.

15. Lewis A. Drummond, "The Puritan-Pietist Tradition: Its Meaning, History, and Influence in Baptist Life," *Review and Expositor,* 77 (1980), pp. 485-86.

16. C. Peter Wagner, "Recent Developments in Church Growth Understanding," *Review and Expositor,* 77 (1980), pp. 516-17.

17. See the excellent biography of Finney by Lewis A. Drummond, *Charles Grandison Finney and the Birth of Modern Evangelism* (London: Hodder and Stoughton, 1983).

18. Karl Barth, *Church Dogmatics,* IV/3, p. 874.

PART TWO:
Evangelism and Contemporary Issues

What are the critical contemporary issues in evangelism? In this section the writers examine five issues which have generated a plethora of discussion in recent years. C. Peter Wagner provides a look at the Church Growth Movement, and how that viewpoint relates to evangelism. Robert E. Coleman discusses the critical need for evangelism to be an integral part of theological education. Paige Patterson offers an insightful perspective into the discussion and debate on lifestyle evangelism. Delos Miles writes with great hope that the divide that has often existed between social work and evangelism is closing as this century concludes. And Don Cox looks at the relatively recent phenomenon of the mass media as an instrument for evangelism.

3

EVANGELISM AND THE CHURCH GROWTH MOVEMENT
C. Peter Wagner

C. Peter Wagner is the Donald McGavran Professor of Church Growth at Fuller Theological Seminary. The author of over thirty books and numerous other publications, Dr. Wagner is considered to be the leader of the American Church Growth Movement today. Two of his books, Your Church Can Grow *and* Your Spiritual Gifts Can Help Your Church Grow, have over 100,000 copies in print.

I welcome the opportunity to contribute to this volume in honor of Lewis Drummond, a giant among today's leaders in the field of evangelism. His passion for holding high the great commission of our Lord in times when many others are attempting to twist it or ignore it has been a substantial contribution to the expansion of God's Kingdom.

Not only do I feel honored by this association with Lewis Drummond and the other outstanding figures who are sharing in this book their thinking and their passion for the lost, but I am glad for the opportunity to systematize my own thoughts on how the fields of evangelism and church growth intersect. Even though the Church Growth Movement is thirty-five years old, few attempts to do this have been made.[1]

What Is the Church Growth Movement?

The insights and emphases of church growth thinking have now been well enough defined and widely enough disseminated so that the Church Growth Movement is commonly recognized as a permanent feature on the religious landscape of America and the world. Its development can be traced through four periods.

1. The 1950s: the birth of the movement.
While Donald A. McGavran, the father of the Church Growth Movement, traces
the development of his thought back to 1936, church growth theory began to take
shape in 1953 when, after almost thirty years as a missionary to India, he penned
the manuscript of *The Bridges of God.* This Magna Charta of church growth was
published in 1955, the commonly accepted date for the beginning of the movement. McGavran, then fifty-seven, spent the balance of the 1950s as a research
fellow in Yale Divinity School and as a peripatetic professor of missions in the
seminaries of the Christian Church, Disciples of Christ.

2. The 1960s: the formative years.
Realizing that unless he settled down to a permanent base his ideas would spread
very slowly, Donald McGavran established the Institute of Church Growth at
Northwest Christian College in Eugene, Oregon in 1961. There he picked up
Australian missionary Alan Tippett as a colleague and received a number of
experienced career missionaries as resident students. This program, however, was
not part of an academic curriculum, so McGavran welcomed the invitation to
become the founding dean of the Fuller Theological Seminary School of World
Mission and Institute of Church Growth in Pasadena, California in 1965. Starting
with himself and Tippett, he built the faculty to six full-time professors by adding
Ralph D. Winter in history, Arthur F. Glasser in theology, Charles H. Kraft in
anthropology, and C. Peter Wagner in church growth.

   During the latter part of the 1960s McGavran systematized his ideas and wrote
the classic textbook in the field, *Understanding Church Growth,* which was
published in 1970.[2]

3. The 1970s: the era of expansion.
Through the 1960s the Church Growth Movement had been focused primarily on
the Third World. No one did more to spread church growth teachings around the
world than Vergil Gerber, executive director of the Evangelical Missions Information Service based in Wheaton, Illinois. Between 1972 and 1980 Gerber conducted grass roots church growth workshops in over fifty nations of the world. His
book, *God's Way to Keep a Church Going and Growing* (Regal Books) went
through five printings in English and was translated into over forty other lan-
guages.

   Meanwhile in 1972 the first Fuller Seminary course in church growth geared to
American churches was held. I had the privilege of teaching it along with Donald
McGavran. One of the members of that class was Win Arn, who later founded the
Institute for American Church Growth and began spreading the word about church
growth in America much as Gerber was doing in the Third World.

4. The 1980s: refining the concepts.

During the 1970s the dialogue precipitated by church growth ideas at times became intense. But by the 1980s the polemics had largely subsided. A rapidly growing number of church growth leaders have been dealing with issues such as the application of management theory, the role of pastoral leadership, the megachurch (several thousands) and the metachurch (several tens of thousands) phenomena, organic growth, church planting, lay ministry, professional consultation, philosophy of ministry, the quality of the church, spiritual gifts, prayer, supernatural signs and wonders, and other important dimensions of church growth.

Relating Church Growth to Evangelism

How does this upstart Church Growth Movement relate to the venerable field of evangelism? Before anyone had heard of Donald McGavran, hundreds of evangelists with names like John Wesley and George Whitefield and Reuben Torrey and Dwight L. Moody and Billy Sunday had lived and died. I think the answer to the question can be dealt with under seven headings.

1. Organizational aspects.

The fields of evangelism and church growth are distinct enough for each to have its own professional society. The Academy for Evangelism in Theological Education was founded in 1973. The North American Society for Church Growth was founded in 1985. While there is some overlap such as George G. Hunter III who has been president of both, most of the members belong to one or the other. They see their professional involvement as either evangelism or church growth.

Because it is such a relatively new movement, the North American Society for Church Growth felt it was necessary to define its field as precisely as possible. Incorporated into its constitution is the following definition of church growth:

> Church growth is that discipline which investigates the nature, expansion, planting, multiplication, function, and health of Christian churches as they relate to the effective implementation of God's commission to "make disciples of all peoples" (Matt. 28:18-20).

Students of church growth strive to integrate the eternal theological principles of God's Word concerning the expansion of the church with the best insights of contemporary social and behavioral sciences, employing as the initial frame of reference the foundational work done by Donald McGavran.

For years many denominational headquarters have featured evangelism desks, and many free-standing evangelistic organizations have been established such as the Billy Graham Evangelistic Association, Evangelism Explosion, Campus Crusade for Christ, Jews for Jesus, and numerous others. Likewise some denominations have more recently begun to include church growth desks. Furthermore, organizations such as the Charles E. Fuller Institute for Evangelism and Church Growth and Church Growth, Inc., both of Pasadena, California; the Church Growth Center of Corunna, Indiana; the Church Growth Institute of Lynchburg, Virginia; Church Growth Designs of Nashville, Tennessee, and others have come into being. Many of these church growth agencies have developed resources specifically to promote evangelism as part of their ministries, but their total interest is broader than evangelism alone.

Organizationally speaking, church growth includes evangelism, but evangelism traditionally has not included church growth.

2. Educational aspects.

Chairs and professorships of evangelism have been part of the seminary and Bible school scene for generations. However, very few chairs of church growth, as such, exist. Two examples which come to mind are the Donald A. McGavran Chair of Church Growth at Fuller Seminary and the Ki Dong Kim Chair of Church Growth at Southwestern Baptist Seminary of Bolivar, Missouri. Other institutions have professorships of "evangelism and church growth," an indication that, in the minds of some educators, the fields are closely linked, which they are. Even at Fuller when the Charles E. Fuller Institute was formed in 1975, the powers that be insisted that it be called an institute of "evangelism and church growth," despite the fact that its ministry was designed to specialize in church growth.

While it is true that some educators continue to think of evangelism and church growth as virtually synonymous, it is also true that the literature emerging from the two fields is quite different. So much church growth literature is now being produced that one can sense the frustration of professor Russell Staples of Andrews University who says:

> The line of books in my library dealing directly with church growth, all published during the last fifteen years, now threatens to reach the two-yard mark—and this in spite of considerable resistance to acquire new books on the topic.[3]

I am not aware of any graduate degrees in church growth per se, although several institutions offer them in evangelism. The heaviest concentration I know of is the Fuller Doctor of Ministry degree where students may elect to take thirty-six of forty-eight units in church growth, including twenty-four of them in classroom experiences.

3. Theological aspects.

Evangelism and church growth are not easy to separate when the goals are the same. But not all leaders in the field of evangelism agree on the goals.

There are three major theologically-based views of evangelism current today, each advocating different goals. I like to call the three presence, proclamation, and persuasion.

The *presence* view of evangelism argues that evangelism consists of helping people in some way, especially if the help is offered in the name of the Lord. Feeding the hungry, abolishing apartheid, joining a picket line to defend the rights of the oppressed, caring for AIDS patients, educating teens on drug abuse—all these and many other good deeds are considered proper evangelistic activities for those who adopt a presence approach. Success is gauged on how many persons are helped by the efforts.

Needless to say, few evangelicals hold a presence view of evangelism. Among evangelicals the major debate on evangelistic goals revolves around the differences between proclamation and persuasion. *Proclamation* advocates recognize that presence is necessary, but is not the goal. The goal is to verbalize the gospel so that unbelievers hear it and understand it. If people come to a stadium or answer the telephone or converse across an airplane seat, and especially if they respond by raising a hand or signing a card or praying a prayer, then evangelism as evangelism has been accomplished. While other ministry such as "follow up" is yet needed, the evangelism has been done according to this view. Among others, theologian J.I. Packer presents a strong theological argument for this position in his *Evangelism and the Sovereignty of God.* In it he says that the essence of evangelism is not producing converts, but rather it is faithfully making known the gospel message.[4] Researcher David Barrett, editor of the prestigious *World Christian Encyclopedia,* is another who holds to the proclamation definition of evangelism.[5] From his premise he deduces, for example, that the United States, Brazil, France, South Africa, and Zaire (to select a few) are now 100 percent evangelized.

While few evangelicals hold the presence view, most of them, including professors of evangelism, do hold the proclamation view of evangelism. This raises an important issue in understanding the relationship of evangelism to church growth. So far as I know, no church growth leaders adopt either the presence or the proclamation view of evangelism. Church growth argues for the *persuasion* view of evangelism.

Persuasion does not reject either presence or proclamation. Both are regarded as necessary for biblical evangelism. But it does not accept either as a goal. The goal of evangelism for the Church Growth Movement is to persuade unbelievers to become followers of Jesus Christ and responsible members of a Christian church. No matter how many times they hear the gospel, if they do not become confessing and practicing disciples of Jesus Christ they are still regarded as being unevangelized.

Church growth advocates consider this view to be the biblical view, based on a correct understanding of the Great Commission. In Matthew 28:19-20 we find the most complete statement of the Great Commission. Jesus instructs his disciples with four action verbs. Three of the four are participles: go, baptize, and teach. One is imperative: make disciples. Thus, the biblical goal of the Great Commission is to make disciples of all nations. Establishing a Christian presence, doing good, and earning the right to be heard are good and necessary. Verbalizing the message of salvation through Jesus Christ and proclaiming the gospel is essential. But neither is seen as the goal of the Great Commission. The Great Commission is fulfilled only when disciples are made.

What are disciples? They are people who confess Jesus Christ as Savior and Lord and who demonstrate this confession through responsible church membership. They are committed both to Christ and to the body of Christ.

As I have mentioned, many who are leaders in the field of evangelism do not agree with this definition. Church growth leaders do. Herein is one of the differences between the two fields.[6]

4. Social aspects.

As we have seen, the field of evangelism allows for more variety in the definition of the term "evangelism" than does the Church Growth Movement. A similar situation exists in regard to views of the relationship between evangelism and social ministries. In this context I am not intending to discuss the position of some liberals that the basic mission of the church is humanitarian rather than conversionist. Rather, let's move directly into the evangelical camp where we do agree with each other that the best favor we can do for Muslims or Hindus or agnostics or whatever is to lead them to a saving knowledge of Jesus Christ.

Among evangelicals, a significant number of leaders advocate what they often call "holistic evangelism." They argue that evangelism and social ministries are so intertwined that it is illegitimate first to make any distinction between the two and secondly to prioritize evangelism over social ministries.

In advocating that position they disagree with the Lausanne Covenant which does both of the above. In Article 5 it states that "reconciliation with man is not reconciliation with God nor is social action evangelism, nor is political liberation salvation." In other words, it separates evangelism from social ministries. Then in Article 6 it affirms that "in the church's mission of sacrificial service evangelism is primary." In other words, it prioritizes evangelism over social ministries. This is not to say that the Lausanne Covenant fails to regard social ministries as a legitimate part of the total mission of the church or that social ministries are unimportant. It simply means that evangelism is more important.

Church growth leaders agree with the Lausanne Covenant and not with proponents of "holistic evangelism." As a field, then, it takes a more narrow view than does the field of evangelism.

5. Missiological aspects.

The word "evangelism" to most Christians signifies monocultural evangelism. Most of the books on evangelism which I have in my library deal with winning to Christ those who are members of the same cultural group. Most professors of evangelism are monocultural. They have never experienced being immersed in another culture and becoming fluent in a vernacular not their own. Such experiences and such teaching are usually left to the department of missions.

The Church Growth Movement intentionally deals with both monocultural and cross-cultural evangelism. As I have previously mentioned, the movement was born in a missiological context and dealt almost exclusively with what we would call the mission field for the first fifteen years of its history. The school which Donald McGavran founded offers degrees in missiology.

In order to sharpen the conceptual differences between these various types of evangelism, church growth leaders use the technical terminology E-1, E-2, and E-3. E-1 (evangelism one) refers to monocultural evangelism. Both E-2 and E-3 involve cross-cultural evangelism, with E-3 crossing a more radical cultural bridge than E-2. E-2 and E-3 evangelistic ministries require different strategies, different planning, different gifts, different training, and different insights from E-1. In the minds of most Christian leaders, the field of evangelism specializes in E-1, while the field of missions specializes in E-2 and E-3. Church growth includes all three.

6. Ecclesiastical aspects.

As one can gather from the name itself, the church is central to church growth. In many forms which evangelism has taken the church is peripheral at best, although most evangelism is also local church based.

The Church Growth Movement has found it helpful to label the three ways by which new members come into the church as follows:

Biological growth refers to the process of the children of church members being socialized into the church. Some do this by dedicating infants and baptizing them when they become believers. Others do it by baptizing infants and confirming them when they become believers. One way works about as well as the other with a mixture of good and bad results. Biological growth is a very important kind of church growth. Worldwide, it is the most frequent way of gaining new church members by a magnitude of something like 80 or 90 percent. Where it has been neglected or taken for granted, as is the case in many of America's mainline denominations today, serious growth problems can emerge.

Transfer growth. Many churches grow because believers are transferring their membership from one church to another. While this does not add new people to the Kingdom of God, it is a very important source of new members of most rapidly-growing churches. People naturally look for new churches when they move their residence from one location to another. But also many who do not move find that their current church affiliation is not meeting their spiritual needs or those of their families, so they decide to switch churches. With few exceptions the growing megachurches in the United States today which have dynamic programs targeted toward meeting people's needs are growing largely by transfer growth.

Conversion growth describes unbelievers who have no church affiliation being saved and brought into church membership. Obviously, in terms of the expansion of the Kingdom of God, conversion growth is the most important of the three.

While church growth embraces all three of these, evangelism deals primarily with conversion growth, secondarily with biological growth, and only occasionally with transfer growth. Some church members, in the process of joining a local church, discover that they have never really been born again, and conversion becomes part of the transfer process. But, percentage wise, this is relatively rare. As the children of believers grow up, they themselves need to be born again, and leading them to Christ is the evangelistic dimension of biological growth. Conversion growth, however, is virtually synonymous with evangelism. Most books on evangelism are books on conversion growth.

As I pointed out earlier, the very definition of evangelism which is advocated by the Church Growth Movement (persuasion evangelism) holds that integral to the evangelistic process itself is not only saving souls but being sure they become responsible members of local churches. Few evangelistic programs give the church such a central emphasis. Those which do could be called "church growth evangelism," where marriage of two fields clearly takes place.

Because the church is central, the Church Growth Movement gives much attention to the health of churches themselves, something which traditional evangelism has scarcely touched. The assumption is that healthy churches will grow. Therefore the Church Growth Movement has identified the vital signs of a healthy church[7] and the major growth-obstructing church diseases.[8] Many aspects of church growth, such as pastoral leadership, new church planting, management principles, diagnostic procedures, preaching, small groups, physical facilities, philosophy of ministry, Christian education, lay ministries, spiritual gifts, stewardship, and others which have not been central to the concerns of evangelism, are very important to church growth leaders. In the ecclesiastical area, then, the field of church growth is broader than the field of evangelism.

7. Methodological aspects.

Evangelism is carried out through a multitude of methods. The Church Growth Movement has always been pragmatic. When it looks at a variety of evangelistic methods, it evaluates each of them according to whether it accomplishes the goal or not. From the church growth point of view, the goal of evangelism is, as the famous Anglican archbishop's definition of 1918 states, "so to present Christ Jesus in the power of the Holy Spirit, that men and women shall come to put their trust in God through Him, to accept Him as their Savior, and serve Him as their King in the fellowship of His Church." In other words, church growth accepts evangelistic methods which make disciples of Jesus Christ, while rejecting those which are supposed to but don't. Effective evangelism results in church growth.

For instance, considerable research has been done in recent years to determine whether city-wide cooperative evangelism has actually helped increase the growth rates of participating churches. Lewis Drummond, to whom this book is dedicated, has been one of those most active in this research. Although there are some notable exceptions, many local church pastors who have cooperated fully in the city-wide efforts have been disappointed that they have not been able to detect a cause and effect relationship between the evangelistic program and the growth of their churches. To the extent that this is true, the Church Growth Movement says, let's reexamine the methodology. If it is a good method poorly applied, let's adjust it and fine tune it until it works. If it is a poor method, let's scrap it and look for another one. As the farmer in Jesus' parable said about the fig tree which did not accomplish its goal of producing figs, "Cut it down; why does it use up the ground?" (Luke 13:7).

I must emphasize that those who hold the proclamation definition of evangelism will not feel comfortable with the preceding two paragraphs. They feel that, so long as people hear and understand the gospel, the evangelism is successful. That is their prerogative, and I respect them. My only purpose in raising it again here is to point out that they differ from church growth advocates on this issue.

Methodologically I see three major distinctives of the Church Growth Movement. Let me list the three:

1. *The goal of evangelism.* This has been covered under the section on theological aspects as well as in what has just been said. But it needs to be included as the first point in this list of distinctives.

2. *The target of evangelism.* Church growth is highly receptor-oriented. It believes that the way the message of salvation is presented must be adjusted or, to use a technical term, contextualized, for each cultural unit. Church growth research has shown that the way churches grow differs from one people group or homogeneous unit to the next. Individuals making up different people groups have different sets of felt needs, and evangelism becomes more powerful if the audience perceives the gospel message to be directed specifically to those needs. Methodologically speaking, many evangelistic efforts have been less than successful because they so present the gospel that accepting Christ is perceived to be a social rather than a spiritual decision. We see it in the New Testament times when many Jewish Christian leaders wanted to require that Gentiles take the social step of being circumcised and becoming Jews in order to follow the Messiah. The Council of Jerusalem put a stop to it then, but it continues in other forms today.

Church growth leaders interpret the *panta ta ethne* of the Great Commission in Matthew 28:19 as literally meaning "all the peoples." As such the prime target for evangelism is what has come to be called the people group.

3. *The sequence of evangelism.* Since no one can evangelize everybody and it is only possible to use the time and resources available to evangelize some, the question becomes: where to begin? Church growth research has developed what is known as resistance-receptivity theory. Methodologically, once people groups are identified, it is important to discover which of them have been prepared by the Holy Spirit to receive the message of the gospel in the way that God has equipped our particular church or mission organization to preach it, and to focus our evangelistic efforts there.

This is not to deny that the gospel must be preached to every creature as Jesus said, but it is to zero in on the harvest field. Jesus told us to pray the Lord of the harvest that he send laborers into the harvest. As any farmer knows, not all crops ripen at the same time. While some fields are ripe, others are green. What makes them ripe? One plants, another waters, but only God gives the increase. To discover a ripe harvest field is to discover where God is currently at work. And to focus evangelistic effort there is simply to join what God is already doing. Studies show that this results in the most effective evangelism possible.

Recent Developments: Power Evangelism

The Church Growth Movement in the 1980s is tuning in more and more to what John Wimber calls "power evangelism."[9] He points out that much of our evangelism in the past has been "program evangelism." The assumption is that if we develop the right program we will therefore be effective in our evangelism. While Wimber is not opposed to evangelistic programs, he does bring to our attention that the New Testament more frequently combines miracles, healings, signs and wonders, and casting out of demons with evangelism than do most of today's evangelistic efforts. Wimber affirms strategy planning but suggests that a more intentional interjection of supernatural power might accomplish evangelistic goals more effectively.

Not all church growth leaders affirm the direction in which Wimber is pointing. They fear, among other things, that the Church Growth Movement may "go charismatic." Some, however, myself included, are open to seeing if we who are not Pentecostals or charismatics may nevertheless learn something important from the vigorous worldwide church growth that these movements are experiencing. There is little question that on a global scale the most effective evangelism at the present time is seen in the Pentecostal/charismatic movements. I believe that power evangelism will become increasingly acceptable to non-charismatics in the decade or so to come. As a non-charismatic evangelical myself, I have tried to aid this process through my book *How to Have a Healing Ministry Without Making*

Your Church Sick. I bring this up just to glance into the future and to surface one potentially fruitful area for the advancement of both evangelism and church growth.

Summary

The fields of evangelism and church growth are distinct, but they enjoy a close and often symbiotic relationship. The field of evangelism is broader than church growth in educational, theological, social, and methodological aspects. The field of church growth is broad in missiological and ecclesiastical aspects. The two intersect and become synonymous when the goal of evangelism—the bottom line on which success or failure is evaluated—is to bring unbelievers into a personal relationship with Jesus Christ and into responsible church membership.

Endnotes

1. Two previous attempts at relating church growth to evangelism on the theoretical level are W. Charles Arn, "Evangelism or Disciple Making?" *Church Growth: State of the Art,* C. Peter Wagner, ed. (Wheaton, IL: Tyndale House Publishers, 1986), pp. 57-67; and a section "Are Evangelism and Church Growth the Same?" in C. Peter Wagner, *Strategies for Church Growth* (Ventura, CA: Regal Books, 1987), pp. 114-30.

2. Understanding Church Growth (Grand Rapids, MI: William Eerdmans Publishing Company) was revised and expanded by McGavran in 1980 and revised and updated by C. Peter Wagner in 1990.

3. Russell Staples, review of *Exploring Church Growth,* Wilbert R. Shenk, ed. *Missiology: An International Review,* July 1984, p. 382.

4. See J. I. Packer, *Evangelism and the Sovereignty of God* (Downers Grove, IL: InterVarsity Press, 1961), p. 40.

5. See David B. Barrett, *World Christian Encyclopedia* (Oxford: Oxford University Press, 1982), p. 199.

6. I elaborate on this theological aspect in some detail in my *Strategies of Church Growth* (Ventura, CA: Regal Books, 1987), pp. 113-132.

7. See my *Your Church Can Grow: Seven Vital Signs of a Healthy Church* (Ventura, CA: Regal Books, 1984).

8. See my *Your Church Can Be Healthy* (Nashville, TN: Abingdon, 1969).

9. See John Wimber with Kevin Springer, *Power Evangelism* (San Francisco, CA: Harper and Row, 1986) and John Wimber with Kevin Springer, *Power Healing* (San Francisco, CA: Harper and Row, 1987).

4

EVANGELISM IN THEOLOGICAL EDUCATION
Robert E. Coleman

*Robert E. Coleman is the Director of the School of World Mission and
Evangelism of Trinity Evangelical Divinity School. The author of many
books, Dr. Coleman has written extensively in the areas of evangelism
and spiritual awakenings. He has also served as president of the
Academy for Evangelism in Theological Education.*

Jesus wove education into the fabric of the Great Commission by sending forth his
church to "make disciples of all nations" (Matt. 28:19). Disciple means "learner,"
as in the sense of an apprentice or student.[1] By nature, then, disciples of Christ are
always learning, even as they teach all that he commanded (Matt. 28:20). Following the Master carries the obligation to reproduce what is learned.

Herein lies the essence of our Lord's plan to raise up a holy people who will
praise him forever. Learning ever more of Christ, disciples grow in his likeness,
not only in cognate understanding of his message, but also in personal involvement in his ministry. Disciples, thus, inevitably become "fishers of men" (Matt.
4:19; Mark 1:17; Luke 5:10), and teach converts in turn to do the same, for that is
what their Teacher did.

The Great Commission simply brings this strategy of multiplication into focus,
not as an option among many choices, not the vocation of a few clergy, but as the
controlling mission of every Christian. It is not a particular gift of the Spirit or a
special call to service; it is a command—a lifestyle Christ chose when he came to
live among us, and now the way he expects his disciples to follow.

This is why making disciples lies at the heart of ministerial training. Walter C.
Kaiser, dean of the faculty at Trinity Evangelical Divinity School, wisely points
out:

> Without this lodestar in theological education, neither the church nor
> the academy will be successful. In fact, it is impossible to define the

mission of the seminary (or related theological schools) without giving
primary attention to the urgent command of the Lord.[2]

Legitimate Academic Study

Evangelism is the cutting edge of the Commission, for it concerns the work of
actually bringing persons to Christ and incorporating them into the fellowship of
believers. Sometimes this ministry is referred to as "soul-winning," a somewhat
limiting term, though it properly locates the issue that must be faced. Men and
women are spiritual creatures, and in their natural state are separated from God—
lost in sin, condemned to death and hell—and apart from the gospel of redeeming
grace they have no hope. There can be no training in the Christian life until people
are saved. Since evangelism brings the church into existence and creates the
environment for valid theological education, it must have priority in ministry.
"Only by first teaching our students how to make disciples will there be a
subsequent need to go on and teach those disciples."[3]

Strangely, though, this priority too often is not recognized as a legitimate
discipline in theological study. The tendency has been to relegate training in
evangelism to experience one gets after seminary. Some evangelistic expertise
may come into the curriculum through related subjects, like preaching or parish
administration, but seldom is Christ's mandate to reach a lost world given adequate attention. Looking at the course offerings and degree requirements today we
would have to agree with Dr. Donald A. McGavran that "a maintenance mentality
still dominates most seminary faculties."[4]

This defensive mentality doubtless has been accentuated in the academy
through an inordinate preoccupation with purely theoretical interests. "Students
become adept technicians of the Bible, theology, and church history, but with too
little appreciation for the scope and meaning of this knowledge for pastoral and
churchly vocation."[5] Proliferation of specialized concerns complicates the problem. In the ensuing fallout the unifying purpose of Christian education can be lost.
It is not that practical ministry is negated, but that the heavy academic atmosphere
in which students and faculty live works against active involvement with people
in the world, a situation particularly distracting to evangelism.

Hopefully this condition is changing. There seems to be increasing awareness
among educators that theological education must take more seriously the full
dimensions of Christian discipleship. Addressing the Academy for Evangelism in
Theological Education last year, Dean Jim L. Waits of Candler School of Theology said:

> The reform of the theological curriculum toward a more coherent
> religious purpose and a more churchly mission is itself an acknow-
> ledgment of the evangelistic task of the seminary. To bring together

heart and mind and spirit—in a new kind of pastoral "wisdom" is to touch the deepest instincts of an evangelical faith. Those of you who teach in this area can be encouraged that the questions of personal faith and practice . . . are at the center of discussion about the reform of the curriculum today . . . The signs are more positive than ever before for acceptance of evangelism as a legitimate discipline in the theological curriculum . . . The best of our seminaries have not learned that passion and vigorous theological scholarship are not inimical to each other, but go hand in hand if faithful to mission.[6]

Integration of Evangelism into Curriculum

How this balance can be achieved in the curriculum has to be worked out by each institution according to its own statement of purpose and accepted philosophy of ministry. The governing board of the school must set the policy, and the administration is responsible for carrying it out. With these directives in mind, faculties should be selected and programs designed to get the job done.

Some schools have established departments of evangelism in which courses leading to the Master's degree are offered in this specialization, and two seminaries, Southwestern Baptist Theological Seminary and the Southern Baptist Theological Seminary, have even moved to the Ph.D. level. In most places where formal instruction in evangelism is available, however, the courses are included in other departments of the institution.

An introductory course in evangelism increasingly is standard fare in seminaries and, depending on teaching resources, a variety of other courses may be available.[7] For example, in the School of World Mission and Evangelism at Trinity, which I direct, no less than twenty regularly scheduled courses are listed in the catalogue,[8] not counting nearly twice that many in world missions. Related courses, of course, can be found in the extension offerings of other departments, such as Christian Education.[9]

Availability of classes, however, does not assure that students will take them. This raises the touchy issue of degree requirements. If evangelism is deemed important, should it not be in the basic curriculum for all students? Most evangelical seminaries agree that it should, and accordingly require a minimum of three or four hour academic credits in this discipline. The allotment may not satisfy everyone,[10] but at least it acknowledges that training in evangelism should be an integral part of formal theological training.

Non-formal Evangelism Training

In the more non-formal aspects of education, however, the seminary has its greatest opportunity to mold the thinking of students. Learning the heartbeat of the gospel and making it meaningful to a lost world is not likely to be caught sitting in a classroom, even when the presentation is supported by relevant readings and video tapes. These tools of the trade may facilitate acquisition of knowledge, but the real work of making disciples requires personal association with mentors as well as fellow learners.[11] Jesus has given us the pattern, and we will never improve upon his method.

This truth, of course, is not forgotten by theological educators, as is attested by the abundance of off-campus field work and internship programs for seminary students—practical work assignments under supervision that provide hands-on experience in ministry. There are, also, any number of extracurricular activities going on during the year that afford opportunities for service involvement. On our campus, as an illustration, every Friday night students can join a group that goes to the inner city for street witnessing. Or they may elect on a different day to participate in an evangelistic visitation at a nearby university or local church. These are only representative of the kind of activities that can help integrate the theoretical and practical aspects of theological study.

Leadership, the Key

Key to the whole enterprise is leadership. An institution may have a well-defined policy, but unless the people entrusted with its implementation personally exemplify the vision, students will have a hard time embracing it.

Administrators are probably in a position to set the tone of a school more than anyone else. Since they have a high degree of visibility, as well as authority, when they are known as zealous disciple makers, it gives considerable impetus to an evangelistic thrust.

Naturally the faculty plays the largest role in teaching. Though the skills and interests of these professional scholars may not pertain directly to soul-winning, their love for the gospel and its proclamation will not go unnoticed by students. Evangelism, like everything else in curriculum, requires a team effort. In my case, it has been reassuring to sense the support of colleagues who, I believe, sincerely try to relate the information of their specializations to this task.

Not all schools have academic Chairs of Evangelism, but the number is growing. In a particular way, these professors serve to accent this field of study in the seminary community, while also bringing broader evangelistic training into the curriculum. Because some academicians may have reservations about this discipline, it is well that evangelism professors have teaching credentials second to none. But impeccable scholarship will mean little unless these persons demonstrate through their lives competence in evangelistic ministry. Above all, in close contact with students, through the power of the Holy Spirit, they must show what the Great Commission is all about. With such teachers, even when resistance may be encountered from unyielding segments of the institution, I am confident that laborers for the world harvest will multiply.

A Look to the Future

The priority given to evangelism in the future of seminary education remains to be seen. In many ways, this will be determined by the resilience of evangelical theology in the academy. A concern to reach lost souls generally accompanies steadfast faith in the Word of God. If this commitment is compromised, there is no basis for a credible witness, however noble the effort.

Yet intellectual assent to the gospel is not enough. Christ's command is to follow him. There is a cross in it—the renunciation of our own way in loving obedience to his mission. If we miss the cross, we will miss evangelism, and in so doing, we will lose the heartbeat of discipleship.

Reflecting upon the evangelistic challenge before us, Walter C. Kaiser, with prophetic insight, writes:

> Should the seminary fail at this critical movement in history, there will be more serious consequences than the Ichabod that will be written over her gates. We will have missed one of the earth's finest hours in the program of God; yes, finest because never was so much committed to so few with such great resources and with such epic proportions of promise in terms of results . . . By now our case is clear. The seminary must take the lead in providing the most original, most spiritually sensitive, most creative discipleship program in evangelism the church or world has ever witnessed.[12]

That, it seems to me, sums it up. The peril of inertia is surpassed only by the opportunity for advancement. We must face the issue, and upon our response hangs the future of theological education.

Endnotes

1. *Theological Dictionary of the New Testament,* ed. Garland Kettel, trans. and ed. Geoffrey W. Bromley, IV (Grand Rapids, MI: Eerdmans Company, 1967), p. 441.

2. Walter C. Kaiser, Jr., "Leadership for Evangelism in Theological Education," *Evangelism on the Cutting Edge,* ed. Robert E. Coleman (Old Tappan, NJ: Fleming H. Revell, 1986), p. 144.

3. Ibid., p. 145

4. Donald A. McGavran, *Effective Evangelism: A Theological Mandate* (Phillipsburg, NJ: Presbyterian and Reformed, 1988), p. 3.

5. Jim L. Waits, "Evangelism and the Theological Curriculum," *Journal of the Academy for Evangelism in Theological Education,* Vol. 3, 1987-88, p. 42.

6. Ibid., p. 44.

7. A fairly complete listing of these courses and their syllabi may be obtained from the Academy for Evangelism in Theological Education, or from the compiler of this information at MARC, 919 W. Huntington Drive, Monrovia, CA 91016.

8. The courses in the 1987-89 catalogue include: Evangelistic Bible Study, Ministering to Jewish People, Theology of Mission and Evangelism, Personal Evangelism, Current Studies in Evangelism, Evangelism in the Local Church, Revival in the Bible, Principles of Discipleship, Principles of Church Growth, Power Encounter, Cross-Cultural Communication, Evangelism of the Early Church, Discipleship Evangelism, Evangelistic Preaching, Jesus and Evangelism, Urban Evangelism, Church Planting in America and Overseas, Church Planting Programs of the E.F.C.A., Sects and Cults, and Contextualization.

9. Trinity offers a MA Specialization in Youth Ministries through the Christian Education Department, in which evangelism is given primary attention. Included in the programs are such courses as Student Evangelism and Evangelistic Communication to Youth.

10. One person that this arrangement will not satisfy, among others, is Dr. Donald A. McGavran who believes that five courses in evangelism, each for four hours of credit, should be required for the M.Div. degree. The first, he contends, should "teach the theology of finding and holding the lost and multiplying congregations of the redeemed . . . The second course would teach how to train laymen and laywomen for evangelism . . . The third course would teach how to multiply congregations in North American Anglo and minority populations . . . A fourth course would accurately describe the state of the churches and denominations in other continents . . . The fifth course would deal with the ways of evangelism that God was most greatly blessing to the redemption of women and men." Donald A. McGavran, *Effective Evangelism,* pp. 6-7. Some of the content envisioned in these courses might be covered in other required courses, but if not, his point is certainly well taken.

11. How this relates to a program for seminarians is discussed in an article, "Discipleship Evangelism at Trinity," by Robert Coleman and John Nyquist, *Trinity World Forum,* Spring, 1987, pp. 11-13.

12. Walter C. Kaiser, Jr. "Leadership for Evangelism in Theological Education," pp. 153, 155.

5

LIFESTYLE EVANGELISM
Paige Patterson

Paige Patterson is the president of the Criswell College and the Criswell Center for Biblical Studies in Dallas, Texas. He also serves as associate pastor of the First Baptist Church of Dallas. Dr. Patterson is the author of numerous books, commentaries, articles, and reviews.

The current debate between advocates of lifestyle evangelism on the one hand and confrontational/intrusional evangelism[1] on the other reminds me at first blush of a hypothetical dilemma I might face on a sub-zero, wind-chilled morning when I rise before dawn to embark on a hunting adventure. The question is this: Shall I wear my thermal long johns, or shall I wear my coat? To prepare for every exigency, the obvious and essential answer is "wear both." For a whole list of reasons, the dispute between these two approaches appears to be as unnecessary as the question above. Just as the answer to staying warm on a cold morning is "yes, do all you can in every way possible," so the answer to evangelistic style seems to be "yes, do all you can in every way as long as the means are honest and not in violation of the Scriptures."

After all, just exactly how can you "confront" someone with his or her lost estate and need of the Savior other than "incarnationally"? Can one leave his body, or must one use his body as a vehicle to carry the gospel? And is it actually possible to witness without relating to the recipient in some fashion? On the other hand, do advocates of the incarnational/relational model suppose that sharing a witness is not after all intensely confrontational and intrusional no matter how cleverly approached? Furthermore, is it not really the case that God has been pleased to utilize differing personalities and distinctive approaches to reach a variety of people? And is it not also true that this is precisely the strategy that Paul was advocating in 1 Corinthians 9:22 when he said, ". . . I am made all things to all men, that I might *by all means* save some" [emphasis mine]?

More mature reflection suggests that an answer so facile is not adequate for a subject of such gravity. Although it seems obvious that both methodologies have a place in the Kingdom, participants in the discussion are saying important things and addressing crucial issues. Therefore, this essay will attempt to state the essence of both views, proceed to a brief evaluation of the approaches practiced by Jesus and by the early church, and conclude with an effort to derive an agenda for the evangelistic enterprise.

Incarnational/Relational versus Comprehensive/Incarnational

Incarnational/relational or lifestyle evangelism devotees express concerns about the methods of evangelism often employed by churches and individuals in the modern era. Noting the severe disjunctions between numbers of reported conversions on the one hand and actual numerical growth of committed disciples in the church on the other, lifestylers suggest that the fault resides in part with methodology. Aldrich, for example, is critical of approaches which he labels "ambush" and "spiritual safari" methods, and he points with some accuracy to the "big fisherman" model in which lay persons herd fish into a stained-glass aquarium where the pastor can throw out a lure from the pulpit.[2]

Over against this typical endeavor Jim Petersen advocates what he calls "affirmation of the gospel."[3] This is defined as "a process of incarnating and demonstrating" the Christian message. Lifestyle evangelism recognizes that strangers tend not to communicate as naturally or as effectively as friends. Many advocates of this approach are convinced that there may often be a violation of the recipient's liberties when one "intrudes" uninvited into the lives of others with a "confrontational" question such as those employed by Campus Crusade or Evangelism Explosion.

Aldrich goes so far as to cite favorably the remark of James Jauncey that "buttonholing a stranger," witnessing to him or her, and pressing for a decision will "likely do more harm than good," and demonstrates a "fundamental lack of respect for human dignity and personality."[4] In contrast to this Aldrich proposes that a Christian "becomes good news as Christ ministers through his serving heart."

> As his friends hear the music of the gospel (presence), they become
> predisposed to respond to its work (proclamation) and then hopefully
> are persuaded to act (persuasion).[5]

Legitimate concerns are apparently at the base of the proposals of lifestyle evangelism's advocates. Some of these concerns may be listed as follows:

> (1) The widespread failure of "converts" to become "disciples."
> Many "decisions" appear either to be uninformed or designed to ter-

minate an encounter with an embarrassing evangelist by whatever means necessary—even recording an insincere decision.

(2) The tendency for those gifted in evangelism to enjoy success while the majority of Christians nurse a growing guilt and frustration over their inadequacies in sharing the gospel.

(3) The predominance of the use of gimmicks and memorized approaches which are notoriously impersonal and subject to abuse. Legalism is often the result.

(4) Rejection of the gospel engendered by belligerent and insensitive approaches in which the sharer never attempts to comprehend the culture or circumstances of the recipient.

(5) Shirking of full responsibility for incarnational Christian responsiveness to the total person in exchange for a hit-and-run technique of discharging one's witness.

(6) Improper development of spiritual gifts in the body-life of the church, preventing the whole body from functioning properly.

Lifestyle evangelists, however, are not alone in their concerns. Practitioners of a more confrontational style of evangelism voice their own anxieties about some aspects of lifestyle evangelism. First, any methodology that runs the risk of excluding someone from the evangelistic purview may inadvertently subvert the Great Commission. McCloskey, whose monograph on the subject provides kind but decisive response to lifestyle advocates, states the problem cogently.

> Thus, a philosophy of evangelism that insists on the presence of a relational element (as a normative practice) will unfortunately exclude those not privileged to have meaningful exposure to Christian friends or the corporate witness of the church.[6]

In addition, the urgency of the task seems to be overlooked in much of the lifestyle evangelistic effort. Awareness of eternity, with its yawning, cavernous hell, impinging upon the vaporous days of life often escapes believers and reveals inadequate passion for the souls of people in the process. Furthermore, too little confidence seems to be placed in the ability of the Holy Spirit to create witnessing situations, instill conviction, empower the witness, and ultimately produce conversion in otherwise improbable situations.

The most telling critique of lifestyle evangelism, as far as evangelicals are concerned, is the criticism that the New Testament apparently sanctions a more aggressive and confrontational approach. In the final analysis, if the biblical record supports a more overt form of encounter, the evangelical really has no other choice. Add to this the pragmatic observations that a more immediate approach is often successful. If salespeople ply their terrestrial and temporal trades for the sake of personal gain among people with whom they have passing acquaintance at best, why should Christians fail to develop this art in the sharing of celestial and eternal matters?

Aldrich makes use of the analogy of music to demonstrate how lifestyle evangelism should function. He suggests that the tune represents the appealing life of the believer to which the words of the gospel are later appended.[7] But McCloskey improves the musical metaphor by suggesting that the melody is the gospel and the harmony is the confirming and sweetening addendum of compassion and godliness which enhances the appeal. The melody can and often does exist on its own. It can even do so quite successfully. Harmony, however, only serves to increase the desirability of the sonata.[8]

One final concern is that the means of lifestyle evangelism not infrequently become ends within themselves. A case in point appears in a recent issue of the *Journal of the Academy for Evangelism in Theological Education*. Former President Jimmy Carter's edited address to faculty and students at the Candler School of Theology at Emory University scrutinizes the task of evangelism. The edited rendition contains little actual discussion of bringing people to faith in Christ but rather centers on programs like Habitat for Humanity and the digging of wells in Africa.[9] Whereas one would want to commend all humanitarian activities and express gratitude for a man of renown who would go to Nicaragua with hammer and nails to build houses, it is nevertheless the case that precious little emphasis in the article is devoted to the topic cited, i.e., "The Task of Evangelism." Carter is even critical in a general way of churches who measure their effectiveness in terms of baptisms or total numbers but fail ostensibly in the social ministries.

To summarize, then, the concerns of the comprehensive/incarnational school about incarnational/relational or lifestyle evangelism, the following problems are noted.

(1) Lifestyle evangelism seems to risk bypassing too many people in its attempt to relate better to a few.

(2) A sense of urgency embraced by the authors of the New Testament is apparently diluted among advocates of lifestyle evangelism.

(3) Inadequate confidence seems to be expressed in the powerful work of the Holy Spirit in his convicting and illuminating activities.

(4) Biblical evidence seems to sanction more confrontational means.

(5) Pragmatically, overt approaches are often more successful.

(6) Among some practitioners of lifestyle evangelism there is an observable tendency to progress no further than social assistance and friendliness.

Joseph Aldrich points out that we are "fishers of men" sent to catch fish and not frogmen who are to dive down and swim with the fish merely making our presence known.[10] This poignant analogy is helpful, and it is appropriately employed by an advocate of lifestyle evangelism. But the analogy does focus attention on the potential liability of lifestyle evangelism. One may swim with the fish and catch none. Worse still, it is possible to swim with the fish long enough so as to become indistinguishable from them. Furthermore, fishermen still catch more fish than frogmen catch, even if frogmen generally are more conversant with "fish culture."

New Testament Precedent

A portion of the answer to this vexing discussion can be discovered by a brief analysis of the strategies of Jesus and of the early church as revealed in the Gospels and Acts. A number of personal encounters between Jesus and others are recorded for us. As often as not, Jesus did not personally know these people in the sense of long-term relationships. This would be the case with Nicodemus, Zaccheus, the Samaritan woman at the well, the rich young ruler, and others. Yet, Jesus demonstrated no inhibitions about proceeding almost immediately to the discussion of spiritual concerns. If the objection is voiced that some of the aforementioned broached the subject themselves, and all lived in a culture which valued extensive religious discussion as something of a favorite way to spend a memorable evening, one may grant the insight but point out that these facts do not alter the procedure which was one of direct confrontation. In the case of the Samaritan woman, even "intrusion" might not be too strong a description.

Furthermore, the commissioning of the twelve (Matt. 10:3-15) and then of the seventy (Luke 10:1-16) can hardly be regarded as stellar examples of lifestyle evangelism. The mission was to be that of excursions in numerous towns for the sole purpose of confronting strangers with the dramatic news of the approach of the Kingdom. If this is not construed as "intrusional" and "confrontational," it is difficult to imagine what would be. Add to this the Great Commission demanding that Christ's followers penetrate all regions of the world, making disciples and baptizing them everywhere, and you have a strong case for more than just lifestyle evangelism. Certainly the Great Commission does not prohibit friendship or cultural adaptation, but it does seem to propose evangelistic activity on a broader scale and on a more confrontational level.

Such a conclusion seems to be supported when observing the patterns of evangelism in the early church. Paul gravitates to the religiously prepared in the synagogues, but he does not hesitate to approach the unprepared and hitherto unknown in the *agora* and from house to house. Paul's testimony to the Ephesian elders at Miletus was that he had "showed you, and taught you publicly, and from house to house, testifying both to the Jews, and also to the Greeks, repentance toward God, and faith toward our Lord Jesus Christ" (Acts 20:20-21). Luke records that Paul disputed daily in both the synagogue and the marketplace with all who would listen (Acts 17:16-17). Furthermore, Paul's recorded missionary journeys allow sufficient time for "friendship evangelism" at Ephesus and Corinth, but considerable imagination would be required to make much of a case for that in most of the cities in which he labored only briefly.

On the other hand, cases like that of Philemon, Onesiphorus (2 Tim. 1:16-18), Timothy, and others clearly suggest that much of the most effective and enduring evangelism involved the establishing of meaningful relationships. Perhaps examination of the biblical evidence favors the utilization of multiple means of evangelistic approaches.

A Proposal

With the example of New Testament methodology before us, a resolution of this current debate may be possible. Maybe the solution is not in choosing between two approaches but in doing both—and in doing them better. Actually, advocates of both styles have warned evangelical churches about the limitations and abuses to which both approaches are vulnerable. Good cases have also been presented for the employment of both lifestyle evangelism and a more confrontational evangelistic approach. Without suggesting that Aldrich and Petersen on one side and McCloskey on the other are really saying the same thing, I do not think I would misrepresent them at all to say that they all favor every honest means to get people to Christ. Perhaps it is possible to formulate guidelines which reflect ways of reducing the legitimate liabilities which have been stated in both approaches. The following may provide a way to begin.

(1) *Evangelism with Integrity.* No other endeavor of life demands greater integrity than evangelism for the simple reason that eternal destinies lie in the balance. Abuse of the rights and freedoms of strangers or treasured friends is inappropriate. At the same time one of the most unforgivable forms of abuse is for a believer to receive benefits from an unbeliever, while allowing him or her to continue without warning toward impending judgment (Ezek. 3:17-18). Blending responsibility with absolute truthfulness, avoidance of deceit, transparency of motive, and respect for the liberties of every individual will pay dividends in all evangelism.

(2) *Evangelism with Sensitivity.* My own experience has been that I seldom have to make an evangelistic approach to anyone in an awkward fashion. Generally, friendliness and approachability lend themselves to a situation in which the lost person himself opens the gate for witness. Some have been surprised to see on the syllabus for my classes in Personal Evangelism Barbara Walters's book *How to*

Talk to Practically Anybody About Practically Anything as a text. The value of the book is that it demonstrates that gentle and productive conversation is almost always possible even with the most reticent or the most obstreperous individuals. Naturalness and friendliness pay dividends. The further ability to talk naturally, non-threateningly, and humbly about Jesus seldom turns off even the most antagonistic.

During a private tour in New York's Metropolitan Art Museum, evangelist Jay Strack and I once stood with a museum employee before Rodin's famous bronze entitled "The Gates of Hell." As we examined every incredible figure, we began to talk about how great was God's love for us in sending Jesus. The museum employee, whom we had never met, listened quietly, unable to avoid hearing our conversation. By the time we asked whether or not he had ever responded to God's love, his demeanor had changed from the original hostility (at our intrusion upon his work on a day he had planned to be off duty) to one of curiosity about the things of God. Kneeling at "The Gates of Hell," he entered the gates of eternal life. The incident is shared in no way to boast, which would be most inappropriate, but only to demonstrate the way in which the Lord uses circumstances and sensitivity to evoke consideration of the truth of the gospel.

Petersen said it astutely.

> Now what does this matter of congruence—that is, harmony with God's ways—have to do with reaching the unreachable? It has a great deal to do with it. A congruent life is the secret of naturalness in communication. *And naturalness is the secret of attracting, rather than repelling with our witness* [italics mine].[11]

(3) *Evangelism with Purity*. What is the motivation for evangelism? The lost often sense whether or not motives are altruistic. Motivations for evangelism which arise from desire for recognition, acclaim, or even the success of building a great church or other organization are not only unworthy of the evangelist but also doomed as far as the anointing of God is concerned. Even the desire for heavenly reward reveals a partially flawed motivation. Ultimately the only holy motives are love for Jesus and love for the lost. One may "go on visitation" or "have a home Bible study" or even attend witness training seminars, but only love for Christ and for the lost will produce consistent and successful sharing of the good news.

(4) *Evangelism with Urgency*. More than five billion souls populate our globe. The birthrate continues to soar by comparison to any candid assessment of "new-birth rate." If the biblical message is true, then hell is a tragic conclusion for those who have not come to God through Christ. The potential of forgiveness and eternal life with God demands that all avenues of evangelization be pursued. The urgency of the task is the most compelling of any assignment the believer has been given.

(5) *Evangelism with Accountability.* Jim Petersen is on target when he suggests that "the church is intended to be more like a guerrilla force than a fixed fortification."[12] Some guerrilla forces are, however, more destructive than they are helpful. The reason for that is, as often as not, lack of accountability. Intending no criticism whatever of parachurch ministries, let it nevertheless be stated that the finest context for evangelism is the local church. In that milieu a measure of accountability for methods, materials, and authenticating lifestyle is generally demanded. Balance of ministries is more likely to be a reality within the church.

(6) *Evangelism with Results.* To fail to reach people for Christ is to fail Christ. Evangelism, properly motivated and consistently attempted, will produce results. Jesus did not call us to be fishers of men only to spend time swapping stories about the one that got away. Some areas are more gospel-resistant than others, but, as God told Isaiah, there will always be a tithe response to the message proclaimed (Isaiah 6:13). The church as a whole and the individual believer can never afford to be satisfied with an evangelistic strategy, however brilliantly conceived, which does not get men and women to Jesus.

Conclusion

Initially, I suggested that both incarnational/relational (lifestyle) and comprehensive/incarnational (confrontational) evangelism were essential just as thermal long johns and coats are essential on cold morning hunts. May I conclude with a slightly different analogy though still from the sporting world? It seems to me that evangelistic methodology is a bit like basketball. Good basketball teams patiently work with the ball "inside," hoping for a "lay-up," a "slam-dunk," or at least a short "jump shot." The reason for this is obvious. Though these are less spectacular than the twenty-five foot, long arching swish shots, they are much more sure and, therefore, have higher percentage success ratios. On the other hand, few teams without at least two or three good outside "shooters" win consistently. Indeed those long three-pointers are not only spectacular to behold but also have the tendency to electrify observers and motivate the whole team. So, shall we work it inside or fire away from the perimeter? Obviously, to win we do both.

Knowing that the higher percentage of "connecting" evangelistic efforts are those from inside, naturally we must always be working for the inside position, but there are precious people to be reached from the perimeter also. In the reaching of those who are just casual contacts, we will see some of the more inspiring work of God. We must understand the potentials, pitfalls, and limitations of each method. We must practice both. Is this not precisely what Jude, our Lord's brother, meant when he said,

And some have compassion, making a difference: and others save with fear, pulling them out of the fire; hating even the garment spotted by the flesh (Jude 22-23).

Endnotes

1. This is the descriptive terminology used by advocates of lifestyle evangelism such as Joseph C. Aldrich, *Lifestyle Evangelism* (Portland, OR: Multonomah, 1981), p. 78. For a more descriptive but less memorable term for "lifestyle evangelism," Aldrich suggests "incarnational/relational." Of course, even the terminology selected by advocates of the two views often reflects an effort to prejudice the reader before he hears the arguments. Therefore, Mark McCloskey prefers to describe his own proposal as "comprehensive/incarnational" rather than accepting Aldrich's "confrontational/intrusional" nomenclature. See McCloskey, *Tell It Often, Tell It Well* (San Bernardino, CA: Here's Life Publishers, 1985), p. 154.

2. Aldrich, pp. 17-18.

3. Jim Petersen, *Evangelism as a Lifestyle* (Colorado Springs, CO: NavPress, 1980), p. 43.

4. Aldrich, p. 80.

5. Aldrich, p. 81.

6. McCloskey, p. 171.

7. Aldrich, p. 20.

8. McCloskey, p. 176.

9. Jimmy Carter, "The Task of Evangelism" in *Journal of the Academy for Evangelism in Theological Education*, Vol. 3, 1987-88, p. 6.

10. Aldrich, p. 83.

11. Petersen, p. 79.

12. Petersen, p. 105.

6

CHURCH SOCIAL WORK AND EVANGELISM AS PARTNERS
Delos Miles

Delos Miles is Professor of Evangelism at Southeastern Baptist Theological Seminary in Wake Forest, North Carolina. Dr. Miles has written extensively on the subject of social work and evangelism, including an entire book on the topic. He is the author of a comprehensive introductory textbook for evangelism, Introduction to Evangelism.

Perhaps you have heard the apocryphal story which illustrates the two main schools of thought regarding evangelism and church social work. It tells of evangelism hamburgers made of rabbit and elephant—one elephant and one rabbit. The evangelism hamburger on the left is made of one social work elephant and one evangelism rabbit. The one on the right is composed of one evangelism elephant and one social work rabbit. Donald McGavran sees the evangelism hamburger on the left being offered to the public by the World Council of Churches, and the evangelism hamburger on the right being offered by the Lausanne Committee on World Evangelization.[1]

The Great Divide

That story is indicative of the great divide which exists today between evangelism and church social work. Evangelicals are deeply concerned that as some Christians move toward greater social involvement they seem correspondingly to move away from biblical Christianity. Sherwood Eliot Wirt in 1968 raised the issue this way: "What is there in the present age that seems to make it mandatory for a man to move from orthodoxy to atheism before he can be taken seriously in his quest for the good of humanity?"[2]

Sociologist Dean R. Hoge in a 1982 book review said categorically, "Today the social-action controversy is over." Hoge thinks that those in favor of social action lost the war. Later, in that same review, he wrote: "Most people have apparently accepted Dean Kelley's view that Protestant churches lack the organizational strength to undertake significant social action."[3]

Yet in 1982, even Jerry Falwell spoke of the weaknesses of fundamentalism in regard to social work. "We tend to be negative and pessimistic," said Falwell. "We have almost totally avoided the political process and the social life our country." Then, Falwell continued, "we have neglected reaching the whole person for the cause of Christ."[4] Falwell's indictments apply also to many Christians who may prefer to call themselves evangelicals.

I do not believe an adequate bridge of reconciliation has been built across these troubled waters of evangelism and social work. The great divide is still there in spite of all our best efforts to bridge over it. Nevertheless, I believe this great canyon is bridged in the Bible; that it can be bridged through Christ; and that it is basically a twentieth-century phenomenon which is the result of what David O. Moberg called "The Great Reversal."[5]

Therefore, perhaps the first point we need to make is that if church social workers and evangelists are to be partners in ministry, we cannot ignore or deny the great divide which separates us. Honesty compels us to admit that we do not now have the kind of partnership between church social work and evangelism which many of us desire.

Meaning of Terms

If church social work and evangelism are to be partners in ministry, both disciplines will need to define the terms they use more clearly and accurately . The ways in which we define our terms can either encourage or discourage the partnership.

Evangelism

Evangelist Billy Graham, for example, defined evangelism in 1983 as "the offering of the whole Christ, by the whole Church, to the whole man, to the whole world."[6] If the world-renowned evangelist was right, and I believe he was, then we may conclude that evangelism and social work are two wings of the same gospel bird.

Now take a much older example that comes from the International Missionary Council at Tambaram in 1938: "Evangelism is the transmission of the Gospel of Christ to the whole world with the purpose of the saving of individual souls. . . ." If this definition by Akira Ebiswa, a Japanese Christian leader, had stopped there, it would have unnecessarily limited and discouraged the partnership between church social work and evangelism. But Ebiswa went on to define evangelism as ". . . also the renovation of society; thus finally to bring down the Kingdom of God on earth."[7]

Whether you resonate with Ebiswa's definition of evangelism or not, perhaps you can agree with me that such a definition lends itself to the view that evangelism and church social work are somewhat like two sides of the same coin. Moreover, if one side of a coin is missing, that coin has lost its value. Furthermore, the lack of a social conscience impugns the reputation of a holy God and leads to societal failure. Evangelism is surely a blood brother to church social work.

Before we part company too quickly with Ebiswa's definition, please note that he viewed evangelism as "the transmission of the Gospel of Christ." Etymologically, whatever else we may need to say about the meaning of evangelism, we must say that it is a phenomenon which has to do with the gospel of Jesus Christ. Our very word *evangelism* is built upon the Greek word *euaggelion* [gospel]. Therefore, evangelism and the gospel are connected both etymologically and theologically. The gospel, as the late American Baptist leader Jitsuo Morikawa reminded us, defines the parameters of evangelism. Tell me where the gospel begins and ends, and I shall tell you precisely where evangelism begins and ends.

Nonetheless, we still have to ask whether the gospel is individual or social. E. Stanley Jones, an indefatigable Methodist evangelist, gave the classic answer to that question: "An individual gospel without a social gospel is a soul without a body, and a social gospel without an individualized gospel is a body without a soul. One is a ghost, and the other is a corpse."[8]

We haven't yet learned that what happens in Washington, D.C., and Wake Forest, North Carolina, and everywhere else is related to what happens in every human heart. The confession, "Jesus is Lord," repudiates any bifurcation between one's personal and public life.

Jesus had no problem coupling evangelism and service. It is a warped gospel which does not cover the gamut of human need.

Anglican research missiologist David B. Barrett has recently rendered the whole church a favor with his unparalleled 1987 monograph, *Evangelize! A Historical Survey of the Concept*. Barrett concluded that the word "evangelize" is still not generally understood in the Christian world. He found that in English "over 300 different definitions of the concept 'evangelize' have been proposed in print, using vastly differing terminology and employing over 700 different terms or synonyms or near-synonyms or part-synonyms." Some of these definitions view evangelizing as proclamation of the gospel only, and not as winning converts; while others take the view evangelizing means winning converts, and is not proclamation only. On top of this wide divergence of definitions of evangelization, "each has denounced the other as inadequate or incorrect," wrote Barrett.[9]

Based on more than thirty-five years of full-time evangelistic ministry, ten of those as an evangelistic pastor and the remainder as a denominational state leader and/or teacher of evangelism, I presently define evangelism as being, doing, and telling the gospel of the Kingdom of God, in order that by the power of the Holy Spirit persons and structures may be converted to the lordship of Jesus Christ. This definition sees evangelization as a three-dimensional phenomenon having to do with being, doing, and telling the good news about God's reign over the universe through Christ. It views evangelism as a Kingdom of God enterprise. Therefore, evangelism has both a personal and corporate dimension.

This definition lifts up evangelism as a work of the Holy Spirit. God's Spirit is the great enabler in all evangelization. The discerning eye will also gaze upon the intentionality of evangelism in the definition. Evangelism has a razor sharp cutting edge to it. Its intention is to convert persons and structures to the Lordship of Jesus Christ. It does not apologize for wanting to disciple all the peoples of the planet.

The evangelism which we prize is not only the strong, clear proclamation of the gospel of Jesus Christ. It also involves an intentional Christian presence and a dialogical persuasion. Instead of counting decisions, it counts disciples. Responsible membership in the body of Christ is what we are after. We want real Christians instead of "rice" Christians.

Let us, however, not entertain any illusions about converting structures to the lordship of Jesus Christ. Some entire family structures can be converted. To deny that would be to deny the examples of complete households being saved in the New Testament. But the conversion of most corporate structures is an exceedingly complex matter.

Christians are not apt to change larger social and political structures in those lands and communities where they are a tiny minority. In fact, until they number in excess of ten percent, about the only structures they can change are their own families and neighborhoods.[10]

Talk about the conversion of structures may be strange to most of us. We recognize the corporate nature of society, the corporate dimension of sin and evil, and the corporate character of the Kingdom of God. But we draw back from corporate language because of our Western ideology of rugged individualism, our evangelical captivity to private faith, and our blindness to corporate personality in the Bible.

The abolition of slavery is a prime example of the conversion of structures. Poverty, witchcraft, prostitution, child labor, war, abortion, pornography, racism, sexism, ageism, and nuclearism are but a few examples of other sinful structures which Christians have sought to convert to the lordship of Jesus Christ. The church herself, insofar as she is a human institution, is forever in need of being converted to the lordship of Jesus Christ. Is this not a part of what has been called "the Protestant principle"? A crying need of our time is the evangelization of nominal church members.

If you prefer some other terms like *transformation* or *change*, rather than *conversion*, I shall not quibble with you so long as you seek to do justice to the biblical concept of corporateness. I believe this kind of understanding of evangelism makes much room for a viable and dynamic partnership between church social workers and evangelists.

Church Social Work

Regarding the meaning of church social work, I shall leave the technical definitions of that discipline to those who make it their life's work. Nevertheless, the following will indicate how I am using the term.

Two terms which are frequently used in speaking about church social work are social ministry and social action. Social ministry is feeding the hungry, giving drink to the thirsty, welcoming strangers, clothing the naked, and visiting the sick and the prisoners. In other words, social ministry is doing such deeds of love and mercy as those mentioned four times in the judgment of the nations scene in Matthew 25:31-46.

Christian social action, on the other hand, involves self-conscious attempts to change sinful social structures. Social action includes deeds of love and justice on behalf of society's outcasts and underclasses. Such actions may range all the way from passing a resolution to participating in an armed revolution, although many Christians will draw a line before the use of violence, and some before the breaking of any laws.

The Good Samaritan story of Luke 10:25-37 may illustrate the difference between social ministry and social action. What the good Samaritan did was social ministry. If he had sought to change the conditions which led to the Jericho road robbery and mugging, that would have been social action.

T.B. Matson, who was for many years a professor of Christian ethics, used the analogy of a precipice to illustrate what we need to do in the way of social work. "We want to provide an ambulance at the foot of the precipice," said Matson. That is Christian social ministry to the wounded victims. But we also "want to build a fence and set up warning signals at the top of the precipice," the professor continued. That is Christian social action.

Included in church social work, as I am using the term, are the technical terms *relief, rehabilitation,* and the umbrella word *development.*[11] I also prefer to use the terms *social involvement* and *social responsibility* as practically synonymous with *church social work.*

Bridge Over Troubled Waters

Now that we have confessed the great divide and defined our terms, how shall we bring church social work and evangelism together?

Walter Rauschenbusch knew what he was talking about when he said, "The adjustment of the Christian message to the regeneration of the social order is plainly one of the most difficult tasks ever laid on the intellect of religious leaders."[12]

The World Evangelical Fellowship and the Lausanne Committee for World Evangelization jointly sponsored a six-day meeting in 1982 at Reformed Bible

Church in Grand Rapids, Michigan to consider the relationship between evangelism and social responsibility. Over fifty evangelical theologians from twenty-six countries participated. The meeting was not to rewrite, but to clarify, the statement in the Lausanne Covenant concerning the responsibility of Christians to engage in social and political action.[13]

A number of pressing questions were addressed. What kind of balance is desirable between evangelism and social justice? Which, if either, should have priority? How may the church minister to the spiritual and physical needs of a troubled world? How should the evangelical Christian respond to the insistent demands of liberation theologians that Christians join in the struggle for social justice?

Eight major papers and case studies were presented. These considered ways in which Christians through the centuries have viewed evangelism and social action, how eschatological views may influence social action, and the propriety of using salvation language to describe social or political liberation.[14]

That 1982 meeting stoutly affirmed the priority of evangelism in these words: "Evangelism has a certain priority. We are not referring to an invariable *temporal* priority, because in some situations a social ministry will take precedence, but to a *logical* one."[15] The official Grand Rapids Report concluded:

> Seldom if ever should we have to choose between satisfying physical hunger and spiritual hunger, or between healing bodies and saving souls, since an authentic love for our neighbor will lead us to serve him or her as a whole person. Nevertheless, if we must choose, then we have to say that the supreme and ultimate need of all humankind is the saving grace of Jesus Christ and therefore a person's eternal, spiritual salvation is of greater importance than his or her temporal and material well-being.[16]

This noteworthy 1982 gathering of evangelical leaders said of the relationship between evangelism and social responsibility: "There is no one relationship in which they are joined, but . . . there are at least three equally valid relationships."[17] These are:

- Church social work is a consequence of evangelism.
- Church social work can be a bridge to evangelism.
- Church social work accompanies evangelism as its partner.[18]

Because the Grand Rapids Report is the latest, clearest, and closest thing to an official statement ever made by evangelicals on the proper relationship between these two disciplines, we may linger here long enough to read:

To proclaim Jesus as Lord and Saviour (evangelism) has social implications, since it summons people to repent of social as well as personal sins, and to live a life of righteousness and peace in a new society which challenges the old.

To give food to the hungry (social responsibility) has evangelistic implications, since good works of love, if some in the name of Christ, are a demonstration and commendation of the Gospel. . . .

Thus, evangelism and social responsibility while distinct from one another, are integrally related in our proclamation of obedience to the Gospel. The partnership is, in reality, a marriage.[19]

I agree with the Mennonite leader Myron Augsburger who told a 1986 meeting of six Anabaptist denominations: "If you think you can be New Testament in peace and social concerns without being evangelistic, then you are mistaken."[20] On the other hand, the flip side of that would also be true: If you think you can be New Testament in your evangelism without being concerned with peace and social concerns, then you are mistaken.

"To truncate the Christian mission simply to the changing of social structures," said Carl F. H. Henry, "profoundly misunderstands the biblical view of human nature and divine redemption."[21] I heartily agree. If that kind of reductionism does happen, we could lose all sight of the individual persons for whom all social structures exist. Nevertheless, I should argue just as strongly that to truncate the Christian mission simply to the changing of individuals profoundly misunderstands the biblical view of sin and of the demonic powers and principalities as well as the biblical view of the Kingdom of God.

Henry sees church social work as a result of evangelism and as a partner. It might even be a preparation for evangelization. But he also recognizes the possibility of social work becoming an illegitimate substitute for evangelism.

My personal view is that social involvement and evangelism are partners. If you would see evangelism and social involvement in partnership, look at how Jesus combined the two in his life and ministry. His ministry was characterized by both proclamation (*kerygma*) and service (*diaconia*). The two went hand in hand, with his words explaining his works, and his works dramatizing his words. His words and deeds were expressions of compassion for persons.

There are times when social involvement is a preparation for evangelism. Wherever evangelism occurs, social involvement should follow until the Second Coming. I also see social involvement as an essential element of authentic evangelism. But I do not believe social involvement is a distraction from evangelism. Nor do I believe it should ever become an equivalent of evangelism.

The gospel of the Kingdom of God is compromised and caricatured by those who reduce it to the changing of social structures or to the changing of individual persons. Evangelists are change agents for God, out to change persons and society. They deal first and foremost with that profound change which the Bible calls repentance and reconciliation. And neither repentance nor reconciliation is a private transaction. Both are relational and have huge social consequences.

I am painfully aware that there are those among us whose rhetoric may lead us to believe that evangelism and Christian social involvement do not meet each other, let alone mix together. Nevertheless, I contend that the two should, and do in fact, interface.

The interfacing which occurs when tongued and grooved lumber is fitted together in the construction of a house may provide an apt analogy. Tongued and grooved lumber, when properly fitted together, form such an entity that each piece complements and completes the other.

Robert Hamblin, a former head of the evangelism program of Southern Baptists, spoke my sentiments when he said:

> I feel social ministry and evangelism are inseparable. I've never believed social ministry is evangelism, but social ministry can and should be evangelistic. Neither do I believe we should do social ministries to evangelize. We should do social ministries because we love people and want to meet their needs.[22]

Conclusion and Summary

A few years ago I toured the newly-commissioned USS Nicholas and met a chief petty officer who had been in the U.S. Navy thirty-eight years. He said to us, "I am not *in* the Navy; I *am* the Navy!" Are you a living bridge between church social work and evangelism? There is no better way to close this gap than to stand in it ourselves.

I have said three things that may assist church social workers and evangelists toward partnership in Christian ministry: (1) Be honest about the great divide which separates us; (2) Define church social work and evangelism more clearly and accurately; (3) View the two disciplines as marriage partners.[23]

Endnotes

1. Donald McGavran, "Credible and Authentic Evangelism," *Global Church Growth Bulletin*, Sept.-Oct., 1980, Vol. XVII, No. 5, p. 63.

2. Sherwood Eliot Wirt, *The Social Conscience of the Evangelical* (New York: Harper & Row, 1968), p. 41.

3. Dean R. Hoge's review of James R. Wood's *Leadership in Voluntary Organizations: The Controversy Over Social Action in Protestant Churches* (Rutgers University Press), in *The Christian Century*, Vol. 99, No. 23, July 7-14, 1982, pp. 764-65.

4. Jerry Falwell, "Why I Am a Fundamentalist," *Fundamentalist Journal*, Vol. 1, No. 1, September, 1982, p. 6.

5. David O. Moberg, *The Great Reversal: Evangelism and Social Concern* (Philadelphia, PA: J. B. Lippincott Co., 1977, rev. ed.), especially pp. 28-45. I have developed this bridging idea more fully in my *Evangelism and Social Involvement* (Nashville, TN: Broadman Press, 1986), especially in pp. 27-133.

6. Billy Graham, "The Evangelist and a Torn World," *Decision*, Vol. 24, No. 11, November, 1983, p. 2 of insert "Special Report on Amsterdam '83."

7. Quoted by John R. Mott, "What Is Evangelism?" *Evangelism*, Volume III of the Tambaram Series (Oxford: Oxford University Press, 1939), p. 49.

8. Quoted by Arthur L. Beals, "Of Ghosts and Corpses," *Seeds*, Vol. 5, No. 8, August, 1982, p. 25.

9. David B. Barrett, *Evangelize! A Historical Survey of the Concept* (Birmingham, AL: New Hope, 1987), pp. 9, 76.

10. See D. A. McGavran's editorial note, "Post-script to Leighton Ford," *Global Church Growth Bulletin*, vol. XIX, No. 3, May-June, 1982, p. 184.

11. See J. Alan Youngren, "The Shell Game Donors Love to Lose," *Christianity Today*, Vol. XXVI, No. 11, June 18, 1982, pp. 39-41. More recently among some evangelicals the term transformation has gained favor over development. See Wayne Bragg, "Beyond Development," in Tom Sine, ed., *The Church in Response to Human Need* (Monrovia, CA: Missions Advanced Research and Communication Center, 1983), pp. 37-95 and especially pp. 71-84. I also recommend to those readers who desire a fuller, evangelical perspective on development: Robert Lincoln Hancock, ed. and Carl F. H. Henry, convener, *The Ministry of Development in Evangelical Perspective: A Symposium on the Social and Spiritual Mandate* (Pasadena, CA: William Carey Library, 1979).

12. Walter Rauschenbusch, *A Theology for the Social Gospel* (New York: Abingdon Press, 1945 ed.), p. 7.

13. "The Lausanne Covenant," in J. D. Douglas, ed., *Let the Earth Hear His Voice* (Minneapolis, MN: World Wide Publications, 1975), pp. 4-5.

14. Arthur Williamson, "Evangelicals Study the Link Between Social Action and Gospel," *Christianity Today*, Vol. XXVI, No. 13, Aug. 6, 1982, pp. 54, 56.

15. Lausanne Occasional Papers No. 21 Grand Rapids Report, *Evangelism and Social Responsibility: An Evangelical Commitment* (A Joint Publication of the Lausanne Committee for World Evangelization and the World Evangelical Fellowship, 1982), p. 24. Italics are in the text of the statement.

16. Ibid., p. 25.

17. Ibid., p. 21.

18. Ibid., p. 21-23.

19. Ibid., p. 24.

20. Quoted in "Historic Peace Churches Seek a New Evangelistic Emphasis," *Christianity Today*, Vol. 29, No. 8, May 17, 1985, p. 44.

21. Carl F. H. Henry, "American Evangelicals in a Turning Time," *The Christian Century,* Vol. XCVII, No. 35, Nov. 5, 1980, p. 1062.

22. Quoted by Jim Newton, "Bob Hamblin, Relational Evangelist," *Missions USA,* Nov.-Dec., 1982, Vol. 53, No. 6, p. 56.

23. Originally published as an article in the *Review and Expositor,* Volume 85 (Spring 1988). Used by permission.

7

EVANGELISM AND
THE MASS MEDIA
Don Cox

Don Cox is the pastor of Southside Baptist Church in Athens, Alabama. He was a student under Dr. Drummond during the years 1983 to 1986 at the Southern Baptist Theological Seminary in Louisville, Kentucky.

One of the most joyful and rewarding experiences of my life has been to study evangelism under the tutelage of Dr. Lewis Drummond. In his classes, Dr. Drummond often defined the work of evangelism in linear terminology. In this framework, he explained that every person is somewhere on a line that leads to the cross, and our job as Christians is always to help that individual move closer to the cross and ultimately into a personal relationship with Jesus Christ. We always desire to help prospects on the journey to meet the Lord, and we must seek to avoid any action that might push them further away from the cross. This approach calls for sensitivity to the leadership of the Holy Spirit and to the individual's particular needs. I believe this definition is sound and biblical. It is a definition born out of the Scriptures where Paul said, "I planted the seed, Apollos watered it, but God made it grow" (1 Cor. 3:6, NIV). This definition also has profound implications in discussing evangelism as it is related to the mass media (for the purpose of this essay, I restrict the term "mass media" to refer to radio and television only). To aid our discussion of this topic, I think a brief history of the broad subject of religious broadcasting would be helpful.

Historical Backgrounds

Religious broadcasting has played an integral role in radio and television from the inception of both media. The first regular radio broadcasting service began with the Westinghouse Electric and Manufacturing Company at station KDKA in Pittsburgh. The station went "on the air" on November 2, 1920. The first private sector religious broadcast followed in two short months on January 2, 1921, when

KDKA broadcasted the evening vesper service of Calvary Episcopal Church in Pittsburgh. Reverend Louis B. Whittemore conducted the service in the absence of the rector.[1] As radio grew, so did the role of religious groups, with many owning stations in the early days.[2]

Entrance into the television market by a religious group began on Easter Sunday, 1940. The Protestant telecast was presented in cooperation with the Federal Council of Churches and the Catholic program, presumably, in cooperation with the National Council of Catholic Men. A Jewish service for Passover, most likely under the aegis of the Jewish Theological Seminary of America, was presented a month later.[3]

The milieu of religious broadcasting today, especially television, is a direct product of directions taken in the early days of radio as it related to governmental regulations and different religious groups. By the late 1920s, religious broadcasting was already sparking controversy, with numerous stripes of "preachers" vying for air time. Some were considered highly controversial and problematic. The first radio network, the National Broadcasting Company established in 1926, not wanting to be barraged with requests for time from the various groups and broadcasters, made a decision in 1928 that had profound effects upon broadcasting in our nation. In essence, they sought to work with different councils who would represent "mainline" religious groups in the broadcast industry. By this move, they sought to keep what they considered controversial preachers off the air. NBC asked the Federal Council of Churches (forerunner of the National Council of Churches) to take responsibility of all Protestant broadcasting on NBC. The company also made similar arrangements with the National Council of Catholic Men and the Jewish Theological Seminary of America to represent their respective constituencies. The NBC Advisory Committee on Religious Activities shaped a policy that further set the posture for today's climate. The first principle laid down by the committee stated:

> The National Broadcasting Company will serve only the central national agencies of the great religious faiths, as for example, the Roman Catholics, the Protestants, and the Jews as distinguished from individual churches of small group movements where the national membership is comparatively small.[4]

The second radio network, CBS, formed in 1927, sold network time to religious groups at first, but in 1931 they followed the lead of NBC in refusing to sell time for religious programs. They opted to apportion a limited amount of free air time to these same "major" Protestant, Catholic, and Jewish groups.[5] Mutual Broadcasting Network, formed in the mid 1930s, provided only purchased time to religious broadcasters for a few years. Evangelicals will remember Charles Fuller of the "Old Fashioned Revival Hour" who was Mutual's biggest customer in the

40s. But in 1944 they made certain changes that virtually caused their religious broadcasting to cease.[6] In short, all the major networks that formed eventually followed the lead of NBC, and the network position was followed by local station managers. Thus non-mainline religious groups, such as evangelicals and fundamentalists, were literally derailed from access to the airways of major networks and their local affiliates. This mentality of the networks was expressed by William J. DuBourdieu, who grouped Protestant broadcasting into "conventional," "fundamentalist," and "irregular," when he said in 1932:

> The Conventional Protestant group is the one which has been chosen
> by radio stations and chains [networks] to be their agent in supplying
> religion to the Protestant section of the nation.[7]

In 1934, Congress established the Federal Communications Commission (FCC) with the passage of the Communications Act. To squash an amendment to the Act that would have forced broadcasters to allocate twenty-five percent of their frequencies to nonprofit groups, the broadcasters assured Congress, based on their past performance in serving such groups, they could be trusted to provide this public service time in the future. In 1935, the newly-formed FCC went along with the broadcast companies, saying that no fixed percentages would be required but that religious leaders would be assured by the FCC that the broadcast companies would continue to give them time to be heard on commercial stations. The networks met this obligation by working through the religious advisory committees of the networks which catered to the "mainline" Catholic, Protestant, and Jewish groups.[8] This arrangement kept them from having to deal with evangelicals and fundamentalists. By the time television began to develop, the networks had long-established relationships with these "mainline" groups, and the same practice was extended into this new medium.[9]

This trend continued to dominate the media until around 1960. Thus, one can see that non-mainline religious groups were forced from earliest times to be entrepreneurial in practice. Evangelicals would have to buy time, and their supporters would have to supply the funds.[10] The mainline groups had free access to the airways. The evangelicals and fundamentalists bought time from non-network stations to get the Word out. Whether or not it is true, evangelicals believed they were being suppressed by the Federal Council of Churches, and out of this belief the National Association of Evangelicals was formed in 1942. From this group in 1944 came the National Religious Broadcasters,[11] which now represents over 1,300 groups. Its original purpose was to overcome the barriers to radio and television use.[12] The function of this organization is now very broad-ranging.

In spite of the disadvantages of having to purchase all their air time, raise their own funds, and produce their shows, the paid-time route fared very well. "By 1959, 53 percent of all religious time on television was occupied by programs that purchased air time, compared to 42 percent by all other types of religious programs."[13] This was true even with the paid-time broadcasters confined to smaller markets.

The following year, a change in FCC policy occurred that began the rapid growth of what is now coined the "electronic church."[14] During 1960, the FCC released a programming statement which said "that no public-interest basis was to be served by distinguishing between sustaining time programs (those broadcast on free air time) and commercially sponsored programs in evaluating a station's performance in the public interest."[15] This paved the way for stations to meet FCC regulations in regard to public access with programs that paid for their air time, whereas before this had to be met by providing free air time to certain non-profit groups including religious groups. By this decision and a few other important decisions, the FCC virtually removed itself from the field of religious television and opened the door to those who were able and willing to pay for time to dominate the airwaves.[16] The expansion of UHF frequency television licenses also fueled rapid growth of evangelical programs. By 1977 programs that purchased air time accounted for 92 percent of air time used for religious programs. Also, by 1978 there were roughly thirty religious television stations with another thirty religious groups having applications before the FCC.[17]

The Scene Today

Most of the programs today are evangelical or fundamentalist in nature. "In 1979 more than half of all national airing of religious programs were accounted for by only ten major evangelical programs."[18] Their rapid growth and buying power has virtually eliminated local programming. However, with the growth in the cable industry and Christian networks, local churches can find available spots to purchase air time if they can afford to enter the market. Evangelical presence on the radio is also prominent with numerous Christian stations and purchased time on stations without a Christian format.

In light of the present situation, many liberal religious groups and some secular groups are yelling "foul." While some criticism may be justified, most of these comments are coming from groups who have been disenfranchised and want their power over the airways back. It might be helpful to remember, however, that the present situation developed partially out of their own structural agreements with the major networks.

The growth in the evangelical/fundamental wing of the church and the demise of the "mainliners" in religious broadcasting and the general culture at large also has a theological explanation. The "social gospel" and the "neoliberal theology" presented by mainliners, especially in the 1960s and 70s, emptied the gospel of meaning and power and precipitated their decline. Their message did not give life-changing, life-sustaining answers, and many began to leave their "mainline" congregations for the evangelical sector of the church. Many of them were probably made aware of these differing theologies through broadcast ministry. Further history of this fascinating phenomenon is outside the scope of this essay. The remaining pages will be devoted to discussing evangelism and the mass media in both its present and future forms.

The Growth of Religious Broadcasting

The size of religious broadcasting today is massive and growing. Even with all of the maladies that have surfaced in the past two years, there has still been growth in the religious broadcasting industry. The latest National Religious Broadcasters directory shows increases in television stations from 221 to 259; radio stations from 1,370 to 1,393; and groups producing programs from 1,010 to 1,068.[19] Another perspective says, "There are over eighty syndicated religious series and hundreds of local or regional productions, series, and broadcast church services on television, and many more on radio. It is a vast and varied field."[20] "There are now five Christian cable networks, numerous religious-owned television and radio stations and sophisticated television production facilities."[21] Some are saying that this growth must end, but I believe it will continue, especially if conservative/evangelical congregations continue to flourish. An indication of this continued growth is the fact that many Christian radio stations are now launched and owned by non-Christians. Their motivation for entering the market is obviously because they believe there is room for growth and there is money to be made.

Effectiveness in Evangelism

As there will be with any entity as large as the religious broadcast industry, debate is going on, even in evangelical circles, over the effectiveness of this route per se in evangelism. The reactions are mixed across the theological spectrum. This debate can best be examined by dividing the issue into three broad areas and discussing each separately.

First of all, how effective are those who use the mass media in "getting the Word out"? One of the chief arguments of the proponents of mass media evangelism is that huge proportions of the public are hearing the gospel proclaimed. For example, Ben Armstrong, Executive Director of the NRB, said in 1979 that "every Sunday morning, nearly 130 million Americans tune their radio and television sets to the 'electronic church.'"[22] Antagonists of broadcast ministry point to figures derived form the Nielsen and Arbitron organizations (independent audience measurement organizations) around 1980 and polls done in the late 1970s and early 80s to argue for a much smaller audience. In an article in *Broadcasting*, Stephen Winzenburg from Florida Southern College said about TV ministries: "The total unduplicated audience is closer to five million households, or seven million total viewers."[23] Others, such as Peter Horsfield in *Religious Television,* say:

> While the picture is far from precise, what is apparent is that the audience claimed by paid-time religious programs is far smaller than has generally been thought. It is unlikely that the regular weekly audience for paid-time religious programs exceeds 20 million people. A more realistic estimate is between 10 and 15 million individual viewers, many of whom watch several different programs each week to produce a higher combined audience figure.[24]

Even Horsfield admits, however, the difficulty in estimating the total audience for all religious programs. More recent figures tend to show a larger audience than the original data revealed. For example, in a recent Nielsen study conducted for CBN. the findings show that, of the 84.9 million TV households in the U.S., 40 percent watched at least one of the top ten religious programs during February 1985. This study supported surveys done by Gallup which recorded that between 32 and 43 percent of all adults recalled watching a religious program in the prior month.[25] "These new figures indicate that the electronic church is a national phenomenon as its proponents have claimed, and as the teleministries illustrate for us."[26] William Fore, in his work *Television and Religion,* seeks to dispel these new figures, but I do not think he does so successfully. However, this discussion does tend to show how large the debate truly is.

Figures for radio listeners are not as readily available, but this audience would certainly add substantial numbers to the total participants. Considering the fact that, in the secular market, very little religious programming is ever presented during "prime-time" but is relegated to low viewing/listening times, the broadcast ministry does a good job, overall, of generating an audience.

The Audience of Religious Broadcasting

We must now go another step and seek to find the type of audience being reached. If we are truly seeking to evangelize, then there should be enough diversity among religious broadcasters to elicit an audience from all groups within a given society. It has long been pointed out that viewers of religious TV are disproportionately older and female. Antagonists have been quick to seek and establish that religious broadcasters have been exploiting this group financially. This conclusion is a poor assessment of media evangelism. The reason for this type of audience can be accounted for on the basis of two factors. Number one, females as a group outlive males by 7.7 years and, secondly, as people grow older, they tend to become more involved in their religious matters. Also, most older adults hold conservative religious beliefs as espoused by evangelical and fundamentalist broadcasters as opposed to "mainline" beliefs.

But there are also other listeners to religious media, and it seems that different types of programs attract a variety of audiences. It has been pointed out that children comprise 30 percent of Jerry Falwell's audience, and also that Falwell's program, along with Pat Robertson's program, is appealing to younger men. Furthermore, the programs produced by Jimmy Swaggart and Falwell only attract 43 percent each of the female audience.[27]

The important factor to be considered, though, is whether these programs are having much effect on the burgeoning and growing number of unchurched people in the country. Are these programs truly reaping a harvest, or are they only reinforcing already held convictions? The evidence suggests that the programs are viewed at least occasionally by people of all persuasions, even those who claim to have no religious interest or church affiliation.[28] And it is fair to assume that some of these people do come to the Lord through watching a program, but by and large, the non-Christian society is not being reached through media evangelism. Win Arn, founder and president of the Institute for American Church Growth, said as recently as a year ago: "More than 70 percent of Americans either have no religious affiliation or are Christian in name only. Religious television doesn't seem to impact significantly this group."[29] I assume the same thing could be said in relation to radio broadcasting.

It therefore seems reasonable to conclude that religious broadcasting is primarily reaching insiders (those who already claim to be followers of Christ) rather than outsiders (those who are part of the non-Christian populace or who are Christian in name only). "The research indicates that the dominant functions now being served by Christian programs for the major segments of its audience appear to be personal inspiration, companionship, and support."[30] The primary role of the mass media could be characterized as providing some Christian nurture to people who are already Christians. I also tend to believe that many evangelicals view these broadcasters as sources of information on a variety of subjects they feel are slanted or suppressed by the secular media. There is a place for this type of service in Christian broadcasting.

The Media's Presentation of the Gospel

When considering the topic of "getting the Word out," we must also seek to explore how well religious broadcasters or televangelists score in gospel presentation. A true gospel presentation will verbalize certain points to the potential convert. Biblically speaking, we are to present the *kerygma*. As Paul said in 1 Corinthians 1:21, God chose to save the world through the foolishness of what was preached (*kerygma*). The cross must be preached! A clear gospel presentation should include at least the facts laid out in 1 Corinthians 15:3-4, where Paul said, "For what I received I passed on to you as of first importance: that Christ died for our sins [substitutionary atonement] according to the scriptures, that he was buried, that he was raised on the third day according to the scriptures" [bodily resurrection]. Along with that, a call for repentance toward God and personal faith in Christ as Lord and Savior (Acts 3:19), should be presented, recognizing his work of propitiation on the cross and Lordship over the life of the believer (Rom. 3:25-26). With the proliferation of the "health and wealth" gospel, this message is often hidden to the viewer or listener of certain broadcast ministries. The demands of the Christian life, including suffering (Phil. 1:29), are also ignored by this false proclamation and theology. On the other hand, there are programs that do a good job in gospel presentation, and I am confident that much planting and some reaping occur in this process. The review of "getting the Word out" is therefore mixed.

The Integrity of the Media

A second aspect to consider when evaluating the effectiveness of the mass media in evangelism, is how well the broadcasters are doing in representing the Christian faith. By this, I am referring to personal integrity and Christian piety. Evangelicals and fundamentalists who are involved in evangelistic outreach through the mass media are often stereotyped as hucksters, shysters, and Elmer Gantrys. The events of the recent past year have only reinforced these unfortunate circumstances. The indictments against Bakker, Swaggart, and Oral Roberts have done untold damage. While the vast majority of religious broadcasters are hard-working and honest, seeking to carry out what they perceive as God's will in their lives, the failures of a few in such a high-profile situation can be extremely damaging to all.

The indulgence in affluent lifestyles has also tarnished the image of religious broadcasting. Much of this lavishness is quite unnecessary and shouldbe curbed. A further hampering of evangelistic effectiveness in broadcast ministry has been caused by the type of fund-raising used. Emergency appeals show poor management of resources and planning. They also can prompt the audience to question one's integrity. If the money is not forthcoming in a particular market to meet the needs of the ministry there, then resources should be diverted elsewhere. Many evangelicals do a good job in using low-key fund raising and in managing the resources entrusted to them. These organizations should be commended, along with those who are totally open about their financial situations. Overall, these ministers and ministries are genuine and above board. They represent the faith well through honesty, integrity, and high quality productions. Again, however, the failures of a few cause all to wince.

Disciple Making

A third area in which we need to evaluate the effectiveness of mass media evangelism is the arena of disciple making. After all, the Great Commission commands us to "make disciples," not garner numbers of call-in converts for personal display. In this area, it appears that overall mass media evangelism has failed. The reason is two-fold. First of all, most broadcast ministries do a poor job of follow-up with inquirers of the gospel. A lengthy quote from Horsfield's work, *Religious Television*, captures this point:

> In January 1981, the author wrote to five broadcasters seeking clarification from them of what it meant to become and live as a Christian. In response to this enquiry, he received a total of 54 mailings in a nine-month period. Of these only six mailings were directed specifically at the original enquiry. The remaining 49 were various forms of fund solicitation. The one exception to this was the Billy Graham organization. In response to the enquiry, the counseling department of the organization sent one mailing of various materials directed at answering the questions asked. In contrast to the other broadcasters, no "personal" letter was received from "Billy Graham himself," and no subsequent financial appeals were forthcoming as a result of this enquiry.[31]

Although Dr. Horsfield does not name the other broadcasters, and the number he contacted was quite small, the result is nonetheless revealing. If this survey is representative, I think we can begin to understand why the effectiveness at making disciples or even garnering converts is so low. Dr. Graham is to be commended, as always, and his example should be followed.

A second reason media evangelism has failed in attempts at disciple making is the disjunction between these ministries and the local church. By and large, broadcasters have not done a good job of working with local churches. "A content study of fifteen paid time religious programs by Hilton in 1980 found that in none of them was the local church ever mentioned."[32] Also, when Dr. Horsfield wrote to the media broadcasters, only one broadcaster included the name of a local church where he could gain further information. No local church made a contact with him as a result of his inquiry, even though two churches of the same affiliation as the broadcaster were located on the block where he lived.[33] As a pastor, this disjunction concerns me for the many inquirers who are left on the field with no real contact by a local church. As a result, I am sure many of these inquirers are left, at best, immature believers and, at worst, hostile and bitter toward the faith. Disciple making cannot be accomplished apart from the local church.

Guidelines for Religious Broadcasting

Regardless of where one stands in this debate over evangelism and the mass media, the mass media will continue to be used by Christians in an effort to evangelize. And the predominant route to the airways will be pay-as-you-go. Sustaining time programs will remain in the minority. I therefore think it would behoove us to lay down some minimum guidelines in which Christians, who feel God is calling them to evangelize through the mass media, should operate. To this now let us turn our attention.

As in any ministry, the life of the minister comes under scrutiny. James 3:1 indicates that those who teach will be judged more strictly by the Lord. Paul, in 1 Corinthians 9, indicated the extent to which one should go to maintain integrity before those he or she is seeking to reach. For mass media evangelism to be effective, the first point in the guideline is that the personal integrity of those involved must be impeccable. Let us be reminded that 1 Thessalonians 5:22 can be translated: "Keep away from every outward appearance of evil" (NIV). This is a command for the utmost in personal scrutiny of our attitudes and actions. Affirmation VIII from the 1983 International Conference of Itinerant Evangelists, held in Amsterdam, is a good rule of thumb for persons in broadcast ministry. It states: "We acknowledge our obligation, as servants of God, to lead lives of holiness and moral purity, knowing that we exemplify Christ to the church and to the world."[34] Although stereotypes are hard to overcome, those in broadcast ministry must seek to put away the negative concepts held by many in the general public. If all those who participate in broadcast ministry would follow the example of Dr. Graham, these matters would take care of themselves.

Closely linked with personal integrity is the subject of accountability. The second guideline is that every broadcast minister should be held accountable. Every person in ministry should be held accountable to other Christians whether it be to deacons, elders, denominations, or the Christian community at large through parachurch organizations. This accountability in media evangelism should be required in three areas.

A. Personal Ethics—If a minister fails morally or in other ethical ways he should submit himself to the wise counsel of Christian brethren. For example, if a pastor has a moral failure, it is usually assumed that the pastor will resign and hopefully enter into a long restorative process involving Christian counseling and accountability to others. The attempt at personal comebacks and snubbing of denominational discipline by some broadcast ministers flies in the face of biblical solutions to moral failures.

B. Financial Accountability must also be maintained, and if those who use the mass media do not regulate themselves in this area, the government will find ways to do it for them. U.S. Rep. J.J. Pickle's (D-Tex) oversight subcommittee of the House Ways and Means Committee has already set precedent in this direction by the congressional hearings he headed involving broadcast ministries. The establishment of the Evangelical Council for Financial Accountability (ECFA) in 1979, and the NRB's approval of the Ethics and Financial Integrity Commission (EFICOM) in February of 1988 will help avert a clash with government and, at the same time, insure needed accountability. EFICOM's standards are tough, including requirements of annual independent audit reports that itemize income sources, expenditures, and compensation; files showing fund-raising activities; and decentralization of financial authority from one person. As a matter of fact, "by January 1, 1990 a majority of a member's board of directors (must) be other than family, staff, or employees."[35] All broadcast ministers should affiliate with and comply with these organizations.

C. Message Accountability—Those who preach false doctrine should be exposed through writings, debate, and other available means. Pastors have an obligation to their congregations to inform them of false theology and those who peddle it. The message of salvation should be presented in its wholeness, and those who do not fall within the broad parameters of evangelical theology should be exposed. I am referring only to those who seek to identify with the evangelical community at large. As Kenneth Kantzer has said: "Evangelical commitment to freedom of religion and free speech does not mean that we need to support false religion or that we may not vigorously oppose antievangelical teaching."[36]

A third guideline involves the variety of appeals made. Simply put, we should use every means available to present the *kerygma*. Carl F. H. Henry said that the current upsurge of religion in the mass media is "a destructive trend which neglects a systematic presentation of Christian truth."[37] His warning calls for hard work in this area. Other types of formats can be used in "pre-evangelism." By that, I mean drawing people's attention to Christian perspectives on world events, family matters, mental health, nutrition, etc. CBN's news format and radio programs such as James Dobson's "Focus on the Family" do a good job in this area. We must seek to loose the message from the negative constraints of the medium and give a good presentation of the gospel.

A fourth guideline concerns the realm of politics. While all evangelicals have a responsibility to speak out on issues of importance such as abortion, protection of the family and moral values that cross into the political realm, we must be careful to keep those items separate from the task of evangelism. Evangelicals should exert pressure on politicians to reach desired goals, but we must be careful not to get too cozy with those who might manipulate us for their purposes. Those in broadcast ministry who are seeking to evangelize must help other evangelicals come to the front in the political fights. Those who evangelize must make themselves available to both Democrats and Republicans. With the expansion of Christian networks, programs can be developed that speak to issues directly, and this format would free others up to participate and focus on the task of evangelism. Dr. James Dobson has set the pace for this in a somewhat related fashion by the merger of his Focus on the Family organization with the Family Research Council headed by Gary Bauer in Washington, D.C. Its purpose is to provide a lobbying/research arm for the pro-family movement. A local chapter, directed by local people, will be established in each state to defend and advance the pro-family movement. Dr. Dobson hopes that this will free his time for more direct ministry to the family, and less direct and open involvement politically. I think that the stereotyping of evangelical ministers with the "New Right" has hurt our ability to evangelize all people. I realize that those who do broadcast feel the need to keep us informed, and for that we should be appreciative. But other routes to provide the same information should be explored. We must pray for those who live within this tension.

Finally, if true evangelism is going to take place, those involved in broadcast ministry are going to have to become more directly involved with the local churches. Affirmation XII in the Amsterdam Affirmations of 1983 states: "We are responsible to the church, and will endeavor always to conduct our ministries so as to build up the local body of believers and serve the church at large."[38] With the administrative skills and resources available to large broadcast ministries, a good network can be established for referral to and follow-up by local churches for those who inquire about the gospel or for those who need counseling. The broadcasters will find enough churches of like mind and faith to establish this network. We must remember, as Dr. Horsfield points out, that "under certain conditions a dramatic change may occur within a person's attitudes and behavior . . . ,"[39] but research shows that for the most part these changes do not continue apart from active involvement in a local group, i.e. the church. In local church terminology this is known as the "revolving door." People, if not plugged into meaningful groups, will come into the front door of the church and out the back. Such networking will involve trust and humility from all involved. If it could be implemented, it would also help to alleviate the criticism by some that televangelists are stealing funds away from the local church. Recent studies have confirmed that this criticism is not true.[40] Those in the local church, however, need to be reminded that this networking could only be a minor part of the church's outreach. Let us remember that the evidence shows that 85 percent of Christians say they came to Christ and the church primarily because of a friend, relative, or associate who loved and led them into the Kingdom. Only .01 percent said they attended church as a result of mass evangelism![41]

All of us most work together as evangelicals, where common ground can be found, to help people on their journeys to the cross and then into lives of maturing discipleship. Some of us must plant, others must water, and our great God will bring the increase. The mass media has a part to play in this process.

Endnotes

1. Jeffrey K. Hadden and Charles E. Swann, *Prime Time Preachers: The Rising Power of Televangelism* (Reading, MA: Addison-Wesley, 1981), p. 73.

2. Ibid., pp. 74-75.

3. Ibid., p. 81.

4. Ibid., pp. 77-78.

5. William F. Fore, *Television and Religion: The Shaping of Faith, Values, and Culture* (Minneapolis, MN: Augsburg Publishing House, 1987), p. 78.

6. Hadden and Swann, *Prime Time Preachers*, p. 78.

7. Ibid.

8. Fore, *Television and Religion*, pp. 78-79.

9. Peter G. Horsfield, *Religious Television: The American Experience* (New York: Longman, Inc., 1984), p. 3.

10. Hadden and Swann, *Prime Time Preachers*, p. 78.

11. Ibid., p. 80.

12. Razelle Frankl, *Televangelism: The Marketing of Popular Religion* (Carbondale and Edwardsville, IL: Southern Illinois University Press, 1987), p. 73.

13. Horsfield, *Religious Television*, p. 7.

14. Ibid., p. 53.

15. Ibid., p. 13.

16. Ibid., p. 15.

17. Ibid., p. 9.

18. Ibid., p. 10.

19. Richard N. Ostling, "Cleaning Up Their Act," *Time*, 15 Feb. 1988, p. 95.

20. Horsfield, *Religious Television*, p. x.

21. Frankl, *Televangelism*, p. 145.

22. Ibid., p. 3.

23. Stephen Winzenburg, "On Understanding TV Evangelists," *Broadcasting*, 18 July 1988, p. 25.

24. Horsfield, *Religious Television*, p. 109.

25. Frankl, *Televangelism*, pp. 18-19.

26. Ibid., p. 149.

27. Ibid.

28. Horsfield, *Religious Television*, p. 117.

29. Win Arn, "Is TV Appropriate for Mass Evangelism?" (A debate with Paul Crouch), *Christianity Today*, 16 Oct. 1987, p. 50.

30. Horsfield, *Religious Television*, p. 120.

31. Ibid., p. 33.

32. Ibid., p. 147.

33. Ibid., p. 60.

34. Billy Graham, *A Biblical Standard for Evangelists: A commentary on the fifteen Affirmations made by participants at the International Conference for Itinerant Evangelists in Amsterdam, the Netherlands—July 1983* (Minneapolis, MN: World Wide Publications, 1984), p. 73.

35. "The Media," *Broadcasting*, 8 Feb. 1988, p. 108.

36. Kenneth Kantzer, "Fine-tuning Televangelism," *Christianity Today*, 18 March 1988, p. 42.

37. Horsfield, *Religious Television*, p. 44.

38. Graham, *A Biblical Standard for Evangelists*, p. 103.

39. Horsfield, *Religious Television*, p. 136.

40. Ibid., p. 149.

41. Win Arn, "Is TV Appropriate for Mass Evangelism?," *Christianity Today*, 16 Oct. 1987, p. 50.

PART THREE:
Evangelism and Theological Issues

Any evangelism without a solid theological foundation is like a body without a skeleton. The body has
no structure and is a helpless, quivering mass.
Likewise, theology without evangelism is the body
without flesh and muscles. It is a structure only; it has
neither ability to move nor life flowing within it.
Perhaps one of the more positive trends in evangelism as we head into the twenty-first century is the
realization that theology and evangelism cannot be
divorced from one another. David Dockery addresses
some of the key theological tenets which must be
understood and communicated by bearers of the
good news. Edward C. Lyrene, Jr. cogently explains
that evangelism without prayer is a powerless evangelism. L. R. Bush III reminds us that the foundation
for our theology of evangelism is a firm commitment
to the authority of the Bible. Can apologetics be part
of the evangelistic task? L. Joseph Rosas III looks at
this issue from both a historical and contemporary
perspective. And Gerald L. Borchert offers a fascinating journey into the Gospel of John, where a
clear evangelistic summons is issued.

8

A THEOLOGICAL FOUNDATION
FOR EVANGELISM
David S. Dockery

*David S. Dockery is Associate Professor of New Testament Interpreta-
tion at the Southern Baptist Theological Seminary in Louisville, Kentucky. The author of numerous articles, chapters, and reviews, Dr.
Dockery previously served as a professor at Criswell Bible College,
where he was co-editor of the* Criswell Theological Review.

One of the common mistakes in our time is to think of evangelism more in terms of a method than a message. Such is the case with revivalists or evangelists who have suggested that evangelism can only take place when the "right words" are uttered or the "right prayer" is prayed by the professing respondent. Recently, this thinking has been taken so far as to suggest that evangelism can only take place when the "right music" is played or the right songs sung. What has been lost, or at least misplaced, is the recognition that beneath genuine evangelism must be a firm theological foundation. Evangelism is the proclamation of the good news in words, as well as the manifestation of this good news in deeds, with the purpose of reconciling men and women to God.

In this chapter we shall attempt to show the importance of theology for evangelism by examining some primary theological themes that undergird the gospel message. Prayerfully, a more theologically-oriented evangelism will strengthen the church and advance the cause of Christ. The primary themes we will examine include: 1) God as creator and the place of men and women in God's creation; 2) the fall of humanity into sin; 3) God's provision in Jesus Christ; and 4) God's salvation of men and women from their estranged, guilty, and dreadful plight.

The Place of Humankind in God's Creation

God has created us in his image and likeness (Gen. 1:27). At first this might appear to refer to our physical makeup, that we look like God. That, however, is not what the Bible means by the terms "image and likeness of God." Theologians have differed over whether image and likeness should be separate ideas. They have also differed over the meaning of these terms. It seems best, however, to think of these words as parallel synonyms.

Some have posited that the "image of God" is what enables humans to relate to one another, while others have suggested that it has more to do with personality, spirituality, or rationality. I would suggest that it is best not to choose one among these. Rather, men and women, because they were created in the image of God, have rationality, morality, spirituality, personality, and can relate to God and other humans, while rightly exercising dominion over the earth and the animals (Gen. 1:26-28; Psalm 8).

We must be cautious in our thinking, not to imagine the image of God as some aspect in men and women, but to see that humans are in the image of God. By this we mean that nothing in us or about us is separable, distinct, or discoverable as the divine image. Each person individually, and the entire race corporately, are the image of God, but no single aspect of human nature or behavior or thought pattern can be isolated as the image of God. Since they have been created in the image and likeness of God, men and women are the highest forms of God's earthly creation. All other aspects of creation are for the purposes of serving men and women and are thus anthropocentric. Yet humanity has been created to serve God and is thus theocentric.

The Fall into Sin

Even though men and women are created in God's image, the entrance of sin into the world has had great and negative influences upon God's creation, especially humans created in God's image. As a result of sin, the image of God was not lost (Gen. 9:6; James 3:9), but is severely tarnished and marred. The role of exercising dominion (Gen. 1:28) has been drastically disturbed by the effects of sin on humans and the course of nature. The ability to live in right relationship with God, with others, with nature, and with our very own selves has been corrupted, thus all attempts at righteousness are as filthy rags in God's sight (Isa. 64:6). All ultimately are spiritually dead and alienated from God (Eph. 2:1-3). They are therefore unable to reflect properly the divine image and likeness (Rom. 1:18-32).

It is necessary to see that the fall into sin (Gen. 3) was not just a moral lapse, but a deliberate turning away from God and rejection of him. The day that Adam and Eve disobeyed God they died spiritually, which ultimately brought physical death (Gen. 2:17). The consequences were many as Paul describes in Romans 1:18-32, 5:12-21, and Ephesians 2:1-11. Sin's entrance has brought about a sinful nature in all humanity. Therefore men and women are not simply sinners because they sin, but they sin because they are sinners. People thus act in accord with their natures. No one ever acts in a way that is contrary to his or her nature.

The idea is most significant when reflecting upon our relationship to God. Because of the entrance of sin into the world and our inheritance of Adam's sinful nature (Rom. 5:12-19), we are by nature hostile to God and estranged from him (Rom. 8:7; Eph. 2:1-3). We have wills that do not obey God, eyes that do not see, and ears that do not hear because spiritually we are dead to God.

While we function as free moral agents with a free will, our decisions and actions are always affected by sin. In day-to-day decisions, we have the ability to make free and rational choices, but these choices are always negatively influenced by our sin nature. In regard to our relationship with God, we do not genuinely repent or turn to God without divine enablement because we are by nature hostile to God.

Any proclamation of the Good News must understand the problem of sin. An awareness of the problem of sin helps to clarify frequently misunderstood concepts about the nature of sinful humanity. Our nature is depraved, but this does not mean we are as wicked as we can be. Rather, the idea of depravity refers to the fact that all aspects of our being are negatively impacted by sin. People still can and still do right and good things viewed by society, but these thoughts and actions, no matter how benevolent, are sinful if not done for the glory of God. We can affirm that people choose to do good, but not the ultimate good which is the goal of pleasing God and seeking his eternal glory. Thus depravity involves our total willful rejection of the will and glory of God.

We are therefore totally depraved, but we cannot say that we are totally corrupt. Other factors such as environment, emotional makeup, heritage, and of course the continuing effect of our having been created in God's image, influence the degree of corruption. Yet, all types of immoral actions, whether lying, murder, adultery, seeking after power, homosexuality, pride, or our failure to love one another, are related to our sinfulness, depravity, and alienation from God. The human hearts of all humanity are wicked, corrupt, and deceitful (Jer. 17:9). The degree of wickedness, corruption, and deceitfulness differs from individual to individual and culture to culture, but certainly some are more noble than others (Acts 17:11). Still, all in this world are estranged from God, but the biblical answer is that Jesus Christ has regained what was lost in Adam (Rom. 5:12-21). The grace of God has provided our restoration and brought about a right relationship with God, with one another, with nature, and with ourselves.

God's Provision in Jesus Christ

The gracious redemption that God provided came in the person of Jesus Christ. When we point to Jesus, we see the whole man Jesus and say that he is God. This man Jesus Christ does not only live through God and with God, he is himself God. The confession of the Christian Church has maintained Christ as one person having two natures, the one divine and the other human. This is the great mystery of godliness, God manifested in the flesh.

A. *The Humanity of Jesus*. Jesus' humanity is taken for granted in the synoptic Gospels, but in other parts of the New Testament it seems as if it might have been called into question or its significance neglected (1 John 1:1-2; 4:2-3). In Mark's gospel there is concentration on the humanity of Jesus as much as in any New Testament book. Matthew and Luke focus on Jesus' birth stories as aspects of his humanity including the temptation accounts. John pictures Jesus as the eternal Word who took on full humanity (John 1:1,14; 4:6,7; 11:33-35), a humanity similar to our own which could be seen. While he is a true man, his humanity must be viewed according to his uniqueness. He is a real man, yet sinless and different from other men (Rom. 8:3). His significance is not found through comparison alongside others but by contrasting his perfection with our imperfection (Heb. 2:9, 14-18; 5:7-8; 10:10). This uniqueness is especially seen in his miraculous birth and sinless life.

B. *The Deity of Jesus*. We must approach Jesus as a true man within the context of history, a man who actually said and did certain things. But we will not understand him even in that context until it is recognized that he is also God and that his deity provides meaning for his speech and actions. That was the experience of his disciples and others who encountered him while he was on the earth. As Emil Brunner commented, "Only when they understood him as this absolute Lord, to whom the full divine sovereignty belongs, did Easter as victory and Good Friday as saving fact become intelligible. Only when they knew Jesus as the present heavenly Lord did they know themselves to be sharers in the messianic kingdom as men of the new messianic era."

Paul, in Philippians 2:5-11, affirms that Jesus existed in the form of God from all eternity. This means that he possessed inwardly and demonstrated outwardly the very nature of God himself (Col. 1:15-16; 2:9). Also the opening verse of John's Gospel is a categorized affirmation of Jesus' full deity (John 1:1-2; 14:9; 17:5). Likewise, there are pictures of Jesus' deity in the unique "I Am" statements of John's gospel (John 6:35; 8:12; 10:7-9, 11-14; 11:25; 14:6; 15:1-5). Particularly do we see this in Jesus' statement about his eternal existence which comes during the confrontation with the Jews (John 8:58). Finally, we see Jesus receiving the worship of Thomas (John 20:28) in his confession, "My Lord and my God." These passages, along with others in the New Testament (e.g. Rom. 9:5; Titus 2:13; Heb. 1:1-8) cut across all lesser confessions of Christ's person, showing that any evangelistic proclamation that would make him merely a great teacher or a great prophet is most inadequate.

It was necessary that Christ should be both God and man. Only as man could Jesus be a redeemer for humanity; and only as a sinless man could he fittingly die for others. Yet it was only as God that his life, ministry, and redeeming death could have infinite value and satisfy the wrath of God, so as to deliver others from it.

Christ has a human nature, but he is not merely a human person. The person of Christ is the God-man, the second person of the Trinity. In the incarnation, Jesus did not change into a human person, nor adopt a human personage. He assumed a human nature in addition to his eternal divine nature. With the assumption of the human nature, he is a divine-human person possessing all the essential qualities of both the human and divine nature. This is a mystery beyond full comprehension. We must also confess that Jesus has both a divine and human consciousness, as well as a human and divine will, yet clearly a unity of person. It is always the same person, Jesus Christ the Lord.

C. *The Death of Jesus.* Jesus Christ's life and death exemplified divine love and exerted an influence for good and sacrifice. But more importantly, Christ's death provided for sinners a sinless substitutionary sacrifice which satisfied divine justice. This incomprehensibly valuable redemption delivered sinners from enslavement, and reconciled and restored sinners from estrangement to full fellowship and inheritance in the household of God. Although there are several models of the cross-work of Christ presented in the Bible, we shall concentrate primarily on the models of atonement, redemption, and reconciliation.

1. The idea of atonement is one of the primary models of the biblical idea of the saving work of Christ (Isa. 53:10; Rom. 3:25; 1 John 2:2; 4:10; Heb. 2:17). This understanding of Christ's work on the cross has reference to the effecting of satisfaction on God (propitiation), while effecting the same satisfaction on the guilt of human sin (expiation). Atonement can only be rightly understood in light of the holiness and justice of God—the severity of the reaction of God's holiness to sin. This concept affirms that God's holiness must be satisfied and the sins of humanity must be removed. Atonement is realized when God takes upon himself, in the person of Jesus, the sinfulness and guilt of humankind, so that his justice might be executed and the sins of men and women forgiven. It is mandatory to underscore this idea by affirming that God is moved to this self-sacrifice by his infinite compassion.

2. The idea of redemption is vitally related to the themes of liberation, deliverance, and ransom. Within this model, there is seen a struggle between the Kingdom of God and the hostile powers enslaving humankind. Redemption is the idea of bringing sinners out of such hostile bondage into authentic freedom (Col. 2:15). As redeemer, Jesus breaks the power of sin and creates a new and obedient heart by delivering us from the power of sin, guilt, death, and Satan, bringing about a people who have been bought with a price (1 Pet. 1:18).

3. The idea of reconciliation involves bringing fallen humanity out of alienation into a state of peace and harmony with God. Jesus, as reconciler, heals the separation and brokenness created by sin and restores communion between God and humankind. Reconciliation is not a process by which men and women become ever more acceptable to God, but an act by which we are delivered from estrangement to fellowship with God. Because of Christ's work on the cross, God has chosen to treat men and women in sin as children rather than transgressors (2 Cor. 5:18-20; Eph. 2:12-16; Col. 1:20-22).

Throughout church history Christian theologians have emphasized some or all of these ideas, including some and rejecting others. It is important to see that all of these ideas, as well as the theme of the example he provided for us (1 Pet. 2:21; 1 John 2:6) are necessary. Other religions have a martyr, but Jesus' death was that of a savior. As Christ took our place and died our death, he provided our salvation. By his obedient life, he fulfilled the law for us and by his death on the cross, he satisfied the demands of the law for us. The cross of Christ is the actual execution of justice on God's unrelaxed penalty revealed in the law (Gal. 3:10-13). This means that Christ suffered for our sins (2 Cor. 5:21). In Jesus, God's holy love is revealed, his holiness is completely satisfied, and his love is clearly demonstrated (1 John 4:10). As Martin Luther said, "This is the mystery of the riches of divine grace for sinners, for by a wonderful exchange our sins are not ours but Christ's and Christ's righteousness is not Christ's but ours." Thus, as P.T. Forsyth has so richly stated, "The work of Christ stands not simply for God's sorrow over sin, but for God's wrath on sin." Therefore, we cannot rightfully understand the cross unless we perceive both God's anguish over sin and his inviolable holiness that refuses to tolerate sin.

D. *The Resurrection and Exaltation of Jesus.* The resurrection is the core of the Christian message (1 Cor. 15:3-4) showing that the hope of the gospel is eschatological in nature (Luke 24:45-48; Acts 2:27, 35). The resurrection tells us that the God who raised Jesus from the dead exists. Also, it establishes Jesus' lordship and deity, as well as guaranteeing the justification of sinners which was accomplished at the cross (Rom. 1:3-4; 4:24-25; 5:9-10). On the other hand, it is a pledge of God's final judgment for those who reject Christ as Lord and Savior (Acts 17:31).

Following his resurrection, Christ ascended into heaven (Acts 1:9-11) where he is exalted at God's right hand (Heb. 1:3), a position of great honor. Having sat down, Christ demonstrated that his earthly work was completed. His position at God's right hand signifies his sharing in God's rule and dominion and the power and authority to which he is entitled. At God's right hand, Jesus exercises his priesthood interceding for his own (John 17; Rom. 8:34; Heb. 7:25). Here he serves as the defense advocate of his church (1 John 2:1) over which he is head (Eph. 1:20-21). From here, he will return to consummate God's redemptive plan. The Bible maintains that faith is the means by which we receive and appropriate the salvation purchased for us by the work of our Lord Jesus Christ (Gal. 2:16; Eph. 2:8-9). This brings us to the final section of this chapter.

God's Salvation of Men and Women

Grace and Faith. Salvation is a free gift of God, and it cannot be merited by our good behavior (Rom. 3:22-24). Grace declares that salvation is not the culmination of humanity's quest for God, but that it resides in the initiative of God toward men and women (Eph. 1:4-7). Even our faith by which we receive salvation is a gift of God (Eph. 2:8-9). As a matter of fact, all of life is such (James 1:17). If grace brings us to God, it also enables us to continue and complete our spiritual pilgrimage. This does not deny human involvement in salvation, but it does affirm the primacy of grace. When men and women receive the grace of God, it is a testimony to the impact of grace itself, but when grace is rejected, it is attributable to the hardness and sinfulness of the human heart.

Grace comes to us while we are still in our sins and brings spiritual transformation based on the accomplished work of Jesus Christ. Even the sanctifying work of the Spirit is enacted in those who do not merit or deserve it. In reality, as B. B. Warfield has so aptly summarized, grace is God's free and loving favor to the ill-deserving.

The degree of divine grace and human involvement has been debated throughout the centuries. There have been classic differences expressed between Augustine and Pelagius, Luther and Erasmus, and the followers of John Calvin and Jacob Arminius. This subject continues to be emotionally debated even in our time. We do not or cannot deny that people on occasion seek and ask for God's grace, but even the asking or seeking is the gift of grace. God does not graciously accept us because he sees our change for the better, as if conversion were the basis for receiving God's grace. Instead, the Bible pictures God coming into our lives, taking us just as we are because he is abundantly merciful (Eph. 2:1-10).

We maintain, with Donald Bloesch, that God is the sole source and mainspring of all gracious and redemptive action, but he is not the sole actor. God is the sole efficient cause of salvation, but not the only causal factor in salvation. There are also secondary and tertiary causes that have to be taken into account. Salvation is of God and is not based on the human response, yet men and women must respond to God's grace. Only persons who receive and are transformed by divine grace can make a favorable response to God's salvific invitation, but only those who do respond are indeed transformed by grace. Thus we affirm the priority of initiating grace without neglecting our responsibility to believe.

Far from violating our wills or personalities, God's grace appeals to our deepest yearnings and therefore, when we are exposed to grace, intrinsically we are drawn toward God. As A. W. Tozer has said, "salvation is from our side a choice, from the divine side it is a seizing upon, an apprehending, a conquest by the Most High

God. Our accepting and will are reactions rather than actions." Initiation always remains with God. We, therefore, affirm that in salvific grace, men and women are not merely passive. Neither do we wish to imply that God does some and we do the rest; but rather with Jonathan Edwards we conclude that God does all and we do all. God does not override the will, but releases the will for believing response. It is certain that convicting grace can be rejected (Matt. 23:37; Luke 7:30; Heb. 12:15). Yet, when we receive the gracious gift of regeneration our wills are turned in a completely new direction. When God extends his grace to us, he is the active agent, but he always extends grace through various means. The means of grace include the preached gospel, the written Word of God, the invitation to respond to grace, the prayers of other believers, and the faith of the respondent. Thus we see the imperative of evangelism, the necessity of proclamation and witness, and the need for responding faith.

This discussion leads to the importance of a further understanding of the meaning of faith. As noted above, the Bible maintains that faith is the means by which we receive and appropriate salvation. Faith includes a full commitment of the whole person to the Lord Jesus, a commitment that involves knowledge, trust, and obedience. Faith is not merely an intellectual assent or an emotional response, but a complete inward spiritual change confirmed to us by the Holy Spirit. Faith is altogether brought about by God, and it is altogether the human response bringing about complete submission to God and full liberation from the snare of sin.

The object of faith is not so much the teaching about Christ, but Christ himself. Though faith is more than doctrinal assent, it must include adherence to doctrine. In our belief in and commitment to Jesus Christ, we acknowledge him as Savior from sin and Lord of our lives, even Lord of creation (Rom. 10:9). True conversion definitely involves a belief in Christ's person as the God-man and in his work as Savior. We must remember, however, that it is possible to have an orthodox understanding of Christ without a living faith in him.

Conversion and Repentance. Conversion signifies our turning to Christ initiated by God. It is a great work of God's power changing the heart and infusing life into our dead spirits. It is very important to recognize that the response to the evangelistic message manifests itself differently in each person who experiences conversion. Not all have a "Damascus road experience" like the Apostle Paul. Some are converted quietly like Lydia and others dramatically like the Philippian jailer (Acts 16). But for all it involves a turning away from sin to righteousness and issues both in service to the world and separation, without withdrawal, from it.

The turning away from sin, renouncing sin, and changing our minds about sin and Christ is what we mean by repentance. It is not merely feeling sorry for ourselves, but the forsaking of sin. D. L. Moody was fond of saying that repentance is deeper than feeling; it is action. It is a turning right about, and God commands all people everywhere to turn.

True conversion does not just stimulate our natural abilities to do better, "to turn over a new leaf," rather it is the impartation of a new nature. Conversion must be differentiated from reformation of character; it is a radical, yet progressive, alteration of our very being. In our contemporary evangelism there is a tendency to confuse a person's emotional experience with true conversion. It is true that we must experience conversion, but conversion itself is not the same as the experience. It is not realized apart from experience, but it must be distinguished from experience. Genuine conversion transcends our experience, restoring in us the tarnished image of God as we are more and more transformed into the image of Christ (Rom. 8:29; 2 Cor. 3:18).

Salvation Metaphors. Briefly we must mention some of the important themes and metaphors or models that the Bible uses to picture our salvation. None of these concepts completely present the full understanding of salvation. We cannot in detail note all of these models, but will give attention to some of the more important elements.

1. *Regeneration* is a spiritual change by which the Holy Spirit imparts divine life. The idea is familiar in the writings of John, Peter, and Paul. It is certainly not without Old Testament precedent, but the classic presentation is found in John 3:3-8 (see also 1 Pet. 1:23; Titus 3:5-7). From John 3 comes the popular term "born again" which is better understood as "born from above," whereby God imparts righteousness to us. It is the experiential picture of our entrance into God's family whereby adoption refers to our position in this family.

2. *Adoption* is primarily a Pauline picture and like other elements of Paul's thought, it is a term with eschatological ramifications. It carries the idea of receiving the position of full grown children of God, adopted into God's family with all the corresponding rights, privileges, and duties (Rom. 8:15; Gal. 4:1-5; Eph. 1:5, 14-15). Adoption is not entirely a past event, for the consummation of our adoption awaits the redemption of our bodies (Rom. 8:23), something hoped for as well as something already possessed.

3. *Justification* is predominantly a Pauline concept, though it is found in other biblical writers, especially Luke. Justification is accomplished at the cross of Christ (Rom. 5:10), guaranteed by his resurrection (Rom. 4:24-25), and applied to us when we believe (Rom. 5:1). While regeneration pictures an experiential impartation of righteousness, justification is an eschatological declaration of our righteousness. Experientially we still sin, but God views us as totally righteous, clothed in the robes of our Lord Jesus Christ (Rom. 4:1-8). Because of Christ's sacrifice, God no longer counts our sins against us (2 Cor. 5:19-21). Justification is more than pardon; it is a granting of positive favor in God's sight.

In justifying men and women, God also justified himself. Sin challenged God's holiness, and by taking a position against sin and evil, God vindicated himself and is thereby both "just and the justifier" (Rom. 3:21-26). Justification reveals God as a God of holy love and merciful righteousness. Justification is declared by God, accomplished by Christ, received by faith, and evidenced by works.

4. *Sanctification* involves different aspects of our salvation and is in a sense an "umbrella" term. The Bible speaks of positional sanctification (1 Cor. 6:11), progressive sanctification (Rom. 6:14–7:25), and ultimate sanctification (1 John 3:1-3). It is the work of the Father (John 17:17), the Son (Gal. 2:20), and primarily of the Spirit (2 Cor. 3:17-18). Yet it is also a work of the believer (Rom. 12:1-2). The Bible does not teach a "letting go and letting God" approach to sanctification; rather we are to work out our salvation, striving after holiness. This is accomplished through the transforming means in our lives of Scripture (1 Pet. 2:2), prayer (Col. 4:2), fellowship and worship (Heb. 10:19-25), and the circumstances of life (Rom. 8:28-30).

5. The arrival at the state of absolute righteousness is our *glorification*. Justification is a declaration of righteousness, sanctification is the process of becoming more righteous, and glorification is the final consummation of our righteousness (Rom. 8:28-30).

6. The putting away of sin and its penalty is *forgiveness*. It includes a gracious forgetting (Eph. 4:32), a sending away of our sins (Matt. 26:28), and a putting aside or disregarding of all sin (Rom. 3:25-26). The Bible is the only religious book that emphasizes total and complete forgiveness (Heb. 10:17) as pictured in the account of the wayward son (Luke 15:11-32). Scripture presents the basis of forgiveness as the death of Christ (Heb. 9:22-26) and our faith and repentance (Luke 17:3-10).

7. Our *union with Christ* is the result of the concepts of adoption, forgiveness, and justification, and is pictured as the new sphere in which believers abide (John 15; Rom. 6:1-11; Eph. 1:3-14). Our union with Christ presents us in our new position before God. Experientially the union of believers with Christ is one of the most tender concepts expressed in Scripture. It is invisible and imperceptible to the senses and it is unfathomable, escaping all inward vision. Yet this mystical mystery (Col. 1:27-28) cannot be dissected or denied.

Eternal Security. God is the author and finisher of our faith (Heb. 12:2). Salvation is from sin and involves disarming believers from the rulers and authorities of this world (Col. 2:14-15). Salvation is only in Christ (John 14:6; Acts 4:12), is imperishable (1 Pet. 1:4), and is the source of all spiritual blessing (Eph. 1:3).

Our salvation is secured in Christ, and nothing can separate us from the love of Christ (Rom. 8:31-39). Our response to this truth brings assurance of our salvation. Eternal security is an objective truth, but our assurance of it is experiential and subjective. It is very important not to ground our assurance in an event or a decision. Assurance must be based on the work of Christ (Heb. 7:25), the witness of the Spirit (Rom. 8:14-17), and our obedience (1 John 5:11-13). We must simultaneously remember that God has promised to keep us from stumbling (Jude

24), having sealed us until the day of redemption (Eph. 4:30). Yet we must not neglect or ignore the many warnings that encourage us to persevere (John 15; Heb. 3, 6, 10) so as not to presume on God's gracious salvation. Thus we are responsible to persevere and hold on to God, but ultimately our security in Christ comes because he has a hold on us (John 10:27-30).

Conclusion

A more expanded theological foundation for evangelism also needs to discuss the corporate as well as the individual aspects of salvation. Most significant also are the reliability of Scripture, the ministry of the Holy Spirit, the ministry of angels, the doctrine of the church, our Lord's return, and, of course, a discussion of the trinitarian God. It is likewise extremely important to recognize that salvation has social as well as spiritual dimensions. This book and its space, however, limit our discussion.

We hope that it has become apparent that a firm theological foundation is important for faithful evangelistic proclamation. Pastors, theologians, evangelists, and lay people must work harder at closing the gap between theology and evangelism so that our theology is done for the church and our proclamation is grounded in biblical theology. Our evangelistic message need not include every aspect of our discussion, but a faithful evangelist will seek to be faithful to a firm theological foundation.

In summary, we affirm that our evangelistic proclamation is informed by the truth that God has created men and women in his image. Humans have sinned and are alienated from God apart from salvific grace. In grace, God takes the initiative in bringing sinners to Christ through the proclamation of the gospel message and the human response of faith. As a result of God's grace, believers experience salvation from sin which involves conversion to God. All of salvation is of God, yet we respond in faith and commitment. The Bible expresses these truths in various metaphors and underscores throughout that God is the author and finisher of our salvation.

We trustingly confess and affirm that Jesus Christ, as the God-man, has fully revealed God to men and women. Having lived a sinless life, Christ died in our place for our sins. He now sits exalted at God's right hand, a position of honor and exaltation, exercising his rule and dominion. We gladly acknowledge as Lord, our prophet, priest, and king who has completely revealed God, reconciled humankind with God, and who sits enthroned as ruler of God's kingdom and head of his Church. In him we place our trust and hope, offering our thanksgiving for the salvation he has provided for us.

9

PRAYER AND EVANGELISM
Edward C. Lyrene, Jr.

Edward C. Lyrene, Jr. is the pastor of Trinity Baptist Church in Foley, Alabama. Dr. Lyrene received his Ph.D. in evangelism while studying under Dr. Lewis Drummond. He has written extensively on the role of prayer in evangelism and spiritual awakenings.

The melancholy aspect of the times and the deplorable state of precious souls should much excite and quicken prayer. When things look discouraging, we should pray more, and then we should complain and fear less. . . . All that love Christ and souls, should show it by their earnest prayers to God.[1]

—Matthew Henry

If we are earnest about world evangelization, if we take the Great Commission seriously, an awakening is vital. It is going to take nothing less than a mighty surge of the Spirit to get the church going. If we have any hope of evangelizing our world in our generation, we must have revival.[2]

I have become absolutely convinced that lack of prayer is the only reason revival has not yet come in our day.[3]

—Lewis A. Drummond

There is something missing in the way many Christians carry out the task of evangelism. Somehow many have come to believe that in learning a few Scripture verses pertaining to the plan of salvation and by polishing their personal testimonies, they will be prepared to lead lost people to Christ.

There can be no question that Scripture truths concerning the gospel are absolutely essential in speaking with a person about the matter of his or her salvation, and that the influence of a personal testimony is of undeniable value. But there is something missing if we have not first approached the task of evangelism with prayer. The work of evangelism is a far greater undertaking than many Christians realize.

Evangelism is a spiritual work which requires spiritual resources. Prayer is the divinely ordained means by which these resources are made available to God's servants.

For too many, prayer is looked upon as a mere adjunct to the task of evangelism. We make our plans and then ask God to bless us. In a study course in evangelism, entitled *How to Witness,* the authors, Joe Ford and Robert M. Saul, point out:

> Prayer is the forgotten force in evangelism today. Few witness training courses devote major emphasis to the necessity of prayer for fruitfulness in witnessing. Yet, all evangelism must begin with prayer. Unless the role of prayer in evangelism is recaptured, the church will only plod along in a world racing swiftly toward hell. Prayer is our greatest need.[4]

Prayer should be the first order of business in the task of world evangelization. Whether it is mass evangelism or personal witnessing, prayer must precede our evangelistic efforts. Whether a Christian seeks to witness to his or her neighbor or plans to go as a missionary to a foreign country, he or she must be assured of the Spirit's power and presence. Prayer brings God and his resources into the work of winning the lost. Without the power of God nothing of eternal value can be accomplished in the work of the Kingdom. The gospel must be preached, and Christians must testify to the life-changing power of Christ, but the Spirit is the one who brings about the conviction necessary for salvation, and the Spirit is the one who brings about conversion.

In the work of evangelism the Spirit is the main object of our prayers.[5] After Jesus had given the Great Commission, he instructed his disciples, "Tarry in Jerusalem till ye be endued with power from on high" (Luke 24:47-49). Following his ascension the disciples gave themselves to prayer and praise for ten days prior to the coming of the Spirit. Not until the coming of the Spirit were the disciples ready for the great task of world evangelization. Even after the initial coming of the Spirit the Christians met regularly for prayer. We too need prayer in order that we may cooperate with the Spirit in winning the lost.

A good example of the priority of prayer in the work of evangelism is found in the ministry of Jesus. In the closing verses of the ninth chapter of Matthew's gospel, there is a summary of his ministry:

> And Jesus went about all the cities and villages, teaching in their synagogues, and preaching the gospel of the kingdom, and healing every sickness and every disease among the people. But when he saw

the multitudes, he was moved with compassion on them, because they fainted, and were scattered abroad, as sheep having no shepherd. Then saith he to his disciples, "The harvest truly is plenteous, but the laborers are few; Pray ye therefore the Lord of the harvest, that he will send forth laborers into his harvest" (Matt. 9:35-38).

In his earthly ministry Jesus was involved with the great task of introducing the Kingdom of God to the Jewish people (and to the world). He preached the gospel of the Kingdom to people who desperately needed to hear the good news of God's love. He taught the people the necessity of repentance and the importance of faith in him. He taught them many things about the Kingdom and how citizens of the Kingdom should live. He ministered in the power of the Spirit to those who needed the healing power of God for physical and spiritual afflictions.

Despite his great power, within the limits of his earthly ministry, Jesus was not able to meet the needs of the multitudes who were as helpless as sheep without a shepherd. Help was needed if the multitudes were to be reached.

The suggestion of Jesus for meeting the needs of the multitudes seems so simple that many may dismiss it as unrealistic and impractical. Nevertheless, it is noteworthy that Jesus did not suggest any of several possible human approaches to meeting the needs of the people: a recruitment campaign to enlist more disciples, a fund-raising effort to secure money for meeting the needs of the people, or a committee to study the matter. He simply turned to his disciples and asked them to pray that the Lord of the harvest would send forth laborers into his harvest. Jesus knew that prayer was the first action that the disciples must undertake in order that the multitudes could be reached. Apparently the disciples did heed the Lord's instructions and they experienced the joy of answered prayer. The disciples themselves became part of the answer to meeting the needs of the multitudes. They were the first workers that the Lord sent out to do the work of the Kingdom (Matt. 10:1ff).

Despite Jesus' teachings on prayer and the great things that come through faith, not many Christians are willing to undergo the discipline needed for a life of effective prayer. Probably not many consistently pray that God will raise up, equip, empower, and send out laborers for the harvest. It could very well be that the chronic shortage of committed Christian workers needed in almost all churches as well as on mission fields everywhere is due to the lack of earnest, consistent, and prevailing prayer. When Christians don't pray, the work suffers. Yet, some do pray, and God answers.

Through Prayer: God Calls People into His Work

Some years ago, when I was a student at Southwestern Seminary, a professor in one of the classes asked for a show of hands of the students who had been dedicated to the service of the Lord by their parents before they were born. To my amazement about 75 percent of the students in a fairly large class (about seventy students) raised their hands.

Thank God for Christian parents who are interested in reaching the world for Christ! God saves through the atoning blood of Christ. But he uses human instruments to bring the saving message of Christ to the multitudes of lost people. How does God send out the messengers? He does it in response to the prayers of his people.

Contrasts in the Effectiveness of Evangelism

Despite the call of God to many persons for full-time Christian work, the progress of evangelism languishes on the American scene. Affluent lifestyles, secularism, and liberal theology have had devastating effects upon the mainline Protestant denominations. Evangelical denominations who have been traditionally strong in evangelism and missions have witnessed a decline in growth.

As an example, the need of the power of God in the evangelistic efforts of the Southern Baptists, the world's largest Protestant denomination, is clearly revealed in the statistics for the year 1987. The convention's 37,000 churches reported a total of 338,495 people baptized. Of these, 175,000 were children reared in Southern Baptist churches. Another 50,000 came from other denominations, and 26,000 were "rebaptisms." Only 87,495 were converts from the unchurched population. That averages approximately two converts for each Southern Baptist church. It is clear that Southern Baptists, along with other evangelical Christians in North America, need to do some serious soul searching and praying regarding the impact they are making on the pagans of America.[6]

By way of contrast, evangelism is booming in South Korea. The Yoido Full Gospel Church of Seoul, Korea, pastored by Paul Y. Cho, is committed to revival and church growth until the Second Coming of Jesus Christ! In 1982, this church led 110,000 people to Christ. In 1983, they had a total of 120,000 converts. How is it possible that so many people could be reached by a single church? Pastor Cho's answer is, "We have seen the importance of developing and keeping a prayer life. If we stop praying, the revival will wane. If we continue praying, I believe that all Korea can be saved"[7]

It should be apparent that prayer is the channel through which God blesses the evangelistic efforts of the church. Without fervent and persistent prayer, God's work does not go forward and people are not saved. It is clear that the church in America must learn to pray. The need for prayer calls for an army of committed intercessors who will learn how to pray and who will persevere until God's blessings come.

Prayer Teaching Tools

In the mid-1970s, in an effort to undergird its ministry of putting Christian literature into every home in the world, the World Literature Crusade sponsored "Change the World" schools of prayer. Eight hours of helpful teaching on prayer and an excellent manual were provided.[8] At the end of the course, participants were given the opportunity to make a commitment to intercede daily for the cause of world evangelization. Follow-up was done by means of monthly cassette tapes containing prayer requests and additional teaching on prayer. This effort appealed to Christians of many denominations. It had many commendable features and was especially helpful in leading a person into a disciplined prayer life. Its chief deficiency was the lack of opportunity for group prayer with people of like vision and commitment.

Larry Lea, pastor of the rapidly growing Church on the Rock, in Rockwall, Texas, has an approach to prayer which follows the outline of the Lord's Prayer. Lea is attempting to enlist 100,000 prayer warriors to intercede for Kingdom concerns. Through prayer clinics, books on prayer, and teaching tapes, Lea has been effective in encouraging prayer. Prayers are being answered, as evidenced by the phenomenal growth of the Church on the Rock. Beginning with just thirteen members in 1980, the church had grown by 1987 to a membership of 11,000.[9]

Southern Baptists have a new teaching aid entitled *Prayer Life*. Coauthored by T. W. Hunt and Catherine Walker, *Prayer Life* promises to be an effective tool in teaching Christians the basic principles of prayer and encouraging a personal ministry of intercession. Of special interest to prayer and evangelism is a section entitled, "Praying for the Lost." Because many Christians do not know how to pray for the conversion of non-Christians these principles are listed as guidelines.

Principles of Intercessory Prayer for the Lost

The authors of *Prayer Life* suggest five steps in praying for the lost:

1. Cultivate a genuine concern and love for the lost.

2. Discover specific people in your concentric circles of relationship who are lost.

3. Pray appropriately and in detail for these specific persons:

—Lord, bring effective witnesses, including me, across their paths.

—Savior, arrange circumstances in their lives in such a way that the very details of their living will point them to Christ.

—Lord, send your Holy Spirit in great power to convict them of their sin and their lostness.

—Father, cause them to understand, through your Holy Spirit, that Jesus is adequate for their salvation from sin.

4. Persist in prayer.

5. Thank God for each step he takes in moving them to salvation.[10]

The Importance of Persistence in Prayer

Of all the lessons which an intercessor needs to learn, that of perseverance in prayer is one of the most important. The Bible has many examples of people who won significant victories through persevering prayer. Jacob (Gen. 32) and Elijah (1 Kings 17 and 18) were examples of men who prevailed in prayer. In the New Testament, Jesus' parable of the importunate widow and the unjust judge (Luke 18:1-8) and the parable of the man borrowing loaves at midnight (Luke 11:5-8) are encouragements to persevere in prayer. Paul Billheimer in *Destined for the Throne* suggested an explanation for the dynamic power of intercessory prayer for the lost: the persistent, faithful prayers of intercessors may so release the influence of the Spirit of God upon a sinner that he or she will find it easier to submit to God than to continue in rebellion.[11]

Lessons from Those Who Have Prayed

Many important lessons can be learned from those who have labored much in prayer and have experienced the fruits of prayer. The surprising thing about prayer is that the more a person prays, the more he or she wants to pray. There is great joy in seeing God answer specific prayers. There is also the deep satisfaction of fellowship with God and the knowledge that one is truly a laborer together with God in the work of the Kingdom. Church history is filled with numerous examples of people whose lives and ministries have been greatly blessed by God through persistent and believing prayer. The church is richer for having had these men and women of faith, courage, and vision. From the many who could be chosen, I have chosen three to consider—mainly because of their important contributions to the cause of evangelism.

Charles Finney. Much of the philosophy and many of the methods of contemporary evangelism stem from the thought and practice of Charles Finney. Beginning with his dramatic conversion in 1821, his long and fruitful ministry resulted in the conversion of thousands and influenced untold numbers of people. Finney, who has been called "the father of modern evangelism," spent most of his life and ministry in the context of revivals and spiritual awakenings.[12]

In his book, *Lectures on Revivals of Religion,* Finney stressed that true prayer prevails with God. In a lecture entitled, "Prevailing Prayer," he defined prevailing prayer as "prayer which obtains the blessing that it seeks. It is prayer that effectively moves God." The modern intercessor would do well to consider Finney's teachings for effective prayer. He gave several guidelines by which a person might prevail in prayer. These principles, tested in the fires of personal experience by this great man of God, are shared with the prayer that many today will experience the joy that comes from answered prayer and realize that a life of prayer and service for God is the highest possible life.

1. The person who prays must pray for a definite object. Finney was convinced that random prayer was totally ineffectual.

2. Prayer, to be effective, must be in accordance with the revealed will of God. A person's request must: 1) be in accord with promises or predictions in the Bible; 2) be in line with the providence of God; and 3) be subject to the Spirit's guidance.

3. Effective prayer requires absolute submission to the will of God.

4. Effective prayer seeks first of all the glory of God. The glory of God is the highest motive in intercessory prayer for the lost.

5. For prayer to be effectual, it must be by the intercession of the Spirit. Without the work of the Holy Spirit in prayer there is not the faith which is necessary for prevailing prayer.

6. Effective prayer is prayer which perseveres. Anxiety of mind and agony of desire concerning a situation or person leads to prevailing prayer. Without intense concentration, prayer will not be effective. Jacob's prayer before his reconciliation with Esau is an example of that type of prayer (Gen. 32:24-30).

7. For prayer to be effective, it needs to be offered in the name of Christ. Finney believed that to pray in faith in the name of Christ means that a Christian can prevail and receive "just as much as God's well-beloved Son would if he were to pray himself for the same things" (John 14:12-13).

8. In order to prevail in prayer a person must "renounce" all sins and intend to leave them forever. Finney demonstrated through Scripture the necessity of a pure conscience, heart, and life in effectively prevailing in prayer.

9. To pray effectively one must pray in faith expecting to receive the things asked for. There is no need to look for an answer to prayer if there is no expectation of obtaining it.[13]

John Hyde. John Hyde, known as "Praying Hyde," served as a Presbyterian missionary to India during the years 1892 to 1911. He was one of the founders of the Sialkot Convention in 1904. Under the leadership of Hyde, a small number of missionaries and students met together for prayer for revival. Out of this simple beginning a movement arose through which literally thousands were won to Christ. The Sialkot Convention met annually for prayer, praise, and serious soul-searching.

Out of the Sialkot Convention arose the Punjab Praise and Prayer Union. Anyone who wished to become a member had to sign a pledge in which five questions had to be answered affirmatively. These questions are presented here with the hope that the readers of this work will seriously consider them and meditate much upon the price which our Savior paid for our salvation:

1. "Are you praying for quickening in your own life, in the life of your fellow workers, and in the Church?"

2. "Are you longing for greater power of the Holy Spirit in your own life and work, and are you convicted that you cannot go on without this power?"

3. "Will you pray that you may not be ashamed of Jesus?"

4. "Do you believe that prayer is the great means for securing this spiritual awakening?"

5. "Will you set apart one half-hour each day as soon as possible to pray for this awakening, and are you willing to pray till the awakening comes?"[14]

At the 1908 convention, John Hyde began to pray that the Lord would save one soul a day through his prayer and witness. These converts had to be people who were willing to profess Jesus Christ publicly and who were willing to be baptized.

Asking such a great thing meant that Hyde had to do his part. It meant long journeys, spending whole nights in prayer, fasting, pain, and conflict. Yet victory came. God heard his prayers, and at the end of the year, four hundred people had been won to the Lord.

A picture of Hyde as a personal worker in evangelism is given by one of his friends in India.

> As a personal worker he would engage a man in a talk about his salvation. By and by he would have his hands on the man's shoulders, looking him very earnestly in the eye. Soon he would get the man on his knees, confessing his sins and seeking salvation.[15]

During the 1909 Convention John Hyde again prayed, this time asking God for two souls a day. That year eight hundred were won to Christ.

At the 1910 Convention, Hyde received the assurance that four souls a day would be won to the Lord. That year he was called to help in revivals and conferences in Calcutta, Bombay, and many of the larger cities in India. Prior to this Convention he spent much time in prayer. "One saw the long sleepless nights and weary days of watching with prayer written on every feature of his face."[16] If ever a day passed that four people were not won to the Lord, he would ask the Lord to show him what the obstacle was in him to this blessing. Invariably he found that it was the lack of praise in his life. He would immediately confess this sin and receive cleansing. As he praised God, souls would come to him, and the numbers would be made up.[17]

Billy Graham. No one would question that Billy Graham has been and continues to be the most influential evangelist in the twentieth century. No other person has preached the gospel face-to-face to so many—over 100 million. Over two million have made decisions for Christ through his preaching.[18] The ministries of the Billy Graham Evangelistic Association have influenced untold numbers throughout the world for many years. But Billy Graham would be the first to acknowledge that the success of his ministry is due to God's blessings which come through prayer. Every crusade, every meeting, every project, and every ministry is held up to God in prayer by faithful intercessors. The results are apparent: When people pray and seek God's blessings, God answers.

A Current Illustration: Pine Grove Baptist Church

No doubt many "ordinary Christians" are intimidated if not overwhelmed by the prayer lives of those whom most would acknowledge as spiritual athletes of Olympic stature. Yet we must realize that God is no respecter of persons (Acts 10:34), that all are encouraged to run the race (1 Cor. 9:24; Phil. 3:14; Heb. 12:1), and that in due season "we shall reap if we faint not" (Gal. 6:9b). Any Christian can make a significant impact upon his or her community if he or she will. Only God knows the influence of the faithful prayer warriors who approach his throne on behalf of the lost, day after day and week after week.

Consider the experience of Pastor Mike Bedford and the Pine Grove Baptist Church. Nestled in the piney woods on the outskirts of Bay Minette in southern Alabama, the Pine Grove Church has come alive in the Spirit. Unlike many churches which are stuck in dead traditions or troubled by unrest and division, Pine Grove has a sweet fellowship with a wonderful unity. When Brother Mike came to the church three years ago, one of the first things he asked for was a men's prayer meeting. The men decided to meet on Tuesday evenings. At this meeting the men asked God to provide for the general needs of the church as well as for the sick and lost. Though the attendance has varied, Brother Mike and the men have continued to pray. There have been times when the Spirit has come down in such power that there has been weeping and confessing of sin.

In addition to the Tuesday Evening Prayer Meeting, the men began to meet at 5:30 on Sunday afternoons for intercessory prayer for lost persons. From an original list on which were recorded the names of unsaved persons or people not in fellowship with the church, there have been seventeen specific answers. Nine have professed Christ, and eight have come back into the fellowship of the church. Many other people added later to the list have also made decisions for Christ. In September of 1988 the church had twenty-two decisions for Christ, including thirteen professions of faith. In every service there is an air of expectancy, and it is now believed that any lost person whose name is added to the prayer list is sooner or later going to be reached for Christ.

Until recently the church did not have an organized program of visitation. The secret of evangelistic efforts has been prayer. When Christians prevail in prayer, souls are saved and lives are changed. Why could this not happen in many churches, large and small, across America?

Missionary Evangelism

As Christians pray for the lost, they should not forget the broader vision of God for the lost around the world. It is estimated that ninety-seven of over 200 countries in the world, with a combined population of over three billion people, are virtually closed to conventional ways of spreading the gospel.[19] The only way to reach these people is through prayer. Christians must pray that God will open the doors to these nations so that these people may have opportunity to hear the gospel. Whether it is a closed heart and mind of an individual or a closed nation, the power of prayer reaches where we cannot go. Therefore we must pray!

Several years ago God laid it on the hearts of various Christians to pray for China. It seemed almost impossible that the doors of this great nation would ever be opened again to the gospel. But Christians prayed, and the doors began to open. President Nixon's ping-pong diplomacy with the Chinese leaders signaled a new openness in China's relations with the West. Along with this openness came increasing opportunities for renewed fellowship with Chinese Christians and for opportunities to share the gospel. God made this possible. God's people had a part in this through their persistent prayer.

Do we really want the lost to be saved? Do we want to see the multitudes reached with the gospel message? Our first responsibility is to pray that God will raise up the laborers who will labor in God's harvest fields!

Prayer is needed: For preachers! For evangelists! For teachers! For missionaries! For the money needed to send them! The need for workers and resources calls for faithful prayer warriors who will earnestly and persistently pray that the job might get done. Of those who pray, all will be quickened to do something about reaching the lost multitudes around them and some will be called into full-time service for the Lord.

Those who study history will discover that persevering prayer is behind every revival movement, every successful mission effort, and the salvation of every lost person. Somewhere, someone has "prayed the price" that people might be saved.

That is why we pray!

The Concert of Prayer

The role of Jonathan Edwards in the revivals of the First Great Awakening in America is well known. Many know him primarily for his famous sermon, "Sinners in the Hands of an Angry God." Yet his treatises on revival established him as the premier theologian of the First Great Awakening. After the initial excitement of the revivals had diminished, Edwards together with a number of evangelical Scottish ministers conceived and promoted a "Concert of Prayer" for worldwide revival. Edwards wrote a lengthy treatise supporting it, entitled *An Humble Attempt to Promote Explicit Agreement and Visible Union of God's People in Extraordinary Prayer for the Revival of Religion and Advancement of Christ's Kingdom on Earth.* The title itself sets forth the basic aim of the prayer movement.[20]

While the Concert of Prayer never really caught on to a great extent during Edwards's day, the idea was revived prior to the Second Great Awakening in America. This time the many prayer meetings were instrumental not only in promoting revival in North America, but were used of God to provide the spiritual impetus for the modern foreign mission movement.

British Baptists were at the forefront of missionary endeavor. Prior to the establishment of the British Baptist Foreign Mission Board, a concert of prayer was organized in 1784. John Sutcliffe read a copy of Edwards's book and issued a call to prayer. Eight years later, at the encouragement of William Carey, the "Particular Baptist Society for Propagating the Gospel Among the Heathen" was established.

In that renewed concert of prayer, John Sutcliffe in 1789 set forth his vision for the success of the prayer meetings:

> O for thousands upon thousands, divided into small bands in their respective cities, towns, villages, and neighborhoods, all met at the same time, and in pursuit of one end, offering up their united prayers, like so many ascending clouds of incense before the Most High! May He shower down blessings on all the scattered tribes of Zion![21]

A Modern Day Concert of Prayer

Considering the priority of the Kingdom of God, the prospect of eternity, the desperate situation of the lost, and the tremendous needs all around us, is it not time that Christians awake from their slumber and answer a call to pray?

David Bryant, a missions specialist with Inter-Varsity Christian Fellowship, is one of a growing number of Christian leaders who are calling for concerts of prayer in our day. He suggests that concerts of prayer should have a two-fold thrust. First, Christians should meet regularly to pray for awakening in the Church. He calls this prayer for "fullness." This term represents all that comes as individual Christians and churches rediscover the joy of the power and presence of God in their lives. Second, Christians should pray for "fulfillment," which is evangelism among the nations.[22]

Responding to the critical needs of our time, Keith Parks, President of the Southern Baptist Foreign Mission Board, has issued a call to prayer. This call to prayer is repeated here with the hope that the spirit of prayer will be poured out upon God's people and that many will come to comprehend the grand vision of a world under the lordship of Christ:

> Let's designate a Sunday every month as a day of prayer for global evangelization.
>
> Let's pray now that the world's untold billions may know Jesus.
>
> Let's pray in every class, in every gathering, in every worship service, in every home, that the gospel may be presented to all people before the year 2000.
>
> Let's pray for nations and national leaders. Let's pray for missionaries and for Christian witnesses who travel and work abroad.
>
> We call on every Christian and every Christian church to join in this new concert in prayer as we keep the world in view—from our knees!

Can We Do It? Will We Do It?

The first foreign mission board in the United States was the American Board of Commissioners for Foreign Missions. It was founded at the insistence of some young college students who caught a great vision for foreign missions.

The leader of the group was Samuel J. Mills, Jr. He was converted in a revival meeting in 1798 in his father's parish in Torringford, Connecticut. While he was a student at Williams College, his spirit was drawn to missions in a powerful way. His thoughts, prayers, and conversations were constantly taken up with thoughts of missions to the heathen.

One day in late August of 1806, he led a group of students to a meadow near the college where by the side of a haystack they devoted the day to prayer, fasting, and conversations which were constantly taken up with thoughts of missions to the heathen. A driving thunderstorm came up and Mills and his companions took refuge from the storm on the lee side of the haystack. After the storm was over and the skies had cleared, a proposal was made to send the gospel to the heathen. Some of the group was reluctant. Others were hesitant, but Mills pronounced the decisive word, *"We can do it if we will!"*

Will we complete the Great Commission in our day?

—Many laborers are needed. Expenses will be great.

—But we have the life-saving message.

—The power must come from God. The power of the Holy Spirit!

—But it starts with prayer.

Will we undertake this great enterprise?

We can do it if we will!

Endnotes

1. Matthew Henry, Matthew to John, Vol. 5 of *Matthew Henry's Commentary on the Whole Bible* (New York: Fleming H. Revell, n.d.), p. 129.

2. Lewis A. Drummond, *The Awakening That Must Come* (Nashville, TN: Broadman Press, 1978), p. 65.

3. Ibid., p. 120.

4. Joe Ford and Robert M. Saul, Member's Booklet from Equipping Center Module: *How to Witness* (Nashville, TN: Sunday School Board of the Southern Baptist Convention, 1979), p. 56.

5. See John 16:7-11 and Luke 11:9-13.

6. "Revived Again: Students Challenged to 'Cast Nets,'" *Southwestern News*, November 1988, 8. Citing these statistics during Fall revival services at Southwestern Baptist Theological Seminary in Fort Worth, Texas, Ed Young, pastor of Second Baptist Church of Houston, Texas, asserted that "never in their history have Southern Baptists done so little with so much" to reach the lost.

7. Paul Y. Cho, *Prayer: Key to Revival* (Waco, TX: Word Books, 1984), p. 20.

8. Dick Eastman, *Change the World School of Prayer* (Studio City, CA: World Literature Crusade, 1976).

9. Larry Lea, *Could You Not Tarry One Hour?* (Altamonte Springs, FL: Creation House, 1987), book cover.

10. T. W. Hunt and Catherine Walker, *Prayer Life: Walking in Fellowship with God* (Nashville, TN: Sunday School Board of the Southern Baptist Convention, 1987), pp. 183-84.

11. Paul E. Billheimer, *Destined for the Throne* (Fort Washington, PA: Christian Literature Crusade, 1975), pp. 17, 63-64.

12. See the excellent biography of Finney by Lewis A. Drummond, *Charles Grandison Finney and the Birth of Modern Evangelism* (London: Hodder and Stoughton, 1983), p. 11.

13. See Finney's lecture on "Prevailing Prayer" in Charles G. Finney, *Lectures on Revivals of Religion* (New York: Fleming H. Revell, 1988), pp. 49f. Finney's works are available today from various Christian book publishers.

14. E. G. Carre, ed., *Praying Hyde* (South Plainfield, NJ: Bridge Publishing, n.d.), p. 11.

15. Ibid., p. 33.

16. Ibid., pp. 37-38.

17. Ibid., p. 39.

18. Kenneth S. Kantzer, "The Evangelist of Our Time," *Christianity Today*, 32, November 18, 1988, p. 14.

19. "Dick Eastman Heads United Effort for World Evangelism by Year 2000," *Every Home*, Vol. 2, No. 10, 1988, p. 1. *Every Home* is a publication of Every Home for Christ, World Literature Crusade.

20. This treatise can be found in its entirety with a historical introduction in Stephen Stein, ed., "Apocalyptic Writings," Vol. 5 of *The Works of Jonathan Edwards* (New Haven, CT: Yale University Press, 1977). An evangelical analysis of this treatise may be found in

Edward Charles Lyrene, Jr., *The Role of Prayer in American Revival Movements, 1740-1860* (Ph.D. dissertation, Southern Baptist Theological Seminary, 1985).

21. David Austin, *The Millennium* (Elizabethtown, NJ: Shepard Kollock, 1794), p. iv. John Sutcliffe was the pastor of the church which William Carey joined after his baptism. He also helped to ordain Carey. The Concert of Prayer and the concern for the advance of God's kingdom undoubtedly influenced Carey and produced a favorable climate for the rise of the mission societies.

22. David Bryant, *With Concerts of Prayer* (Ventura, CA: Regal Books, 1984), pp. 41, 45, 185-94.

10

EVANGELISM AND BIBLICAL AUTHORITY
L. R. Bush III

L. R. Bush III is the academic vice president and dean of the faculty at Southeastern Baptist Theological Seminary, serving under its president, Lewis A. Drummond. For several years, Dr. Bush was associate professor of philosophy of religion at Southwestern Baptist Theological Seminary. Among his many writings is a history of the Baptists' beliefs about the Bible, Baptists and the Bible, *co-authored with Tom J. Nettles.*

Biblical prophets often said, "The Word of the Lord came unto me . . ." Unfortunately they do not always give much of a description of the process by which that happened.

Scripture says that God appeared to Moses in a rather explicit way (cf. Exod. 33:11). Isaiah had a direct vision of the personal presence of God (Isa. 6) as did Daniel (Dan. 7:9-14) and a few others (cf. Gen. 28:12-13; Ezek. 1:26-28; Rev. 4-5). But there is no indication that all biblical writers had experiences in which God manifested his personal presence to them. Often we have no description of the manner in which God revealed himself to the prophets (cf. Joel 1:1).

Divine Revelation

Communication (in whatever manner by whatever means) between God and his prophets is known as divine revelation.[1] Such communication may be a factual message, an insight, a historical event, an interpretation of that event, a moral standard, a prophecy of future events or of future divine actions, or any number of other matters that the sovereign God may choose to reveal to his prophet (cf. Amos 3:7).

At times this communication was direct and verbal. For example, God spoke to Moses out of the burning bush (Exod. 3–4). One night he called young Samuel so distinctly that Samuel thought it was the voice of Eli (1 Sam. 3). Apparently God spoke directly to Noah (giving him specific dimensions and instructions for the ark, Gen. 6). He spoke to Isaiah about the rejection his (Isaiah's) preaching would receive (Isa. 6:9ff).

At other times God communicated indirectly through angelic messengers. Abraham spoke with a "man" whom he called "Lord." Many interpret this to have been a pre-incarnate appearance of Christ, while others think it was an angelic messenger speaking on behalf of God. In either case, the message was delivered verbally because Sarah overheard the conversation and laughed (Gen. 18). Scripture is not always ambiguous about the identity of the messenger, however. The angel Gabriel delivered God's message to Daniel (Dan. 9:21) and he also delivered a message to Zechariah (the father of John the Baptist, Luke 1:19). The "Angel of the Lord" came and sat down under the oak in Ophrah in order to speak to Gideon (Judg. 6:11).

Thus we see that the means of divine revelation is, at times, clearly made known by the writer of the biblical material. Nevertheless we often have no such description and thus no direct knowledge of the process (or processes) involved in divine revelation.[2]

Biblical Inspiration

If revelation is the communication from God to the prophet, inspiration is the work of God's Spirit that guarantees the accurate recording of the content of the divine revelation and the truthful description of the circumstances in which it came. Thus inspiration completes the purpose of divine revelation by getting God's message accurately delivered from the prophet to the people.

Inspiration applies also to the written expressions of worship in the Psalms. Praise in response to the revealed goodness of God's creation or to his revealed providence, songs of repentance or of thanksgiving, or even the collection of proverbial wisdom can be elicited under the inspiration of God's Spirit just as well as the ethical and political preaching of God's prophets can.

Inspiration also refers to the teaching ministry of the Spirit (John 16:13-15). Inspiration is a personal relationship between the Holy Spirit and the biblical writer. It functions in a multitude of intimately spiritual ways. It is never impersonal or mechanical, even in cases when the focus is primarily fact gathering.

Inspiration is as mysterious and as multi-faceted as is divine revelation itself. In every case, however, inspiration refers to the spiritually-guided process of writing out the message God wanted communicated to his people through the Bible. Inspiration produced Scripture.[3]

Human Authors

Those who wrote the biblical text were not supernatural beings. They spoke normal language. They had normal knowledge. They worked, loved, lived, sinned, worshiped, failed, and made mistakes as do all humans.

They lived in particular cultures, in certain geographical locations, had friends, went to visit their grandchildren, and did all the other things that normal people do. They spoke (and wrote) with figures of speech and idioms just as their original hearers did. Their writing style was uniquely theirs.

But because they were willing servants or because of certain qualifications they had, or perhaps for reasons known only to God, reasons of his sovereign will, God chose to give them a message and a commission to communicate that message to others. God's Holy Spirit then guided them and enabled them to accomplish God's purpose.

Biblical Infallibility

There is no evidence that God accomplishes his revelational purpose through error or accident. Revelation comes through truth and providence. Truth is an essential element of God's nature, for he is the only ultimate by which truth could ever be measured.

His Scripture-writing prophets and apostles were not inherently infallible nor always truthful in their personal lives. They were sinful people in need of redemption, just like we are. But as they wrote Holy Scripture, delivering the message God had placed in their hearts and minds to be delivered, God spiritually guarded them from both deliberate lies and unintentional errors.

If this were not so, then we who look to God for his guiding word of truth would not be able to find it simply by turning to Scripture as such. We might still look to Scripture as a source of traditional teachings, but we would be left to our own rational abilities to discover the truth itself. Only the intellectually gifted, however, could ever hope to sift out all of the truth and thereby recognize all of the "human errors" in the Bible. It is naively optimistic to think that even they could do it.

the bible was written in and comes to us from the ancient Middle-eastern world. the masses of ordinary people today surely could never hope to have the academic expertise to recognize in the ancient thought forms all possible human errors that the writers could have made and thus, by a process of elimination, locate and come to know the sum total of revealed truth. Moreover, the truth we seek is about matters as important as the will of God for our lives or teachings that concern our eternal destiny. Thus if Scripture were not protected from fallibility and error, God would have failed in his basic purpose of revealing these truths to his people generally.

Truth cannot be finally located in the individual human mind. Truth is located in the character of God. Unfortunately even the superior human intelligence standing alone may fail. Only God and his Word may be properly regarded as infallible. Truth may be known by men, but truth is established by God alone.

Though weak and liable to err as humans, the biblical writers were guided by God's Spirit as they conveyed the content and the context of God's revelation. Scripture itself was providentially produced (2 Pet. 1:20-21). What Scripture says is what God intended for it to say (cf. 1 Thess. 2:13; Ps. 119:89). The literary genre, the vocabulary, and the style were as human as the many human authors, but the teaching, the message, the information conveyed ultimately had God as its author, and thus truthfulness as an essential quality (cf. 1 John 5:6).

In this way, God's revelation was not lost or dissipated in the life of the prophet or the apostle (Isa. 40:8). Rather it was inscripturated and thus marvelously preserved for us (1 Kings 8:56). It is only God and his Word that is by definition inerrant (Ezek. 12:25). God speaks only the truth for he is true (1 John 5:20).

The Blessing of God upon Biblical Faith

Our foundational assumption, then, remains. Scripture is assuredly truthful. We can trust it to reveal God himself to us. We appropriately build our doctrine from it. We do not deny that some parts are hard to understand (cf. 2 Pet. 3:16), and we do not claim to have solved every problem. Evangelicals do not claim omniscience nor infallibility for themselves or for their interpretations. Only God has those characteristics, and thus we expect God's Word to manifest nothing else but truthfulness.

Church history records the common faith in the utter truthfulness of the Bible by almost every theologian of note until relatively modern times.[4] I have done extensive research in the writings of Baptist theologians, pastors, and missionaries.[5] Their defense of biblical truthfulness has been pervasive and persuasive. Scripture, they claim, has truth, without any mixture of error, for its matter, because its author ultimately is God.

Those pastors and church leaders who have been blessed with unusual evangelistic success have almost always been quick to affirm their complete trust in the total truthfulness of the Holy Scripture. Such belief does not guarantee evangelistic success (the belief is not a pragmatic tool with which to manipulate God's favor), but it is notable that God has so often chosen to bless those who do believe the doctrine of biblical inerrancy. Is God not saying something to the Christian community by bestowing this most significant manifestation of his grace on those pastors and churches that unequivocally trust and obey his revealed Word, the Bible?

Why Evangelism Depends upon Divine Revelation

Evangelism is the sharing of the "Good News" about Christ with others. We testify that Jesus is the Christ (the Messiah of the Hebrew Old Testament), the true and unique Son of God. Moreover, we say that by coming to believe and by continuing to believe that Jesus is who we testify that he is, and by believing that he died for our sins and rose from the grave the third day according to the Scriptures, we can, are, and will be saved from everlasting punishment. In what way does biblical authority impact this testimony?

1) The whole premise of evangelism is that the biblical story about Jesus is true, that he is who the New Testament writers claim that he is. If the New Testament is not by inspiration guaranteed to be fully truthful but in fact is fallible, then it may be that Jesus was not the unique Son of God. Then it would make sense to ask whether or not he always told the truth (or whether he ever said any of the things the New Testament reports him as saying), and one's answer to this question would lie in subjective opinion based on personal experiences.[6] Epistemologically speaking, "opinion" is a notoriously poor source of assured knowledge.

2) "You must be born again" clearly requires a change (a new beginning). For Jews, "birth" was a divine gift, a blessing from God, an act of beneficent providence. The New Testament calls for this new start in everyone's life and makes it a requirement. It is such a drastic requirement that one would dare not proclaim its necessity unless (fully truthful) Scripture taught it. Modern psychologists may counsel patients to "try to turn over a new leaf and pick up the pieces and try again," but never would they say "you need to die and be born all over again if you ever expect to have any hope of success." Modern counsel does not tell us that the problem is inherent within us. the "problem" is always external circumstances and pressures that make us the way we are. Scripture teaches the necessity of the new birth, however.

3) It should be clear that, technically speaking, Christianity does not depend upon an inerrant Bible. Christ could still be the Son of God even if Scripture were to say that he were not the Son of God. But to have such a contradiction between who Christ actually was and who Christ's disciples wrote that they thought he was, would mean either that he did not teach them very well, or that they seriously misunderstood him, or that they lied about him and about his teachings about truth. In either case one would hardly want to be depending upon their testimony in matters of eternal destiny. If, however, they are inspired by God and thus write with divine authority, it is correct to believe them and to obey our Lord's Great Commission which they report.

4) In America one cannot legally enter and search someone's house without a legal warrant. Neither should one enter the mind and heart of another person without a sound basis for doing so; nor should one expect that they repent, change

their ultimate commitments, and put their faith exclusively in Jesus. We make such demands only on the premise that we are under obligation to do so because God, the creator of law and the creator of a person's heart and mind, has taught us to do this in his Word.

5) The basic truths on which evangelism is based are not intuitive but are counter-intuitive, and thus they must find their basis in objective truth. For example, we would intuitively think that there should be many ways to reach God, that good works could contribute to our salvation, and that Christ's death serves primarily as a moral influence upon us to teach us to be self-sacrificing in our love for others. But these intuitive principles do not motivate evangelists and do not lead people to repentance and faith. Biblical principles do.

How Scripture Supports Evangelism

Matthew begins with the genealogy of Jesus, tracing his ancestors through King David back to Abraham (1:1). Thus Matthew begins with the original "Jew," the patriarch of the nation of Israel. Jesus then is the Jewish messiah fulfilling Jewish law and prophecy. But Matthew ends with the Lord's Great Commission (28:19-20) commanding his followers to make disciples of all nations, not just Israel.

Mark (in vs. 1) tells us that he is writing a "gospel" about Jesus Christ (i.e., he is proclaiming the good news that Jesus is the promised messiah). He ends his book (16:20) telling us that the disciples went out and preached everywhere about Jesus.[7]

Luke is concerned to give a full account of this "synoptic" tradition so that Theophilus could know the certainty of the things he had been taught about Christ. Luke traces the Lord's genealogy back to God's creation of Adam (3:38), and he ends his account with the Lord's reminder to his disciples that they are witnesses of the truth that must be preached (24:45-49).

John identifies Jesus as the incarnate, creative Word of God who brings grace and truth and makes the Father known to us. His gospel ends (20:28-31) with the affirmation of Thomas (that Jesus is both Lord and God), and the promise that such belief will bring salvation and life.

Acts traces the evangelistic progress and success of the early church. In the end (28:31) we find Paul boldly and without hindrance preaching the kingdom of God and teaching about Jesus Christ.

Romans sets out "gospel theology" in its most comprehensive setting. Paul has a sense of obligation about his preaching of this gospel. He affirms that it is the power of God for salvation, and thus he is not ashamed of it (1:14-16).

First and Second Corinthians deal with a "problem church," but even there Paul is quick to affirm that his success was not due to his eloquence or special intelligence, but was due to God's power (1 Cor. 2:1-5). His message, of course, concerns Jesus Christ the crucified one. the ministry of the gospel is described as a treasure that we have been given (2 Cor. 4:1,3,7).

To the Galatians Paul writes in astonishment that they had so quickly turned to a false gospel, and he warns them in the strongest terms to remain orthodox (1:6-9). To the Ephesians he writes of our having been chosen in Christ before creation itself (1:3-14). Paul offers thanks to God that the Philippians have been such important partners in the gospel ministry (1:3-6), and that the Colossians have faith, love, and hope through the gospel which is producing fruit worldwide (1:3-6).

Paul wrote to the Thessalonians about the gospel coming to them in the power of the Spirit, not in words alone (1 Thess. 1:5), and about the perseverance of their faith through persecutions and trials (2 Thess. 1:4). To Timothy Paul urged sound doctrine that conforms to the glorious gospel of the blessed God (1 Tim. 1:10-11), and the memory of Jesus Christ raised from the dead, Paul's gospel (2 Tim. 2:8). The reason Paul left Titus on Crete was for him to appoint elders who could encourage others by sound doctrine (Titus 1:5-9). Even Philemon is remembered in prayer because of his faith in the Lord Jesus (vs. 4-5).

The writer of Hebrews urges us through Jesus to offer to God a sacrifice of praise — the fruit of lips that confess his name (13-15). James is quite aware of the crucial importance of turning a sinner from his or her error (5:20).

As a consequence of God's great mercy, Peter tells us that we have been given a new birth into a living hope through the resurrection of Jesus Christ from the dead (1 Pet. 1:3). His divine power has given us great and precious promises (2 Pet. 1:3-4). John's message is that God is light, and the blood of Jesus purifies us from sin (1 John. 1:5-7). Antichrists may come, but we are to have nothing to do with them (2 John 7-11). Christians are to work together for the truth (3 John 8). Jude tells us that we may at times need to contend for the faith that has been entrusted to us (Jude 3).

No one can miss the evangelistic theme of the book of Revelation. It is Christ who has freed us from our sins (1:5), and it is he who is coming with clouds (1:7) to reign (11:15). The invitation is clear (22:17). Come to Christ. He will save. Behold, he is coming soon!

Summary

Our doctrine of Scripture is not arbitrary but is drawn from the Bible's own documented content. We claim no more than Scripture itself claims: that the teachings of the Bible are the teachings of God to his people, and that these teachings have been revealed to and recorded by divinely inspired authors. Inscripturated truth is the result of this providential work of God, and the blessing of God is associated with belief in his Word.

The only valid basis for sharing the gospel with others is the fact that it is true, and that Jesus really is who the New Testament says that he is, the Messiah (Christ), the unique Son of God. If the gospel is not God's command that we repent and believe in Jesus as the risen Lord, then we are acting presumptuously and arrogantly when we witness and evangelize. We are not, however, basing our "Good News" on our subjective opinion of what people should think and do but rather on what we are presented with in the text of fully truthful Scripture.

It is the common testimony of the New Testament that the resurrection of Jesus the crucified one is a historical reality and is the sole basis upon which gospel testimony is based. Thus evangelism is nothing other than the application of New Testament teachings. the authority that lies behind the authority of Scripture is the authority of Christ himself (Matt. 28:18). Authentic evangelism is a divine mandate mediated to us through the teachings of the Bible. Thus the invitation we offer is not ours. It is his.[8]

Endnotes

1. The doctrine of divine revelation is very carefully treated by many evangelical theologians. I would urge an interested, beginning student to study Leon Morris, *I Believe in Revelation* (Grand Rapids: William B. Eerdmans Publishing Co., 1976).

2. Based on the references we do have (a few of which are mentioned in the preceding paragraphs), we can surely assume that God could and did use whatever means were necessary in order to guarantee that his message was adequately communicated to these prophetic spokesmen. This communication, as even our brief survey shows, was not necessarily done through ecstatic experiences or even through mystical or meditative procedures. In 1 Samuel 3, little Samuel assumed that Eli was calling him. He did not discover God through ecstasy. God simply initiated a relationship unexpectedly (though Samuel's circumstances had undoubtedly prepared him for such a relationship). Samuel experienced what at first he took to be an ordinary communication from an ordinary man. We have no other example, however, exactly like that (though cf. Genesis 32:24-30; John 9:35-38; Acts 9:5-7; and other places where apparently the truth was not fully realized at first). The means of divine revelation, then, seem to have varied from case to case.

3. We know even less of the actual process involved in inspiration than we do of the process of revelation. God once wrote the Ten Commandments himself (Exodus 31:18), but that was hardly typical of the Scripture-writing process. Normally those who knew God's mind (because God had made his thoughts known to them) wrote down that which God wanted us to know.

Because God revealed himself in events and in historical circumstances as well as in direct verbal messages, the writing of biblical history was as important as the writing of the covenant laws. The same principle applies to the New Testament. What Jesus did was as important as what Jesus said (though even with several accounts we do not have an exhaustive report, cf. John 21:25).

Like all history, biblical history is selective. It is a thematic history in which the relationship between God and man is the main theme. God's kingdom is of central interest. The promise and fulfillment of messianic prophecy is a connecting thread. Sin and salvation, rebellion and redemption, agony and atonement provide the dramatic contrasts that move us toward the heart of reality.

4. For extensive primary source documentation (in contrast to the less reliable work offered by Jack Rogers and Donald McKim) see John D. Woodbridge, *Biblical Authority* (Grand Rapids: Zondervan, 1983).

5. See L. Russ Bush and Tom J. Nettles, *Baptists and the Bible* (Chicago: Moody, 1980). All of the references found in the main body of this book are from primary source materials. Our goal was to provide an objective scholarly reference work drawn from Baptist writers from the seventeenth century until the modern day. In my mind, the historic position of mainstream Baptists is not in doubt. Affirmations of the total truthfulness of the authentic canonical text of the sixty-six books of the Old and the New Testaments are as characteristic of Baptist theology as are affirmations of believer's baptism.

6. Critical scholars may claim that their negative conclusions are based upon evidence and human reason. Whether or not Jesus existed or said what the New Testament claims that he said, however, is a historical matter. The New Testament is the authenticated documentary evidence, and thus scholarly denials of biblical claims are themselves "rational" rejections of the available evidence. It is difficult in principle to see how human reason can determine the non-facticity of historical matters in the absence of alternative, substantiated claims from equally authentic documentary sources. Such sources are not readily obvious, and thus I claim that denials of biblical claims about Christ remain in the realm of subjective opinion, and that the negative critic should at the very least consider Pascal's Wager.

7. For those who do not accept the longer ending, 16:6-7 imply the same thing.

8. Portions of this essay were originally printed in L. Russ Bush, *Understanding Biblical Inerrancy* (Fort Worth: Columbia Publications, 1988), used here with permission.

11

EVANGELISM AND APOLOGETICS
L. Joseph Rosas III

*L. Joseph Rosas III is the pastor of the First Baptist church of Fisher-
ville, Kentucky. He recently earned a Ph.D. in Christian Philosophy at
the Southern Baptist Theological Seminary, where he also took evangelism seminars under Dr. Lewis Drummond. Dr. Rosas has written
recent articles on sanctification and on Edward John Carnell.*

Evangelism is one of the major perennial tasks of the Christian community—nearly all evangelicals would agree in that. There exists, however, a wider variety of
opinions on the need, value, and desirability of an apologetic strategy in presenting and commending the gospel to the world. Some have even repudiated
apologetics as destructive to authentic Christian faith.

The Nature of Apologetics

The average Christian may not even understand the meaning of the term
apologetics. One could conjure up the image of a half-hearted or even an embar-
rassed (i.e., "apologetic") presentation of the gospel. Many Christians will never
encounter formal philosophical skepticism. But all Christians hear questions like:
"Why did my baby die?" or "Why is life so difficult?" or "What is the purpose of
life?" or "Is God real?" Peter encouraged believers to "be ready to give an answer
to every man that asketh you a reason of the hope that is in you with meekness and
fear. . . ." (1 Pet. 3:15).

The etymology of the concept "to give an answer" is traced to the ancient
Greek legal system.[1] In ancient Athens the plaintiff would bring an accusation
(*kategoria*) before the court. The accused had the right of making a reply
(*apologia*) to the accusation. The reply sought to show the falsity of the accusation; hence the accused attempted to "speak off" the charge. This gives the

derivation in the verb *apologesthai* "to give an answer, legally to defend one's self"; and the noun *apologia*, "the answer given, the defense made"; and *apologetikos* which refers to the art of making one's reply or giving an answer.

Thus, there is a distinction between an apology and apologetics. An apology refers to a specific defense whereas apologetics refer to the science of making an apology. More precisely, apologetics is that branch of Christian theology which seeks to develop principles for making a specific apology. Some have even argued that apologetics is a way of doing theology, as opposed to kerygmatic theology which is concerned with doctrinal exposition.[2] The danger in this approach is that some confessional aspects of theology are sometimes jettisoned to appease the modern mind. Others have argued that Christian apologetics is done only for the Christian community, but this would make Peter's exhortation meaningless.

A Christian apologist is simply one who actively seeks to defend the Christian faith. One's view of Christian apologetics is determined, in large measure, by a variety of secondary questions. What, if any, capacity does the non-believer have for knowing truth? What is the relationship between faith and reason? What is the relationship between the truth claims of Christianity and other world religions? Are there good reasons for believing in the existence of God or accepting the truth claims of the Bible? How does the believer respond to objections to the Christian world view—such as the challenges posed by the problem of evil, advances in scientific knowledge that seem to preclude divine activity, Marxist materialism, ethical relativism, or secular humanism? These and a host of other questions are, or at least ought to be, of some concern to any Christian seeking to share the truth of the gospel that "God was in Christ reconciling the world unto himself" (2 Cor. 5:19).

There is both a positive and negative aspect of the apologetic task. Positively, theological interpretation must take place before any defense can be given. The basic affirmations to be defended must be set forth. Negatively, an apologist must seek to counter false charges and misconceptions raised by the detractors of the Christian faith, as well as expose the weaknesses of other worldviews.

An apologist will actively seek to present the claims of Christ in the best possible light. However, in no sense should apologetic concerns cause one to "water down" orthodoxy's truth claims simply to accommodate current intellectual fads. Indeed, both the accommodation to and granting the absolute status of the "modern" perspective by Schleiermacher, Bultmann, and others in the liberal wing of the Church have no doubt contributed to some of the suspicion with which apologetics has been viewed by more orthodox Christians.

The Case against Apologetics

Those who deny any cognitive meaning to "God-talk"—denying either the objective existence of God or our ability to speak meaningfully about God—are obviously not interested in apologetics of any sort. Further, religious relativists and universalists who see opposing belief-systems as if they are but various paths leading up the same mountain to the Eternal would admit only a marginal role for apologetics. However, these critics are not our concern.

There are many good evangelical Christians who are either ambivalent toward or totally reject the legitimacy of apologetics. Often this rejection is founded upon a suspicion or open hostility toward philosophy in general. At a popular level, there is a widespread resistance to an overly "intellectual" faith. Many, perhaps most Christians, have come to faith in Christ without ever having heard an apologetic discussion.

Nor can all those who oppose such inquiry be dismissed as simple and uneducated persons lacking intellectual sophistication. Both some Christians and some philosophers would find the notion of a "Christian philosophy" a contradiction in terms.[3] Various significant Christian thinkers have weighed-in in the battle against philosophy. The early Church father Tertullian asked, "What has Jerusalem to do with Athens, the Church with the Academy, the Christian with the heretic?" Luther called philosophy a "harlot." Kierkegaard lamented that "philosophers turn wine into water."

Paul's warning against "vain philosophy" is cited as biblical proof of wisdom's folly. Paul said, "Beware lest any man spoil you through philosophy and vain deceit, after the tradition of men, after the rudiments of the world and not after Christ" (Col. 2:8). To be sure, there are numerous false philosophies in the world. But a more careful examination of this verse indicates that Paul is warning against "intellectualism or high sounding nonsense" (Phillips), the "worthless deceits of human wisdom" (TEV, or, better still, "hollow and delusive speculations" (NEB).

Paul appears to have been concerned ultimately with the kind of idle speculation that detracts from Christian living. Surely more than philosophy is in view here. "Hollow and delusive speculations" may abound in everything from the gossip of the supermarket tabloid to overly speculative obsessions with the details of eschatological events and chronologies that go beyond the clear teaching of Scripture.

Another aspect of the case against apologetics is based upon the biblical teaching that the unregenerate or natural mind is incapable of perceiving the things of God (1 Cor. 1:13). The Bible does describe the mind of the unbeliever as darkened and bound by the fear of death (Eph. 4:18; Heb. 2:15). With eyes that are blind and ears that are deaf, the individual is pictured as dead in trespasses and sins (Rom. 11:8; Eph. 2:1). The Bible says that "faith comes by hearing and hearing by the Word of God" (Rom. 10:17). Apologetic arguments cannot generate faith, but the Christian can answer the false charges of the unbeliever so that obstacles to hearing the gospel are removed. Apologetics arguments, like sermon illustrations, personal testimonies, drama, art, and Christian music, can provide a context for a hearing of the Word that results in faith.

The Case for Apologetics

Philosophy is simply a way of looking at life. The basic questions about God, humankind, the good, the true, and the beautiful all fall within the purview of classical philosophy. Etienne Gilson, in *A History of Christian Philosophy in the Middle Ages*, argued that the concerns of pagan Greek philosophy as encountered by Christians of the first century and the concerns of philosophy in the eighteenth century, after 1700 years of Christian influence, were radically different. Christianity reshaped and redirected the philosophical enterprise. As long as there are Christians with philosophical inclinations, there will be Christian philosophy. To abandon completely the dialogue with philosophy is to concede the false answers (and even false questions) of modernity by default, before the intellectual has even been addressed.

As has been mentioned, Peter encouraged Christians to be prepared to give an *apologian*, "But sanctify the Lord God in your hearts: and be ready to give an answer to every man that asketh you a reason of the hope that is in you with meekness and fear: Having a good conscience; that, whereas they speak evil of you, as of evildoers, they may be ashamed that falsely accuse your good conversation in Christ" (1 Pet. 3:15-16). This "proof-text" for apologetics has sometimes been overused, much the same way as the warning of Paul against "vain philosophy" is abused by detractors of apologetics. It is inconceivable that Peter was commanding Christians to go brandishing about with theistic proofs or a formal theodicy firmly in tow. Rather, he simply encouraged the kind of godly life that invites curiosity in order that one might commend the gospel. This included answering the false charges frequently leveled against the early Christians.

There are in fact numerous New Testament examples of this kind of apologetic activity. In the book of Acts, Paul defends himself before the mob in Jerusalem (Acts 22:1ff), before the Jewish council (Acts 23:1ff), before Felix (Acts 24:1ff), and before Festus and Agrippa (Acts 25:1ff). Paul also sought to establish an apologetic point of contact in his discussion with the Athenian philosophers (Acts 17:16-34). The synoptic Gospels, the Gospel of John, and the book of Hebrews all give evidence of apologetic activity. As J. K. S. Reid observed:

> There is in fact no difficulty in identifying apologetic elements in the New Testament. They appear both early and prominently. Apologetic activity is built into the foundations of the apostolic witness.[4]

Further, the whole of Christian history since the apostolic era is filled with numerous examples of the importance of apologetics. Origen's *Contra Celsum*, Augustine's *De Civitate Dei*, Aquinas's *Summa Contra Gentiles*, and Butler's *Analogy of Religion* are among the classic works in Christian apologetics. As human questions have grown in complexity, apologetic responses have also become more sophisticated. There was a dearth in apologetic activity during the second quarter of the twentieth century, due in part to the influence of Karl Barth. However, this trend now seems reversed.[5] The real issue is what kind of apologetic approach the Christian should employ.

Apologetic Approaches

Throughout the history of the church a wide variety of apologetic methods have been employed. Broadly speaking these can be divided into two categories: subjective and objective apologetics.[6] Theologians of all confessional positions have utilized or been influenced by these approaches.

The subjective school tends to stress the need for personal encounter. The limits of human reason and the impossibility of "metaphysics" (that which is beyond the physical) is emphasized. God is viewed as radically transcendent. In its existential expression, great emphasis is placed upon the paradoxical nature of the incarnation. A "leap" must be made from the objective and historical to the truth with which faith is concerned. Indeed, rational speculation can only provide an approximation—and this is wholly unacceptable for faith. Grace and faith are operative because of Divine activity. Therefore one cannot be "argued into faith." Luther, Pascal, Kierkegaard, and Barth are among the major Christian thinkers who would share this interest. There are numerous subtle differences among "subjectivist" thinkers. Many Christians, however, resonate with crucial aspects of this approach.

The objective school tends to deal with verification from the standpoint of objective fact. St. Thomas Aquinas, following Aristotle, stressed the human mind's ability to draw general conclusion based upon observation of particulars. In other words, there is much truth about God and his relationship to the world that is available to persons apart from revelation. Thus, Thomism stressed natural theology. Great confidence was placed in the classical theistic proofs. The ontological, cosmological, teleological, and moral arguments have been the subject of much debate and for a time fell into disrepute. Reformulated for a contemporary audience, they still have appeal to some Christians.[7] However, even Thomas argued that a faith based solely upon rational proofs was not sufficient for salvation.

St. Augustine, following Plato, argued that certain presuppositions must be accepted before the observable world can make sense. He stressed that faith must precede understanding. Reformed thinkers have tended to follow Augustine. They contend that belief in God is a properly basic belief—a presupposition that the Christian has good grounds for basic beginnings. The arguments for the existence of God are seen as little more than Christian reflections. They cannot lead one to faith. Apologists of this model would stress the consistency of the Christian world-view or the emptiness of non-Christian alternatives.

Old Testament prophecies, miracles, the life and teachings of Jesus, the resurrection of Jesus, the history of Christianity, and arguments from religious experience are often developed as apologetic arguments showing the coherence and integrity of the Christian faith. Responses to the problem of evil are also a major concern of most objective-type apologists. Of course, there are also numerous subtle differences among "objectivist" thinkers (i.e., Thomists, neo-Thomists, Christian rationalists, presuppositionalists, foundationalists, and evidentialists).

Some Positive Suggestions

Although I have written this essay with certain presuppositions (i.e., I am in the orthodox evangelical "camp," influenced and informed by the Reformed perspective), the best apologetic strategy would be to avoid excessive system loyalty and appropriate the best elements of the approaches outlined above.

All Christians acknowledge the existence of God. The Reformed thinker, however, accepts as a basic presupposition that God exists and has revealed himself as the Living Word, through the Lord Jesus Christ, and in the written Word—the Bible. The Bible says, "he that cometh to God must believe that he is. . . ." (Heb. 11:6). Further, the Holy Spirit is the only one who can make this Word intelligible and applicable to the human heart.

This does not mean that the Christian is an irrationalist or that the Christian position cannot be defended. Although knowledge of God is occasioned by an act of faith—a faith graciously given by the Holy Spirit, the believer has adequate epistemic grounds for holding the Christian worldview. Further, these grounds may be coherently presented and rationally defended. Thus, while the Christian is convicted by more than mere rational argumentation, it can be shown that Christians have reasonable grounds for belief.

A wholistic Christian philosophy of religion asserts that God is the ultimate source of all truth. Thus, while faith is different from mundane knowledge, all genuine knowledge is properly grounded in the nature, character, and works of the triune God revealed in Scripture. For example, it is his providence and governance of his creation that gives order, meaning, and content to the reality of observed phenomenon. While the non-Christian may have access to many fragments of knowledge, one must know God in order to have the proper perspective upon all truth.

Christian apologetics is a legitimate enterprise to the extent that it answers questions, resolves difficulties, and removes obstacles to the hearing of the gospel. Such an apologetic should also show the emptiness of non-Christian worldviews, and underscore the simplicity, beauty, and truth of the Christian worldview. In no sense, however, can one be intellectually persuaded to believe apart from the regenerating work of the Holy Spirit. Any "faith" that rests solely upon apologetic evidences is a "work" and is not of grace nor would it be sufficient for salvation.

One should study a number of apologetic resources and develop an approach that is consistent with his or her larger theological system. A very readable thematic popular approach to a number of apologetic problems is given in Dr. Drummond's (and Paul R. Baxter's) book, *How to Respond to a Skeptic*.[8] One of Dr. Drummond's former colleagues at The Southern Baptist Theological Seminary in Louisville, Kentucky, Dr. Richard B. Cunningham, has recently had published an excellent apologetic for the Christian in dialogue with competing worldviews.[9] The apologetic classics are always worthwhile reading.[10] C. S. Lewis, Josh McDowell, Francis Schaeffer, and a host of other contemporary popular writers have proven useful to many.

In the evangelistic encounter every effort should be made actually to hear and to understand the non-believer's concerns, doubts, or questions. A good way to insure that this has in fact happened is for the Christian witness to repeat the non-believer's position to his or her satisfaction. The Christian should not be afraid to concede the truthfulness or value of aspects of the non-believer's position. The goal is not simply to win the argument but to share the gospel.

Drummond and Baxter have well said, "Caustic debates between believers and non-believers always tend to degenerate into fruitless verbal battles that do little to enhance the image of Christianity."[11]

Focus on major issues! One wag responded to the question of where Cain got his wife with the retort, "You are a married man and a married man ought to leave other men's wives alone." We do not have to deal with every obscure question that rolls down the pike in giving a reasoned defense of the faith.

Further, the non-believer does not have to be persuaded of all the tenets of orthodoxy to hear and believe the *kerygma*. If it will help to deflect an objection or problem by observing that there are numerous interpretations of a particular passage of Scripture or doctrinal point then do so, even if you have a strong personal view, as long as gospel truth is not at stake.

In dealing with a major challenge to the Christian position, focus on the strongest point articulated by the non-Christian. It does little good—and can do great harm—to attack opponents of straw. Be intellectually honest—if you do not know how to respond, say so.

If the non-believer does not express doubts or difficulties at an intellectual level, adjust your apology accordingly. Don't launch a full-scale but unnecessary apologetic attack simply because you are able to do so. You are seeking to impress the lost with Jesus, not your intellectual prowess.

Sharing the gospel is not parroting someone else's sales pitch; it is, like preaching, truth shared through personality. The battle is not with flesh and blood (Eph. 6:12). The weapons of our warfare are not fleshly. Some years ago I heard Josh McDowell's testimony about how he came to Christ. He worked in all the intellectual doubts he had and how they were resolved one by one as he came to faith. But the most impressive thing about his testimony to me was that after his conversion, Josh, for the first time in his life, was able to show love to his unworthy father. Indeed, love is the key. Jesus said that love would be the mark of true discipleship (John 13:34-35).

In the final analysis, the greatest problem for faith is not doubt but spiritual death and dearth. Spiritual blindness and a darkened human heart can only be reached by "the love of God . . . shed abroad in our hearts" (Rom. 5:5). A prayerful, loving Spirit-energized sharing of the gospel is a mighty weapon in the hands of a sovereign God.

Endnotes

1. Bernard Ramm, *Varieties of Christian Apologetics* (Grand Rapids, MI: Baker, 1961), p. 11.

2. Paul Tillich, "The Problem of Theological Method," *Four Existentialist Theologians*, ed. Will Herberg (New York: Doubleday, 1958), p. 278.

3. An excellent evangelical response to these critics is offered by Richard B. Cunningham, "A Case for Christian Philosophy," *Review and Expositor*, 82 (1985), pp. 493-506.

4. J. K. S. Reid, *Christian Apologetics* (London: Hodder and Stoughton, 1969), p. 15.

5. Avery Dulles, *A History of Apologetics* (London: Hutchinson and Corpus, 1971), p. 240.

6. As suggested by A. J. Hoover, "Apologetics," *Evangelical Dictionary of Theology*, ed. W. A. Elwell (Grand Rapids, MI: Baker, 1984), pp. 69-70. Cf. Ramm, *Varieties of Christian Apologetics*, and John P. Newport, "Representative Contemporary Approaches to the Use of Philosophy in Christian Thought," *Review and Expositor*, 82 (1985), 507-519.

7. For example, Oxford philosopher Richard Swinburne has given a very technical restatement to several of the classical arguments in *The Existence of God* (Oxford: Oxford Unviersity Press, 1979). C. S. Lewis's *Mere Christianity* remains among the most readable popular examples of the Thomistic approach.

8. Lewis A. Drummond and Paul R. Baxter, *How to Respond to a Skeptic* (Chicago, IL: Moody, 1986). Cf. also Lewis A. Drummond's pamphlet, "A thinking layman's guide to the question: Who Was Jesus?"

9. Richard B. Cunningham, *The Christian Faith and Its Contemporary Rivals* (Nashville, TN: Broadman, 1988).

10. Cf. L. Russ Bush, ed., *Classical Readings in Christian Apologetics: A.D. 100-1800* (Grand Rapids, MI: Zondervan, 1983).

11. Drummond and Baxter, *How to Respond to a Skeptic*, p. 16.

12

OUR EVANGELISTIC SUMMONS: PERSPECTIVES FROM JOHN
Gerald L. Borchert

Gerald L. Borchert is Professor of New Testament Interpretation at the Southern Baptist Theological Seminary. He is the author of ten books including Dynamics of Evangelism *and* Assurance and Warning. *Dr. Borchert is presently writing a new commentary on the Gospel of John.*

In an era when insecurity reigns throughout our world and people are threatened by revolution, bombing, economic disasters, food shortages, rampant immorality, grasping greed, growing poverty, and multitudes of problems associated with drug trafficking, it is imperative for the church to be absolutely clear on the nature and characteristics of its evangelistic summons. Since no book of the Bible is perhaps more precise in defining the Scripture's mission imperative than the Gospel of John, it may be strategic for those interested in evangelism to gain some perspectives from this core text of Christianity. The purpose of this gospel is none other than engendering believing which issues in new life through Jesus (John 20:20-31). Every story and every sign has been set down in writing to lead readers to life in Christ.

After having taught this book for over a quarter of a century in many parts of the world, I still remain awed and very excited by the power of its stories and its unequivocal call for transformation.[1] Even though it is a book of the first Christian century, it still today envelopes the spirit of human beings in a unique way. Perhaps, that is the reason why Clement of Alexandria early called it "the spiritual gospel."

In the context of the first-century world, where compromise with the political powers was regularly advocated and where syncretism was a way of life, the writer of the Johannine gospel and epistles was absolutely convinced that a living confession for the incarnation (in-flesh-ment) of Jesus was a key to his reader's transformation.[2] The presence of the Spirit of God was, as he indicates in 1 John

4:2, evident in that person who confesses that Jesus Christ "has come in the flesh." For people to fail to acknowledge that reality in their lives was for the Johannine writer an evidence of the spirit of antichrist (1 John 4:1-3). We of the twentieth century must become keenly aware that such a confession was hardly to be equated with a statement of orthodox faith. Certainly confessing "Jesus come in the flesh" is an orthodox statement, but it is a reality that must be apprehended in the context of life. Only then will it fulfill the Johannine sense of confession.

It is at this very point that persons concerned with evangelism need to be absolutely clear what is meant when they confront Johannine words like truth, witness, believing, knowing, and life. All of these terms are very dynamic words. Further, since the Gospel of John is regularly given to new converts as a book to be read, it is vitally important that some instruction be given to those reading the book for the first time. In making this statement, I am not advocating that only sophisticated educators ought to teach the gospel. Indeed, I am greatly fearful of that option because I have heard many tangential academic papers on the Fourth Gospel. But I believe that a little guidance will help new Christians to uncover the marvelous message of the book. Moreover, it might even prevent well-intentioned evangelists from drawing wrong conclusions out of the great stories of John. Remember, the early church writers recognized that there was a great depth to this book, and that is why Clement designated it as the "spiritual gospel." Great care, therefore, must be taken in reading it in order not to misread it.

The Importance of Believing

As I indicated in the *Dynamics of Evangelism*, to believe or to know Jesus is a basic premise of the Johannine writer.[3] But John is not talking primarily about information or head knowledge. He is talking about relationship or relational knowledge. In his time there was a growing tendency to categorize belief in terms of information acquisition. On the Jewish side it led to the various rabbinic parties laying down multitudes of legal perspectives which finally became codified in works like the Mishnah and the Talmud. On the hellenistic side, it led to strange, complicated mythological formulations associated with groups conveniently labeled under the heading of gnosticism. While both of these groups sought for a relationship with God, it was presupposed that having detailed information was fundamental to establishing the relationship. Now John takes pains to make clear to his readers that while information is important, it is not primarily *what you know* but *who you know* that is important in Christianity.[4]

Because of problems associated with the words for knowledge and belief or faith, John completely avoided the Greek nouns *gnosis* and *pistis* in his gospel and used *only the verbs!* The reason is that he did not want his readers to focus on *information about* Jesus but on a *relationship with* Jesus. Now that concept of dynamic relationship is crucial for every evangelist to understand. A person may have gained a great deal of information about Jesus such as having attended confirmation classes or pastoral instruction classes, and that person may have readily asserted to all of the correct formulas; yet that person may still not have experienced a transformation in living.

John illustrates this phenomenon very well in the story of Martha and Lazarus. When Lazarus had been dead for four days, Jesus returned from Galilee to Judea. Martha met him and after stating "if only you would have been here, my brother would not have died" she added, "still I know that whatever you ask of God, God will provide" (John 11:21-22). When Jesus answered that Lazarus would rise again, she countered with the fact that she knew Pharisaic theology and *knew* that he would rise at the end of time. Then Jesus told her that he was the resurrection and the life, and that the dying one should live. She replied that she believed that Jesus was the Christ, the Son of God, the expected one—the Messiah (11:25-27).

For many persons involved in evangelism, such a confession would be sufficient to guarantee entrance into the church. Indeed, many preachers use this confession as the point of their sermons. Moreover, many churches would readily baptize someone with such a confession. But that confession is not the end of the story! It continues with Mary and it involves a repetition of the "if only" statement. Clearly the dialogue suggests a hopelessness among the people. Jesus, however, finally arrives at the tomb and calls for the stone to be taken away. Then it is Martha who speaks. Notice her words: "Lord by this time he stinks!" (11:39).

The point of the story should then be obvious. Martha can say both "I believe that you are the Son of God" and "It is impossible." We too may confess the right words about Jesus like Martha, and yet lack a real understanding of what those words actually mean. Accordingly, it is imperative to recognize that if evangelism gets no further than correct words, it is powerless for life. The task of the evangelist is to get beyond the words to the reality of life. Such must be our determined goal in the era of word-oriented superficiality.

But such does not exhaust the problem. I have heard evangelists and preachers quote John 1:12 from the King James Version, *"even* to them that believe on his name" and suggest that "all you have to do is believe in the name of Jesus in order to be saved." It is almost as though believing in the name of Jesus is a minimal statement of the "belief" necessary for salvation. My students learn very quickly however, that such is not the meaning of the Greek because *"even"* is not in the Greek! To believe in the name of Jesus, therefore, is not a minimal statement. It is to accept the Lord's nature in one's life—to receive him as God in one's life—and to take on a new authority for life. Believing or knowing Jesus is not gaining more head knowledge about him. It is gaining a new direction for life, finding a new authority for all of one's thoughts, motives and actions. Such is the meaning of believing in the name of Jesus.

Moreover, remember that simply because people may *say* they "believe," it does not automatically mean that Jesus accepts what they say. In John 2:23-25 there is a very interesting summation to this issue. The text says that many believed (*episteusan*) "in his name," but Jesus did not believe (*episteuen*) them. Some scholars have tried to make fine distinctions on the verbal patterns with or without the preposition, but John himself indicates the point of the text—namely, Jesus "knows" what people are like and he knows when authentic believing is occurring. In constructing this gospel, John was not interested in encouraging superficial attachments to Jesus. He was concerned about developing authentic believing. Every evangelist worth gospel salt ought to follow in the footsteps of John by making sure authentic believing is taking place among people. In our concern for witnessing we must take care lest we play the numbers game and fail to gain conversions.

The Model of Witnessing

Witnessing is another of the great concepts in this gospel and the Baptizer (John the Baptist) is portrayed as a *model witness*. When one reads the texts related to the Baptizer, a very interesting picture emerges—one that every evangelist needs to study. The characteristics of the Baptizer can be summarized in four categories.

First, as a witness the Baptizer was one who *came to know* Jesus. Readers who are familiar with the Lukan birth narratives and the clear relationship between the mothers of Jesus and John the Baptist may wonder why the Fourth Gospel pictures the Baptizer as stating not only that his listeners do not know Jesus (1:26), but that at one time he himself did not know Jesus (1:31). In the Johannine sense however, to know the "Lamb of God who takes away the sin of the world" (1:29) is only attained through a God-given experience, and not merely natural perception. To be a witness, therefore, means that one must experience first hand the nature of the divine presence which resides in Jesus—i.e., what John means by the statement "The word became flesh and tented (tabernacled) among us" (1:14). Then one can be a witness.

Second, when one has a correct perception of God in one's life, then like the Baptizer one does *not* have to *make claims* for oneself. One can settle for being merely a voice (1:23). One does not have to be the light, one can accept being a *witness to* the light (1:7-8). Among the greatest temptations which confront ministers and evangelists is the desire to play God in the world and in the church. God, indeed, came down to humanity in Jesus, but our temptation is to rise up and pretend that we possess the insights of God. To be authentic witnesses, however, means that we must accept our humanity and recognize Christ's divinity challenging our lives. To yield to the temptation and play God to others means that we in fact lose our ability to be true witnesses.

Third, John modeled for us the fact that being a witness to Christ means *being a servant*. The call of an evangelist/minister is *not to be boss*, but to be slave. The corporate model of the minister as Chief Executive Officer is hardly the model of the one who feels unworthy even to untie the sandals of Jesus (1:27). The very meaning of ministry is caught up in the term servanthood (*diakonia*)! The concept of servanthood, however, is a very difficult model to follow, and lipservice becomes our usual way of recognizing this element of our calling. Our natural inclination is to seek for honor and recognition because we love to be served. To accept the servant role is a hard pill for ministers to swallow, particularly since we can tell ourselves that people seem to receive a blessing by serving "the servants of Christ."

But if that were not sufficient, the Baptizer evidences a fourth characteristic which may be even more telling. He is the *introducer* of his disciples to Jesus. The concept of being an introducer of people to Christ is well rooted in most books on evangelism and witnessing. But there is one particular aspect of this characteristic that needs to be highlighted. That aspect involves the fact that the Baptizer was actually turning *his disciples* over to Jesus. He was in reality dissolving his little kingdom or group of followers in order that Jesus might build a new following. Among all of the characteristics of the Baptizer this one needs to be especially underlined for the church and ministry which stands on the threshold of the twenty-first century. One of the greatest temptations of ministers, churches, and evangelistic and mission organizations has been the desire for kingdom building. To make a name for ourselves by painting our particular identification marks on other people and on material things is a passion that infects all of humanity and weasels its way into Christianity.

But to discover the freedom of genuinely turning over to Christ what has been marked by our efforts is one sign of being an authentic witness. When we actually begin to turn all we are and have over to Christ, it becomes much more difficult to play the numbers game or to place ourselves in the center of our discussions. Now it should scarcely take any imagination to determine why this type of thinking is not usually a central element in most books on evangelism or ministry. While we may give some attention to humility, the Baptizer's type of self-giving is a very different pattern than most of our lifestyles as Christian witnesses.

Perhaps we need a reintegration of the characteristics of the Baptizer into our considerations of twenty-first century evangelism and mission. Maybe the Johannine picture of the Baptizer can teach us something very important about the nature of being true witnesses for Christ. To think of the Baptizer only as a figure belonging to the old era is to miss the point of why he appears at the beginning of all of our Gospels. Certainly in the first and third chapters of John, the Baptizer is pictured as such an ideal witness that the portrayal of Peter in chapters 13, 18, 20, and 21 pales in terms of consistency by comparison. Only the beloved disciple seems to have a stronger sense of Christian integrity.

The Style of Love

But the mention of Peter brings to mind another important element in the task of evangelism. Among the most moving stories in the Fourth Gospel is the one which deals with the love command (chapter 13), and which introduces the section of the gospel frequently referred to as the Farewell Discourses.

As the hour of Jesus' destiny arrived (13:1), the Lord sought to teach his disciples a lesson through an illustrative act. Wrapping a towel around himself and taking a basin of water, he began to wash the disciples feet (13:4-5). When Peter tried to stop him, Jesus announced that failure to be washed by him would mean exclusion from his company. Whereupon Peter changed his tune and practically asked Jesus to give him a shower. Patiently Jesus dealt with his well-intentioned disciple by telling Peter that feet would be enough to symbolize the relationship. But then Jesus began his explanation. For the disciples to call Jesus teacher and Lord was a correct evaluation. Those titles were a fitting designation. But Jesus was interested in more than titles. He was *concerned* with modeling for his disciples an authentic lifestyle of service which they were called to emulate by serving one another (13:12-16).

This discussion concerning servanthood in the setting of an illustrative act, introduced by the announcement that the hour had come, is linked by John in the closing part of the chapter with another announcement that it was the time for the Son of Man to be glorified (13:31). In this context of the forthcoming departure of Jesus (13:33), John reminded his readers that Jesus had enunciated a new commandment. It is this commandment that gives focus not only to the chapter but to the entire Gospel of John. The best known verse of the Bible (John 3:16) highlights the love of God for humanity, but the great command of Jesus highlights the responsibility of Christians to love one another (13:34).

It is incredibly important for those interested in evangelism to remember: Jesus did *not* say that others recognize Christians by their confessional statements or doctrinal affirmations. Instead, they would understand Christians by their love for one another (13:35). Of course doctrine is important! But doctrine is not the fundamental basis of witnessing to the world. The world is attracted to Christianity principally by love. This thesis is often forgotten by Christians who sometimes fight for minuscule differences in theological orthodoxy and grow harsh and cold in their relationships with their brothers and sisters. They may then wonder why they can win other Christians to their fold but fail to attract genuine pagans (unbelievers) into the Kingdom of God. In my lifetime I have watched a number of well-intentioned evangelistic efforts grind into non-productivity on the wheels of arguments over theological orthodoxy. I wish Christians could learn that non-Christians will recognize us as authentic messengers of God *by our love* for one another!

What has been very interesting for me to watch is how many Christians from conservative, so-called orthodox churches have been attracted to groups like Mormons and their young people have joined organizations like the Moonies and other group-oriented religious cults. Maybe it is time for many of those involved in evangelism to rediscover the importance of a loving Christian community as one of the most *basic ingredients* for engendering evangelistic results which will last. We may talk a good line about love, but the world can easily see whether we actually love one another. The world is honestly looking for *demonstrated love*. It will often settle for *shadows* of true love. But it will not long be deceived by *empty* words of love.

The Nature of the Divine Resource

Now to build a loving community takes the presence of God in the midst of that community. John reminds us that the presence of God in the form of the Holy Spirit is a gift of Jesus to the community (John 20:22). While he was with his disciples, Jesus was their supporter and counselor (*parakletos*). But when it was time for him to go, he promised that he would send another counselor to be with them continually (John 14:16). The idea of God's presence in the life of a believer is one of the most fundamental ideas of Christianity. In the Old Testament this concept is expressed in germinal form in the Exodus experience of the people of Israel. God moved with his people in the moving tabernacle in the wilderness. Then he was seen as inhabiting the temple in Jerusalem. But he was not to be confined to a building as the woman of Samaria had to learn (4:20-24).

For John "God is Spirit" and the believer must recognize what that reality means (John 4:24). When Jesus came, he was not confined to a building. John says that "he tabernacled (tented) among us" (1:14). In his life he gave us a divine illustration of a non-confined God who breaks the boundaries of place, tradition and of our expectations. His pattern in the world is that he was the symbol of presence and that he loved people. He wants them in return to love him and to love one another (John 3:16 and 15:12-17; cf. Mark 12:31-33, Matt. 22:37-40 and Luke 10:27). Even more, he wants them to love their enemies (cf. Matt. 5:43-46).

The reason the Paraclete (the counselor) is so important for John is that the Spirit provides Christians with purpose for life. Moreover, the Spirit keeps them from the desperate loneliness of people who feel abandoned and who have no focus to life (John 14:15-21).

But the Paraclete has another function which every evangelist must understand. The Paraclete is the one to whom is given the task of showing the world the realities of sin, righteousness and judgment (John 16:8). While our task as evangelists is to bear witness, it is not our task to argue. We may possess brilliance in the use of words but conviction of sin is the task of God's Spirit. The Spirit can use us for divine purposes but we must take great care lest we assume that we are responsible for either the conviction of sin, the vision of righteousness or the divine encounter of people with the reality of judgment (16:9-11).

Further, even if we are used by God to touch someone with our witness concerning Christ Jesus, who is the Savior of the world (John 4:42) and our Lord and God (20:28), we must be ready to acknowledge that the ultimate *guide* of Christian converts is not us but the Holy Spirit who will lead them into the life of truth (16:13). Fortunately, although we as mere mortals have some problems with correct perceptions in our lives, we can be sure that the Holy Spirit has no problem knowing how to glorify Christ or to recognize the role of God the Father in the salvation process (16:14-15).

While the teaching concerning the Holy Spirit is thus crucial to the evangelistic process, the doctrine of the Holy Spirit has given rise to many arguments in the history of the church. Some Christians have misread the Scriptures and employed the doctrine as a manipulative vehicle for "using" God. We must remember that the biblical perspective does not advocate people using God but *God using his servants*. Additionally the teaching on the Spirit has often been separated from the initial salvation process and designated to the second stage of salvation. But the teaching of John is that God does not give the Spirit by measure or in partial stages (John 3:34). When one becomes a Christian one gains the presence of the Spirit in one's life.[5] That presence of the Spirit, however, does not mean that one always obeys the Spirit. The Christian must learn how to yield to the leading of the Spirit in one's life. This yielding is a very important part of the on-going process of transformation, and every evangelist needs to recognize the role of the Spirit in his or her life, and in lives of those who by God's grace the evangelist may be able to touch.

But some Christians have become fearful of the Holy Spirit because of the excesses of others. Such was the case with the reaction to the Montanists of the third century and such has been the reaction to other groups throughout history. Yet the presence of various excesses in the church has often become the basis for avoiding a wholesome teaching on the Holy Spirit. Failure to teach and understand the role of the Paraclete in the task of evangelism and in the *process* of transformation is a very serious error—an error which can lead to an overestimation of the human role in salvation and to the proclamation of a powerless faith. Effective evangelism is the result of dependence upon the work of the Holy Spirit—which means in reality the work of God.

God has been active in the word becoming flesh (1:14), in the lamb of God being lifted up and in taking away the sin of the world (1:29 and 3:14-15), in the power of the resurrection, in the post-resurrection declaration of peace and commission to proclaim the forgiveness of sins (20:19-21), in the gift of the Holy Spirit (20:22), in the expectation of the return of Christ (14:1-3) and in our great hope of the resurrection to life (5:28-29).[6]

Conclusion

To proclaim that message by God's grace with an authentically transformed human spirit ought to be the goal of every evangelist who is marked by the name of the Lord Jesus. In carrying out this evangelistic task in our contemporary era the perspectives of the Gospel of John are as vital for us as they were when they were first penned for the early church. To reread these stories as messages for serious evangelists as well as for recent converts is a call I would issue to you. There are of course many more lessons to be uncovered, but I suspect that not even this entire volume of essays would be sufficient to contain the wealth of its untapped resources (cf. John 21:25).

Endnotes

1. For my reflections on the power of the gospel, please see my article "The Fourth Gospel and Its Theological Impact," *Review and Expositor* 78 (1981), 249-258.

2 I am aware that since C. H. Dodd the question of the common authorship of the gospel and the epistle are questioned by some scholars, but I remain unconvinced by those arguments. I am also aware that more recently the entire question of the authorship of the gospel and the epistle are now discussed in terms of the Johannine school. It is not the place in this paper to discuss the involved issue of the pros and cons of such matters. For further information on the matter readers may consult the many commentaries such as George R. Beasley-Murray, *John*, Word Biblical Commentary (Waco, TX: Word, 1987), and the change of position on the part of Raymond Brown between his major works *The Gospel According to John*, 2 vols., The Anchor Bible (Garden City, NY: Doubleday, 1966 and 1970), and *The Johannine Epistles,* The Anchor Bible (Garden City, NY: Doubleday, 1981).

3. Gerald Borchert, *The Dynamics of Evangelism* (Waco, TX: Word, 1976), pp. 57-58.

4. See my discussion in *Assurance and Warning* (Nashville, TN: Broadman, 1987), pp. 96-97.

5. Many people become confused with the Lukan expression to be filled with the Holy Spirit, but as I have pointed out in "The Spirit and Salvation," *Criswell Theological Review* 3.1 (1988), 70-71, Luke uses the expression "To be filled with" for various emotions, etc. such as wrath, awe, fear, wonder, madness, envy, etc. (Luke 4:28; 5:26; 6:11; Acts 3:10; 5:17; 13:45 and 19:29). Great care, moreover, must be taken lest one thinks this idea of being filled with the Spirit is a Christian concept for Luke related to a post-pentecost period

because it was used by Luke of such persons as John the Baptist, Elizabeth and Zechariah prior to Jesus (Luke 1:15, 41 and 67). Being filled with the Spirit is Luke's way of talking about the presence of the Spirit in one's life.

6. For a more complex discussion on the importance of the resurrection in John please see my article "The Resurrection Perspective in John: An Evangelical Summons," *Review and Expositor* 85 (1988), 501-513.

PART FOUR:
Evangelism and the Call to Discipleship

What is the relationship between evangelism and discipleship? Are they part of the same task or are they different disciplines within the Christian life? Two former students of Lewis Drummond approach these questions from different perspectives. Harry L. Poe discusses the debate over the meaning of discipleship and the nature of its relationship to evangelism. James G. Merritt looks at discipleship particularly in the context of following Jesus, and its relationship to evangelism.

13

EVANGELISM AND DISCIPLESHIP
Harry L. Poe

Harry L. Poe is Associate Professor of Evangelism at the Southern Baptist Theological Seminary. He completed the Ph.D. in evangelism under Lewis Drummond at Southern Seminary. An accomplished writer in evangelism and practical ministries, Dr. Poe has also served the Kentucky Baptist Convention as the Associate Director of Evangelism.

Discipleship has grown in importance as an issue in evangelism during the latter half of the twentieth century. Unfortunately, Christians have disagreed over the meaning of discipleship and the nature of its relationship to evangelism. Conservatives and liberals alike have embraced the term, but the absence of a consensus over the concept of discipleship and how it relates to evangelism has resulted in confusion and heated debate.

The Problem of Consensus

Dietrich Bonhoeffer placed discipleship on the front burner of theological interest in his book *The Cost of Discipleship.* In the opening words of his book, Bonhoeffer charged that "Cheap grace is the deadly enemy of our Church. We are fighting today for costly grace."[1] He published his book in 1937 as he saw the Church in Germany accommodate itself to Hitler. A nation full of Christians saw no dichotomy between Christ and Hitler. Something was wrong, and Bonhoeffer reckoned that Christians had adopted "cheap grace" which justified sin rather than the "costly grace" of Jesus Christ which justified sinners. Most of the nation was listed on the church rolls and fully expected to go to heaven, but Jesus Christ the living Lord seemed to play no part in the day-to-day affairs of people.

Perhaps because of his iconoclastic phrase "cheap grace" coupled with his martyr's death at the hands of the Nazis, Bonhoeffer's call for discipleship gained a gradual hearing. With the ferment of the 1960's, however, Bonhoeffer's emphasis on "radical" discipleship came into its own. Some came to identify the essence of discipleship as social involvement. In the wake of the upheavals of the sixties, this understanding of discipleship began to find institutional form. Jubilee, a Christian group committed to peace, justice, and reconciliation, published *The Other Side* with the motto "Justice Rooted in Discipleship." This same emphasis finds expression among the Sojourners and Bruderhof communities who see Christian community as a vital necessity in discipleship. The Community on Communities serves to provide a means of communication between many of these communities. Speaking from this emerging tradition, Jim Wallis has said of twentieth-century Christians, "We have lost that visible style of life which was evident in the early Christian communities and which gave their evangelism its compelling power and authority."[2]

Alarmed by the mortality rate among converts, many of the major denominations have taken steps to institutionalize the concept of discipleship to preserve their evangelistic fruit. The Southern Baptist Convention reports a membership of over 14 million, but half of these members are either inactive or have disappeared without a trace. To highlight the importance of discipleship, the Church Training program of Southern Baptists has taken steps to change its name to Discipleship Training. A variety of groups have developed "discipleship notebooks" that teach Christians the disciplines of the devotional life through a regimented program of study under supervision. Denominations and parachurch groups as well have followed this approach which places discipleship in the context of an educational process.

From its earliest beginnings, the Church Growth Movement has also embraced discipleship as a concept integrally related to evangelism. In his classic work *Understanding Church Growth*, Donald McGavran defined the Church's mission as

> an enterprise devoted to proclaiming the Good News of Jesus Christ,
> and to persuading men to become His disciples and dependable members of His Church.[3]

Win Arn insists that disciples rather than decisions should constitute the goal of evangelism.[4] Peter Wagner takes up this theme and insists that Church Growth leaders "are interested only in *disciples*, validated primarily through commitment to Jesus Christ as Lord and to responsible membership in a Christian church."[5]

The Church Growth Movement led the way to defining evangelism in terms of the goal of making disciples, but not all evangelicals have accepted this approach. Even before discipleship came into vogue, J. I. Packer warned against the "widespread and persistent habit of defining evangelism in terms, not of a message delivered, but an effect produced in our hearers."[6]

Largely through the leadership of John Stott, the Lausanne Congress on World Evangelization adopted a definition of evangelism that focused on the content of the message of the gospel, but it also reflected the concern for discipleship:

> In issuing the gospel invitation we have no liberty to conceal the cost
> of discipleship. Jesus still calls all who would follow him to deny
> themselves, take up their cross, and identify themselves with his new
> community. The results of evangelism include obedience to Christ,
> incorporation into his church and responsible service in the world.[7]

Nonetheless, some of those attending the Congress saw the Covenant as a retrenchment from the kind of discipleship they advocated. In response to the Lausanne Covenant's assertion that "In the church's mission of sacrificial service evangelism is primary," an ad hoc group responded with a statement on "Theology and Implication of Radical Discipleship."[8]

Even the phrase "radical discipleship" means different things to people of different theological persuasions. James G. Merritt, a Reformed thinker and one of the leading young conservative voices in the Southern Baptist Convention declared,

> . . . the evangelistic call of Jesus, simply put, was essentially a call to
> repentance and radical discipleship. . . . and that this discipleship
> entailed self-denial and the willing bearing of the cross.[9]

Merritt raises the issue of repentance as an aspect of this kind of discipleship. In this regard, Merritt agrees with Jim Wallis who links repentance and discipleship but who insists that "repentance is the essential first step of conversion."[10]

From another perspective David Watson brings several other matters to the fore which relate to discipleship:

> In the New Testament, the call to believe is a call to discipleship. It
> involves a clear commitment of the will to the person of Jesus Christ
> . . . a personal and total surrender to Jesus as Savior and Lord with all
> the ethical demands involved in such a discipleship.[11]

Watson stresses commitment and the role of Jesus as Lord as well as Savior. These elements have definite implications for how one communicates the gospel which deserves more attention later.

Facing the Real Issues

Thus, we see a stream of conservative to liberal Christians concerned with evangelism who see discipleship as an essential aspect of evangelism. Everyone seems to agree that true Christians need to be disciples of Jesus Christ, but so far, little agreement has arisen over what that means for evangelism. The various positions presented have arisen from serious concerns related to life situations. The concern for discipleship did not emerge as a theoretical concept in an academic setting, rather it resulted from the phenomenon of people claiming to be Christians who have no interest in the things of Christ. All those concerned with the subject seem to share the common assumption that conversion ought to result in a change in life that makes a person increasingly like Christ. Yet, the way people have approached discipleship has tended to depend more upon them personally and their concerns than it has depended upon the objective question of discipleship.

Discipleship first emerged as an issue in evangelism for me when I served as a prison chaplain. When men first came to the prison, they remained in the reception unit until classified to go out on "the yard" or be transferred to a minimum or maximum security facility. Several church groups came into the prison to conduct evangelistic services in the reception unit, and they reported a number of converts. Unfortunately, very few converts ever appeared in chapel when they entered the general prison population.

I decided to enlist the aid of the visiting groups to strengthen our follow-up procedure. When I spoke with the leader of one of the groups, however, I met with a startling reply.

"It's not my place to tell him to go to church," he said. "I just get him on his knees, get him saved, and move on to the next one. I get him on his knees, get him saved, and move to the next one. That's what I've been doing for twenty years. It's up to them whether or not they go to church. It's not my place to get into all of that."

I was concerned with a formal, structural problem of integrating people into a fellowship of Christians. In the process I discovered a theological problem of evangelism which stood isolated from the church and lacked specific content about Christ. Bonhoeffer's concern centered in a state church that had made peace with Hitler. Wallis has a concern for Christian life that reflects the concern Jesus had for the social and physical needs of people and society. To a certain extent, the confusion over the concept of discipleship as it relates to evangelism has come from the tendency to identify discipleship with one's own immediate concern.

From this brief overview, however, several issues arise. What does the question of discipleship mean in terms of salvation by grace? To what extent is discipleship a human effort and to what extent is it a divine work? Does discipleship precede salvation, coincide with salvation, or arise from salvation? What is the relationship between repentance and faith? What is the difference between having Jesus as Savior and Jesus as Lord? What is the relationship between faith and commitment? What role does the organized church and its education programs play in discipleship? Where does evangelism end and discipleship begin? What is the relationship between discipleship and sanctification? How does the question of discipleship affect the message of the gospel? Can one be a disciple without being a Christian?

Toward a Resolution

Any resolution of the relationship between evangelism and discipleship must come from the gospel message itself. The difficulties in Christian practice cannot be solved by altering the gospel in its demands, rather the gospel ought to contain the clue for the solution. Simply stated, evangelism means proclaiming the gospel. Simply stated, discipleship means following Jesus. Because Jesus no longer walks the earth as God incarnate, we cannot follow him in the sense that Peter, Andrew, James, and John left their nets to follow him. On the other hand, the gospel message presents Jesus to people today.

Following. Whether or not someone follows Jesus depends to a certain extent on who they think Jesus is. The manner in which someone follows Jesus also depends to a certain extent on who they think Jesus is. During his ministry, some followed Jesus as his disciple because they considered him a great teacher, a prophet, or perhaps even one of the great prophets returned from the dead. Judas followed Jesus as a disciple with enough commitment to be counted one of the closest followers. When the crisis came, however, the kind of commitment Judas and his colleagues had did not keep them. They called him "Lord, Lord," but they did so as we would speak of anyone great. The sad fact of commitment is that it failed everyone who set out to follow the great leader. Love kept a few of the women and John at his side as he died, but when the crisis comes, commitment is not enough.

Anyone can commit themselves to a cause or a person. People like to have some worthy purpose to give them a sense of fulfillment. The temptation today, as 2000 years ago, is to offer a cause to which people can commit themselves, rather than presenting Jesus. Following Jesus is altogether different from commitment. Peter had even more commitment than Judas, and his commitment failed him just as miserably. Discipleship rests on a far more substantial foundation than human commitment which ebbs and flows. Discipleship rests on the one who calls us to follow. The one who calls is the one who continually makes it possible to follow. The gospel presents Jesus as the Lord and Savior.

Lord and Savior. To speak of Jesus as Lord does not refer to the quality of our obedience to him. Jesus is Lord regardless of human obedience, and the dreadful day is coming when everything in all creation will acknowledge him as Lord (Phil. 2:10-11), even those who rejected him. When the Bible uses the term "Lord," it does not mean simply a nobleman or master. In the latter days of Israel, the people came to believe the name of God was too holy to pronounce, so they used the title "Lord" in place of the name *Yahweh*. The early church refused to say "Caesar is Lord," because they did not believe they should honor the authority of Caesar and be obedient to him. Both in the intention of the emperor cult and from the tradition of Israel, the phrase meant "Caesar is God." Christians believe that Jesus is God, the only begotten of the Father. To call Jesus our Lord means we realize the divine origin of the one who came to die for us. The gospel insists upon the deity of Christ.

Christ is Savior only because he is Lord. His critics rightly observed that only God can forgive sins (Luke 5:21). Only God could deal with the problem of sin and grant life to people. If Christ is not God, then he cannot save. The gospel bases salvation on the divine intervention of God who came into the world he had created. This fact renders void such statements as "I took Jesus as my Savior when I was fourteen, then I made him my Lord when I was twenty-five." Apart from sounding like commodity trading, statements like this one betray a basic misunderstanding of the gospel.

The promise of salvation rests with those who confess the Lord Jesus (Rom. 10:9-10, 13). One may have embraced the idea of heaven, eternal life, forgiveness of sins, and a thousand other blessings, but until one has confessed the Lord Jesus they do not have Jesus as their Savior. The English Puritans of the late sixteenth and early seventeenth century used to refer to the threefold office of Christ as Prophet, Priest, and King. In his earthly ministry, Jesus performed the work of prophet. He not only spoke the word of God, he was the Word of God. In his death and resurrection, he performed the work of a priest. He made and continues to make intercession for us, having borne our sins himself. In his ascended and exalted state, however, he reigns as King of kings and Lord of lords.

The Rich Young Ruler could not bring himself to give up his security to follow the man he called "Good Teacher" (Luke 18:18). But Zacchaeus immediately proceeded to dispose of his property and settled scores to follow the one he called "Lord" (Luke 19:8). The behavior of both men is perfectly understandable, given who each thought Jesus was. If Jesus was a good teacher, then what he had to say is relative. If, on the other hand, Jesus is Lord, then what he has to say is all that matters. In the gospel, salvation comes through repentance and faith in the Lord Jesus.

Repentance and Faith. For centuries theologians have argued over the place of repentance and faith in the order of salvation. Does faith come first, or repentance? Some would insist that repentance plays no part in salvation, otherwise salvation would be by works. Others argue that repentance is the basis for faith, otherwise salvation would come from cheap grace. An examination of the Bible leaves us perplexed when we try to discover the proper sequence. In his first two gospel sermons in Acts, Peter calls for repentance as the basis for salvation, but he never mentions faith (Acts 2:38; 3:19). Of course, those who repented were called "believers" (Acts 2:44; 4:32; 10:45). Paul told the Philippian jailer to "Believe on the Lord Jesus" (Acts 16:31), but he never mentioned repentance. When Peter gave an account of the conversion of Cornelius, he described how the Gentiles had the same experience as Jews who had faith. The Jewish Christians replied that God had granted repentance to the Gentiles (Acts 10:43; 11:15-18).

Perhaps the Bible is right, and theologians have asked the wrong question for centuries. Rather than two events, repentance and faith seem to occur as a single event. Rather than a cause and effect situation in which one produces the other, the Bible seems to indicate that repentance and faith are the two dimensions of the single experience called *conversion*. The two dimensions are so inseparable that one cannot occur without the other. Thus, to speak of one is to speak of the other by implication.

"Repentance" is a translation of the Greek word *metanoia* which has the idea of turning around or changing one's mind about something. When Zacchaeus met Jesus, he changed his mind about his possessions. The whole view of life, what mattered to him, and where he looked for security changed when he met Jesus. From the point of view of what he left behind, we speak of repentance. From the point of view of what he embraced, we speak of faith. The overall experience of repenting toward God from sin through faith in the Lord Jesus Christ, we call conversion (from the Greek word *epistrephein*, which means to turn).

We see the same idea of repentance and faith at work in the call of Abraham. God told him to leave his family, his friends, his culture, his country, his language, all that he was and all that he knew, and go to a land that he did not even know. God also promised to give him a family and a land and a place in history. Abraham believed God and left and went. He could not go to the new land without leaving the old; he could not leave the old land without going to the new. It occurred as one experience. He did it because he believed God. He had faith in God, and he changed his mind about everything that mattered to him. Abraham had believed in God before. In fact, living in Ur he had believed in many gods. Atheism had not posed a problem for him or very many other people in the history of the world. Faith, however, involves more than believing *in* God. It involves believing God, trusting God. Abraham did not simply turn his back on his old life in order to make a fresh start. He repented in faith toward God.

The validity of discipleship does not rest on the severity of our obedience to our own conception of righteousness as the Rich Young Ruler expected. It depends on meeting the Lord who draws us to follow him as we leave behind our own agendas. Repentance and faith do not occur as the cause/effect result of one another so much as they simultaneously occur as the result of meeting the Lord Jesus. In presenting the gospel, we have the obligation to present the Lord Jesus.

Salvation. In the twentieth century, American evangelicals have tended to equal salvation with justification. Justification refers to the legal dimension of salvation whereby God forgives our sins and declares us righteous. It deals with the negative aspect of salvation whereby God takes away the bad things. Most of the formal plans for presenting the gospel, such as "The Four Spiritual Laws," The Romans Road, and Evangelism Explosion, focus on justification. Unfortunately, the twentieth century has witnessed a neglect of the positive dimension of salvation known as regeneration. This aspect of salvation deals with what God brings into a life by his Holy Spirit. This positive aspect includes the new birth, the new nature, adoption as a child of God, the seal of assurance, guidance into truth, on-going cleansing from sin, holiness, communion with God, and empowering for service. The dynamic continuing dimension of salvation that coincides with and proceeds from justification and regeneration is sanctification.

Whereas justification and regeneration occur in a moment, sanctification extends the entire life of a Christian. The Holy Spirit sanctifies or makes holy. Paul described this process to the Corinthians:

> And we all, with unveiled face, beholding the glory of the Lord, are
> being changed into his likeness from one degree of glory to another; for
> this comes from the Lord who is the Spirit (2 Cor. 3:18, RSV).

By the activity of the Holy Spirit, a Christian grows to spiritual maturity, as they consciously focus their lives on Christ. Paul also compared this life-long process with winning a race (Phil. 3:12-14; 2 Tim. 4:7-8). Jesus himself compared it to a branch that receives its life by virtue of its attachment to the main vine (John 15:1-11). Apart from its connection to the vine, the branch is a lifeless limb that produces no fruit. The vine makes the fruit appear in due season. The New Testament makes clear that the present benefits of salvation God intends for Christians to enjoy during their life only come through the intimacy of a relationship with Christ.

In the twentieth century, a popular conception of eternal life as a commodity has arisen that sharply contrasts with the biblical view. This view portrays eternal life as a possession rather than as a relationship. Paul constantly reminds us that the benefits of Christ belong to those who are "in Christ." John joins this theme and declares bluntly:

> And this is the testimony, that God gave us eternal life, and this life is
> in his Son. He who has the Son has life; he who has not the Son of God
> has not life (1 John 5:11-12 RSV).

Salvation does not consist in our having eternal life, but in Christ having *us*. The Rich Young Ruler wanted eternal life but did not want the Lord. Zacchaeus wanted the Lord and found that he had eternal life as a result. Paul had a parallel experience: "For his sake I have suffered the loss of all things, and count them as refuse, in order that I may gain Christ and be found in him . . ." (Phil. 3:8b-9a, RSV).

By presenting salvation as only a transaction whereby we obtain eternal life, we limit the extent to which discipleship can occur. We present the gospel as though nothing else remains to experience, instead of as the prelude Jesus described to Nathaniel: "You shall see greater things than that" (John 1:50b, RSV). With a faulty view of salvation, Christians have no basis for pursuing Christ.

When Peter preached the first gospel sermon on the Day of Pentecost, he dealt with more than justification. What is more, he never mentioned eternal life. He did not have to mention it. Eternal life comes as the by-product of what he did offer: the forgiveness of sins and the gift of the Holy Spirit. The absence of sin and the presence of God creates eternal life.

When we fail to disclose the role of the Holy Spirit in salvation to someone as we tell them the gospel, we have left out how God applies salvation to our lives (Rom. 8:11). We leave young Christians ignorant of the one who makes discipleship a possibility (Gal. 5:25). We leave them ignorant of the power at work within them (Eph. 1:16-20). We leave them ignorant of the fellowship they can experience with God (Rom. 8:14-16). We leave them ignorant of the guidance available to them (John 16:13-15). We leave them ignorant of their obligation for service (Eph. 4:11-14).

I once asked a denominational leader why his denomination made no mention of the Holy Spirit in their gospel presentation materials. He replied that they did not want to confuse people. They were afraid someone might link the gift of the Holy Spirit with speaking in tongues. Rather than deal with the issue, they left it out entirely. Unfortunately, this attitude has characterized American Christians for the majority of the twentieth century. A fear of the excesses of the holiness movement and later the charismatic movement have succeeded in making the Holy Spirit and sanctification the two lost doctrines of the twentieth century. The implications for evangelism and discipleship are enormous.

Follow-up. When the apostles found faith in their hearers, they immediately drew the new believers into the fellowship of the church. Following the dramatic experience of the Day of Pentecost, the believers devoted themselves to learning what it meant to follow Jesus. They did so through spending time with those who could teach them. They ate together and prayed together. They worshiped together and demonstrated the power of God in their lives through the things they did, so that God used them in the conversion of other people on a daily basis. Luke describes this follow-up process in Acts 2:42-47.

While discipleship necessarily includes being and doing, it also necessarily includes learning. The disciple follows as a learner throughout life. In this respect, reclaiming the idea of discipline might go a long way toward revitalizing the learning dimension of discipleship. The early church practiced the disciplines of prayer, Bible study, and fellowship. They had the intentional habit of making these disciplines a part of their lives. While no program of study constitutes discipleship, the discipline that such a program affords creates a context for discipleship to occur. For most people a discipline must begin as self-consciously painful before it can grow sub-consciously natural.

Prayer, Bible study, and Christian fellowship form the triad through which the Lord continues to speak to Christians and to bid them follow. Through prayer a Christian experiences the leadership of the Spirit, but the objective word of the Bible and the experience of other Christians provide the two witnesses to test one's experience, if it be of God. Likewise, prayer and other Christians form the context of interpreting Scripture, lest there be a private interpretation.

Finally, prayer and the Bible form the basis for determining the direction of the church, that things might be done decently and in order.

Conclusion

Interest in discipleship has grown from a variety of concerns held by a diverse spectrum of Christians. These concerns include the disparity between Christian faith and practice, the accommodation of Christians to worldliness, the high percentage of converts who never become part of a church, the high percentage of inactive church members, the apathy of congregations, the impotence of ministries, and the lack of interest in spiritual matters. All of these concerns relate to a failure in discipleship.

Since the beginning of the church, Christians have had to deal with this problem. Unfortunately, the remedy we choose may intensify the problem rather than remedy it. The concern for spiritual discipline carried many Christians to the cloisters during the Middle Ages, but it carried them away from ministry to a world in need. Often we labor under the temptation of finding a structural solution to a spiritual problem. If Christians do not take the lordship of Christ seriously, then we reason that obedience needs to be stressed in evangelism. If Christians do not have a conscious desire to serve Christ, then we reason that commitment needs a more prominent emphasis in evangelism.

All too often we attempt to correct a spiritual problem with a greater exertion of the flesh. John Hendrick has observed that "the main cause of the current ineffectiveness in our churches, whether in nurture or evangelism or social action, is related to an erosion of faith."[12] Paul dealt essentially with the same problem among the Galatians who had turned to a structural means—the law—for their progress:

> Let me ask you only this: Did you receive the Spirit by works of the law, or by hearing with faith? Are you so foolish? Having begun with the Spirit, are you now ending with the flesh? (Gal. 3:2-3 RSV).

If Christians lack obedience and commitment, they cannot with any validity dredge them up from within apart from faith. Paul understood obedience, for he remained obedient to "the heavenly vision" (Acts 26:19). He told the Romans that the Lord supplied the grace "to bring about the obedience of faith" (Rom. 1:5). Obedience does not result from the effort to be obedient, rather it comes from the grace of God as we trust Christ.

Discipleship will not improve by making the demands of Christianity more vigorous in the presentation of the gospel. Rather, discipleship will grow increasingly more prevalent as we give more attention to the gracious benefits of Christ in the gospel. Christ alone supplies sufficient motive to follow Christ. The love, joy, and peace of the relationship with Christ creates the compulsion to follow. Call it irresistible grace, but never cheap. Paul said of it,

> I have been crucified with Christ; it is no longer I who live, but Christ who lives in me; and the life I now live in the flesh I live by faith in the Son of God, who loved me and gave himself for me (Gal. 2:20 RSV).

As we face the twenty-first century, we have the challenge of recovering the sound doctrine of the Holy Spirit. We have the obligation to restore regeneration and sanctification to our preaching of the gospel. Our churches have the responsibility to take the initiative in embracing new Christians, teaching them the disciplines of Christian life, and modeling the work of ministry. We need to understand that discipleship will take different forms because God has given us different callings—but one Lord, one faith, one baptism.

Finally, apart from a life of discipleship rooted in one's daily relationship with Jesus Christ, a Christian has no substantial motive to evangelize. Even if one has the intellectual belief that everyone needs to know Jesus Christ, that belief does not supply the motivation by itself to evangelize. Guilt will not do it. Only that close communion with the Lord produces the kind of joy that compels a Christian to tell the gospel. New Christians have to tell others what has happened, because their joy is so full. Apart from the maintenance of that close fellowship with the Lord, however, the joy fades. Sin creeps in. Our lives show little resemblance to the one who loved us and gave himself for us. King David well understood this dynamic when, in his great psalm of confession, he prayed:

Restore unto me the joy of thy salvation;
and uphold me with thy free Spirit.
Then will I teach transgressors thy ways;
and sinners shall be converted unto thee (Ps. 51:12-13).

Endnotes

1. Dietrich Bonhoeffer, *The Cost of Discipleship* (Rev. ed.; New York: Collier Books, 1963), p. 45.

2. Jim Wallis, *The Call to Conversion* (San Francisco, CA: Harper & Row Publishers, 1981), p. 19.

3. Donald A. McGavran, *Understanding Church Growth* (Rev. ed.; Grand Rapids, MI: William B. Eerdmans Publishing Co., 1980), p. 26.

4. Donald A. McGavran and Winfield C. Arn, *Ten Steps for Church Growth* (San Francisco, CA: Harper & Row Publishers, 1977), p. 11.

5. C. Peter Wagner, *Your Church Can Grow* (Glendale, CA: Regal Books, 1979), p. 31.

6. J. I. Packer, *Evangelism and the Sovereignty of God* (Downers Grove, IL: Inter-Varsity Press, 1961), p. 37.

7. Delos Miles, *Introduction to Evangelism* (Nashville, TN: Broadman Press, 1983), p. 40.

8. Harvie M. Conn, *Evangelism: Doing Justice and Preaching Grace* (Grand Rapids, MI: The Zondervan Corp., 1982), p. 61.

9. James Gregory Merritt, *Evangelism for Discipleship in the Gospel of Luke: Implications for Modern Day Evangelism* (Unpublished Ph.D. dissertation at the Southern Baptist Theological Seminary, 1982), p. 4.

10. Wallis, p. 4.

11. David Watson, *I Believe in Evangelism* (Grand Rapids, MI: William B. Eerdmans Publishing Co., 1979), p. 11.

12. John R. Hendrick, *Opening the Door of Faith* (Atlanta, GA: John Knox Press, 1977), p. 87.

14

EVANGELISM AND
THE CALL OF CHRIST
James G. Merritt

*James G. Merritt is the pastor of the rapidly growing First Baptist
Church of Snellville, Georgia. He earned the Ph.D. in evangelism at
the Southern Baptist Theological Seminary under Lewis Drummond.
Dr. Merritt's doctoral thesis dealt specifically with evangelism and the
call of Christ in the Gospel of Luke.*

When I was asked to write an article in honor of Dr. Lewis Drummond, my former
mentor, I enthusiastically accepted. First of all, Dr. Drummond has had an inestimable impact upon my life, both as a student and as a preacher of the gospel of
Jesus Christ. I was also excited about the topic, "Evangelism and the Call of
Christ," because this was precisely the subject of my doctoral thesis: *Evangelism
for Discipleship in the Gospel of Luke: Implications for Modern-Day Evangelism.*

It should go without saying that the task of evangelism is at least one *raison
d'etre* of the church.[1] This proposition, however, begs the question of the character and nature of the evangelistic call. Many evangelical leaders have come to
recognize that one of the major drawbacks of evangelism today has been the
tendency, even among evangelicals, to oversimplify the evangelistic message.[2]

Juan Carlos Ortiz, in his refreshing book, *Disciple*, reminds us that the gospel
which we have in the Bible is the gospel of the kingdom of God. It presents Jesus
as King and as Lord of all life. The gospel is a Christ-centered word. Yet today it
seems that the gospel has often become a person-centered message, the gospel of
the "big offer" and the "hot sale," getting people to Christ rather than submitting
to him as Lord.[3] The fact is, Jesus sought more than a superficial following; he
sought disciples. In short, the evangelistic call of Jesus was essentially a call to
repentance and radical discipleship.[4] One could liken the call of Jesus to a

beautiful diamond, through which prisms of light flow. Different shades of light will be seen according to the angle at which the diamond is held. Likewise, the call of Christ to discipleship is a multi-faceted call which demands a singular commitment of faith and obedience.

To examine the call of Christ in an exhaustive fashion is beyond the purview of this article. Hence, I am going to deal with the responsibility of an individual Christian to personal evangelism as one response to the call of Christ. One of the great weaknesses of the church today as it attempts to carry out her evangelistic mandate is the failure of her individual members to realize that each individual Christian has, as a responsibility of true discipleship, the need for being a personal evangelist. This aspect of the call of Christ is seen over and over in Luke's gospel.[5]

Normally, when the word "discipleship" is mentioned, particularly in the context of following Jesus, various thoughts of "denying self," "taking up the cross," and "counting the cost" come to mind. These concepts are intimately attached to the entire call of Christ to discipleship. Yet, the concept of *discipleship as evangelism* has been ignored to the detriment of the modern church. Several key passages in Luke's gospel reveal that the evangelistic task is incumbent upon everyone who would be a follower of Jesus Christ.[6]

Luke's recording of our Lord's calling of the first disciples is most instructive. In Luke 5:1-11 we read the story of how Simon Peter, and the brothers James and John, were summoned by Christ to follow him in a life of discipleship. These men had been fishing all night but had not caught anything. But at the command of a perfect stranger, Jesus, these men cast their nets out into the deep and caught such a gigantic amount of fish that "their net was breaking" (5:6). It was not a "lucky guess" by our Lord, but rather a miraculous manifestation of his divine power. But from a discipleship perspective, the main interest lies not in the miraculous catch, but in the reaction of the disciples and the response of Jesus in verses eight through ten.

Two words are of particular significance in verses five and eight of this chapter. The first is Peter's address of Jesus as "Master."[7] The word is used only by disciples, or near disciples,[8] and here signifies an attitude of obedience, accented by Peter's lowering of the net at Jesus' command, despite a night of fruitless fishing.[9]

The second word is "Lord," Peter's address of Jesus in verse eight. Though the title of Lord is almost entirely absent from the other synoptics as a designation of Jesus, in Luke it is one of the most common. For the disciples the term signifies that the authority of Jesus goes beyond that of a "rabbi"—a significant point.[10]

In verse ten Jesus makes a prediction: "Do not be afraid. From now on you will catch men." This prophecy has the effect of a command[11] representing the fact that the call to intimate discipleship is a call to immediate evangelism.[12]

The verb "catch men" literally means "to capture alive"[13] and was used in the Septuagint for saving persons alive from danger.[14] Obviously here it refers to saving lost humanity from the spiritual danger of separation from God. From this point on, rather than taking fish, the disciples will be taking persons for God and the kingdom. The disciples will be recruiting agents for the new people of God.[15]

Even as Jesus went fishing for these disciples, these disciples are now to go fishing for others. Jesus is calling disciples who, in turn, are willing to gather other disciples in missionary service.[16] This observation is crucial, for as Hahn has stated: "Discipleship therefore means to be totally bound to Jesus' person and His mission. It is precisely this which distinguishes it from any previous idea of discipleship."[17]

The implications of this entire passage are staggering for every Christian. To be a disciple one must follow Jesus. But to follow Jesus, one will become a fisher of men. Therefore, "if you are not fishing, you are not following!" The call to discipleship is indeed a call to evangelism.

In Luke 9:1-6 the full contingency of the Twelve are sent out on their first full-fledged evangelistic mission. Luke has included the narrative of the mission of the Twelve here, for he wishes to record that the Twelve, witnesses and missionaries *par excellence* in Acts, are both fulfilling their earlier calling and prefiguring their later ministry.[18] A proleptic anticipation of further ministry, it is also a pragmatic exercise in "catching men alive."[19]

The disciples are sent out to preach the kingdom of God (9:2). This message ties the missionary task of the disciples to Jesus' own as he was the kingdom-preacher. His message was to be their message, just as his mission was to be their mission.[20]

In the Lukan scheme of things, the passage shows that the purpose behind the choosing of the Twelve in 6:13 is that they might share in the evangelistic mission of Jesus.[21] Jesus makes it plain that at times rejection is to be expected as one response to the evangelistic call of Christ. Still, the message is to be taken everywhere for the response given to the church's message is to be left to the judgment of God. Discipleship means offering to everyone, whether they accept it or reject it, the message of salvation.

In Luke 10:1-16 we have an incident recorded only by Luke. The fact that Luke is the only evangelist to record a further mission by Seventy (-two) other disciples is extremely significant for it serves to highlight his strong interest in mission and evangelism. What is addressed to the Twelve in Matthew (cf. Matthew 9:27ff.; 10:7-16; 11:21-23) is here directed to the Seventy (-two).[22]

This fact is extremely important, for it shows that the task of evangelism is not limited to the Twelve, a point that would not have been lost on Luke's Gentile (or Jewish) readers.[23] The mission is a parallel to the mission of the Twelve in 9:1ff.

Luke's point is this: The mission of the Seventy (-two) is the continuing task of the church.[24]

The events of 9:1-6 are repeated on a grander scale, thus showing that the task of mission was not confined to the Twelve—a crucial fact in understanding Luke's conception of discipleship and evangelism.[25]

The fact that they are sent out "two by two," follows the Old Testament rules for binding corroborating testimony.[26] This detail indicates that evangelistic proclamation was to be their major concern.[27]

Thus, the future work of the church and the present task of the disciples is, in Luke's eyes, seen in the mission of the Seventy (-two).[28] Hendriksen has caught the significance of this perspective:

> ... does not the mention of these Seventy (-two) stress the fact that the kingdom's work is not limited to the few, for example, to Jesus and the Twelve, but that every believer should participate? ... first there was Jesus, then also the Twelve, now the Seventy (-two). And these, in turn are told to pray that the Lord may send forth (still more) laborers into the harvest.[29]

Disciples are sent forth as "laborers into the harvest" (9:2). This "harvest" has as its background the eschatological gathering of God's people which is regarded as occurring in the mission of the disciples.[30] The point is not to be missed: the relation of the disciples to Jesus is fashioned in the mold of witness. Witness to Jesus and his message is the task to which disciples are called.[31] Indeed, Luke closes his gospel with precisely this message from the risen Lord.

The "third mission" of the disciples is recorded in the resurrection commission given by Christ in Luke 24:45-49. This commission is intimately related to the other pre-resurrection missions of the disciples (cf. 9:1-9; 10:1-20), and is a continuation of these preceding missions.[32] This commission is the resurrection command to be "fishers of men." A new element now enters Luke's thought explicitly: a prophetic command to preach the gospel to all nations.[33]

In 24:44 Jesus is referring back to what he told his disciples in his pre-resurrection state. Luke desires to show that Jesus is consistent in his teaching and command, both in his physical presence and his soon-to-be absence.[34] The mission of the church—to evangelize, to preach repentance for the forgiveness of sins—is traced to scriptural prophecy.[35]

Verses 48-49 climax the commission of the risen Lord to his church for all ages. The term "witness" found in verse 48 is first found in Luke's writings here and combines the denotation of the term as a "witness to facts" with that of a "witness" in the sense of evangelistic confession.[36] The understanding is that of one who fully proclaims the message of Christ, not of one who bears witness to the point of death.[37]

The disciples are to discharge their evangelistic task by proclaiming both the facts of the risen Lord and their significance which they have grasped in faith.[38] This strong Lukan view of the disciples to give witness to the risen Christ is not unrelated to the aspect of discipleship understood as "following Jesus."[39] Evangelistic witness to the risen Lord is a continuation of the demands to discipleship of the earthly Jesus.[40]

For this evangelistic task, Jesus invokes the "promise of the Father," a reference to the Holy Spirit.[41] Luke imbues the giving of the Holy Spirit with a particular theological interpretation—it is an empowering for mission.[42] Evangelism is to be done by the disciples of Jesus in the Spirit and the Spirit is given to the disciples for evangelism.[43]

A conclusion salient both to the corporate mission of the church and to the personal discipleship of the individual is drawn: Evangelism is an integral part of discipleship, not just an appendage to it. A true and sincere response to the call of Christ to discipleship will result in the development of a lifestyle in which spreading the gospel of the kingdom is both natural and necessary.

Indeed, evangelism is itself a sign that one has heard correctly the word and demand of Jesus. In other words, it is both a misnomer and biblically incorrect to separate in totality evangelism from discipleship. Evangelism not only results in the making of disciples, but true discipleship always results in personal evangelism. A natural response to the call of discipleship given by our Lord is personal evangelism.

I feel compelled to conclude this article with an experience drawn from the life of the man in whose honor it was written. I was in my Master's degree work at Southern Seminary in Louisville, Kentucky. I was taking a class entitled "Evangelistic Preaching" with a man that I barely knew, named Lewis Drummond. Dr. Drummond was rarely late for class, but in this instance he was twenty minutes late.

Several students were tempted to leave, but deep down we all knew that Dr. Drummond would eventually be there since he never missed a lecture. Finally, twenty minutes late, Dr. Drummond came walking in. He apologized profusely for his tardiness. We all soon, however, forgot his tardiness when he gave us the reason for it. He said, "I am so sorry that I was late; but I just finished leading the telephone repairman to Christ." His testimony set my heart on fire. It was at that moment that I knew that I had found the man with whom I wanted to do doctoral work. I wanted to study under a man who not only practiced what he preached, but also preached what he practiced!

It was Dr. Lewis Drummond who, both by precept and practice, taught me the intimate connection between "fishing and following"—that is between evangelism and discipleship. Would to God that all true professing Christians would heed the call of Christ in becoming personal evangelists—for the essence of true discipleship is in making disciples of others.

Endnotes

1. "The unmistakable priority of God's people, the Church in the world, is to proclaim God's revealed Word. Divorced from this calling, the church and Christians are undurable (sic.) and unendurable phenomena. By stifling divine revelation, they are, in fact, an affront to God. Devoid of motivation for implementing Christ's calls, they become both delinquents and delinquent in neighbor and world relations." Carl F. H. Henry, *God, Revelation and Authority*, II, (Waco, TX: Word, 1979), p. 22.

2. J. I. Packer, *Evangelism and Sovereignty of God*, (Downers Grove, IL: InterVarsity Press, 1961), p. 37. "But the way to tell whether in fact you are evangelizing is not to ask whether conversions are known to have resulted from your witness, it is to ask whether you are faithfully making known the gospel message." Ibid., p. 41. Also see Robert E. Webber, *Common Roots: a Call to Evangelical Maturity*, (Grand Rapids: Zondervan, 1979), p. 156.

3. Juan Carlos Ortiz, *Disciple* (Altamonte Springs, FL: Creation House, 1979), pp. 12-13. Cf. R. B. Kuiper, *God-centered Evangelism* (Carlisle, PA: Banner of Truth, 1979), p. 8, for his acute observation of this problem in the evangelistic enterprise.

4. Jim Wallis, *Agenda for Biblical People* (San Francisco: Harper and Row, 1984), p. 19. He asserts, "A central tenet of biblical teaching is that those who have experienced conversion through the gospel are to enter into a life of serious discipleship." Ibid., p. 9.

5. Donald Bloesch, *Essentials of Evangelical Theology*, II, (San Francisco: Harper and Row, 1978), p. 36. See also Howard A. Snyder, *The Community of the King* (Downers Grove, IL: InterVarsity Press, 1979), p. 104.

6. Michael Green in his outstanding work *Evangelism in the Early Church* (Grand Rapids: Eerdmans, 1970), has flatly stated that "The man who, more than anyone in the early church, has given us his assessments of the factors in evangelism is St. Luke." (p. 148). See also I. Howard Marshall, *Luke: Historian and Theologian* (Grand Rapids: Zondervan, 1979), p. 319.

7. The word "Master" is Lukan, being absent from the Synoptic parallels which use either "teacher" or "rabbi" though here it appears to be roughly equivalent to "rabbi." See I. Howard Marshall, *Commentary on Luke, The New International Greek Commentary on the New Testament* (Grand Rapids: Eerdmans, 1978), p. 203. Also see Joseph A. Fitzmyer, *The Gospel According to Luke*, I - IX (New York: Doubleday 1981), p. 566.

8. George E. Ladd, *Theology of the New Testament* (Grand Rapids: Eerdmans, 1974), p. 338.

9. Marshall, *Commentary on Luke*, p. 202.

10. The word here definitely means more than a mere honorific "sir" though it has perhaps less connotation than the Christology of the early church. Marshall, *Commentary on Luke*, p. 274; Ladd, p. 171.

11. This is exactly how it is presented in Mark 1:17.

12. The phrase "from now on" is Lukan (Cf. 1:48; 12:52; 22:18, 69; Acts 18:6) and stresses the new dimension which comes in one's life when he meets Jesus: priorities are totally rearranged. Leon Morris, *The Gospel According to Luke* (Grand Rapids: Eerdmans, 1974), p. 114. With this phrase, Luke introduces a note of immediacy to the call missing in Mark. Fitzmyer, p. 568.

13. Walter Bauer, *A Greek-English Lexicon of the New Testament and Other Early Christian Literature* (Chicago: University of Chicago Press, 1979), p. 340. Cf. II Timothy 2:26.

14. See Num. 31:15,18; Deut. 20:16.

15. C. H. Dodd, *The Founder of Christianity* (New York: Macmillan, 1970), p. 91; Dietrich Muller, "Disciple," *The New International Dictionary of New Testament Theology,* I (Grand Rapids: Zondervan, 1979), p. 489.

16. A. B. Bruce, *The Training of the Twelve* (Grand Rapids: Kregel, 1971), pp. 12-13.

17. Ferdinand Hahn, *Mission in the New Testament,* (London: SCM Press, 1965), p. 21.

18. Marshall, *Commentary on Luke,* p. 350.

19. E. Earle Ellis, *The Gospel of Luke* (Greenwood, SC: Attic Press, 1974), p. 135, notes: "The Earlier Prophecy of Christ to Peter" (5:10) now finds a partial fulfillment."

20. Marshall, *Commentary on Luke,* p. 352; Fitzmyer, p. 753. This message certainly included for Luke the call to discipleship and repentance. The Good News of the kingdom precedes the call to repent. Marshall, *Commentary on Luke,* p. 350. Cf. 4:16-21. See Bruce, p. 102.

21. Fitzmyer, p. 252. He also states that it is a foreshadowing of the commission in 24:46-47. Marshall makes the salient point that though the various instructions give the impression of being meant for a particular time and place, their preservation by Mark and the other Evangelists signifies that they regarded the basic principles as having lasting value for the church. Marshall, *Commentary on Luke,* p. 351.

22. The question as to whether "Seventy" or Seventy-two" is the correct number of disciples is extremely difficult to determine and is not germane to this article. Hence, "Seventy (-two)" will be the continued reference for the present purpose, thus preserving the uncertainty of the writer as to the correct figure. For a full discussion see Bruce M. Metzger, *A Textual Commentary on the Greek New Testament* (London: United Bible Society, 1971), pp. 150-151.

23. It is thus very possible that Luke regarded this mission as a prefigurement of the church's mission to the Gentiles. Marshall, *Commentary on Luke,* p. 413.

24. Ellis, p. 154.

25. Helmut Flender, *St. Luke: Theologian of Redemptive History* (Philadelphia: Fortress, 1967), pp. 19-23.

26. Cf. Deut. 17:6: 19:15.

27. Marshall, *Commentary on Luke,* p. 416.

28. Marshall, *Commentary on Luke,* p. 416; Ellis, p. 155. This understanding is bolstered by the fact that the message is still the same: in the person of Jesus the kingdom of God has come. Both before and after Easter one could proclaim the presence of the kingdom!

29. William Hendriksen, *The Gospel of Luke* (Grand Rapids: Baker, 1978), p. 572.

30. Bruce Demarest, "Seed," *New International Dictionary of New Testament Theology,* III (Grand Rapids: Zondervan, 1978), 525-527. Marshall, *Commentary on Luke,*

p. 416, states that though the reference may have been to Israel and its original context, Luke may have seen it as a harbinger of the church's world mission.

31. This truth is both theologically expressed by the parable of the lamp (8:16-18) and practically illustrated by the Gerasene Demoniac (8:6-39). These passages undergird and illustrate the call to discipleship as the call to personal evangelism.

32. Ellis, p. 228.

33. The references to preaching "unto all the nations" and the promise of divine power link this material with Matt. 28:16-20. The promise of the Holy Spirit and the reference to "forgiveness of sins" link it to John 20:21-23. Hence, common tradition underlies these accounts with the basic nucleus comprised of Jesus' commission to spread the gospel, the offer of forgiveness of sins, and the promise of divine power. Marshall, *Commentary on Luke*, pp. 903-904.

34. Luke's phrase "while still being with you" is his way of expressing the difference between the periods of Jesus' earthly life and that of his absence. The Lord is primarily referring back to his passion predictions in 9:22,44; 17:25; 18:31 ff.; 22:37. Marshall, *Commentary on Luke*, pp. 904-905.

35. Cf. 13-35. The phrase "in his name" (v. 47) is tantamount to "give an opportunity for repentance," (Acts 5:31). Marshall, *Commentary on Luke*, p. 906. This proclamation is to be done "to all nations" in keeping with Luke's universalism. Thus the passage serves as a proleptic anticipation of the mission to the Gentiles in the Book of Acts.

36. A. A. Trites, "Witness," *New International Dictionary of New Testament Theology*, III, 1044. The fact of a risen Lord intrinsically demands its evangelistic proclamation in Luke's thought.

37. Trites, "Witness,", Ibid., p. 1044.

38. See further A. A. Trites, "The Idea of Witness in the Synoptic Gospels—Some Juridical Considerations" *Themelios*, 5 (March, 1968), 1826. And R. V. Moss, "The Witnessing Church in the New Testament," *Theology and Life*, 3 (1960, 266).

39. Fitzmyer, p. 243. See also Mark Sheridan, "Disciples and Discipleship in Matthew and Luke," *Biblical Theology Bulletin*, 3 (1973), 241-254; See C. K. Barrett, *Luke the Historian in Recent Study* (Philadelphia: Fortress, 1970) , p. 71.

40. Marshall, *Luke*, pp. 200-201 has astutely noted that "evangelism and speaking the word of the Lord were by no means confined to those who were witnesses in the technical sense . . . it was not the messengers who had to be authenticated so much as the message itself. Presentation of the gospel might be done by anybody."

41. Marshall, *Commentary on Luke*, p. 907.

42. Marshall, *Luke*, p. 200. See also Charles Hummel, *Fire in the Fireplace: Contemporary Charismatic Renewal* (Downers Grove, IL: InterVarsity Press, 1979), p. 482. Cf. Luke 12:11. In light of this statement the essence of being a Christian is seen in the activity of mission.

43. Morris, p. 343. For a further study of the Holy Spirit in Luke's thought see K. Stalder, "Der Heilige Geist In der lukanischen Ekklesia Logie," *Una Sancta* 30 (1975), 287-293. Brilliantly, Luke has set the stage for Pentecost and a proper understanding of it in Acts 2.

PART FIVE:
Evangelism and Reaching People

The methodology of evangelism is a diverse discipline. In this section the writers look at four distinct approaches for reaching people for Christ. Bill Bright says that one of the primary reasons people do not do one-on-one personal evangelism is a fear of failure. His chapter addresses ways to conquer that fear. Franklin Graham examines missionary, or cross-cultural, evangelism as a means to reach people for Christ. T.W. Wilson looks at crusade evangelism and the ways this methodology of evangelism can be most successful. Finally, Larry J. Michael discusses general principles for reaching one segment of our world for Christ, the youth of today.

15

PERSONAL EVANGELISM: CONQUERING THE FEAR OF FAILURE
Bill Bright

Bill Bright is a name virtually synonymous with personal evangelism today. He is the president of Campus Crusade for Christ International. The author of numerous books and articles, Mr. Bright's most recent book is Witnessing without Fear.

I am honored to write a chapter for this book in honor of Lewis A. Drummond. Dr. Drummond is a man I greatly admire for his contributions to the exciting field of evangelism.

In my experiences in teaching, writing, and doing personal evangelism, I have observed a looming concern that causes many to neglect the exciting opportunity to witness to someone: the fear of failure. For many people, when someone says "no" to Christ, they feel personally rejected. In this chapter, I hope to alleviate some of these fears so that we may all become bold witnesses for Christ.

When Someone Says "No" to Christ

On a bright, hot day in Oklahoma many years ago, I had concluded a visit with my parents and was driving toward the airport in a rented car. Ahead, I saw a big truck pulling out from a side road, preparing to enter my lane of the highway.

In a flash of a moment, I thought, "I have the right of way—surely, he's going to stop till I've gone past." I was wrong. He pulled right in front of me, and there was no way I could stop or swerve to avoid him.

The crash totaled my car. My only injury was a small scratch on my arm where my watch had moved. But the truck driver, at fault for not yielding the right-of-way, was so scared he almost had a nervous breakdown. We left the car beside the road, and the driver drove me back to Coweta to see his boss.

The boss was the county commissioner, a long-time friend of my family, to whom I had witnessed several times previously with no results. He helped me handle the details and reporting of the accident, then drove me to the airport.

I just knew in my heart that the Lord would use these otherwise traumatic circumstances to allow me to share Christ again with this man. I decided to be straightforward with him.

"You know, I think the Lord may have allowed all this to happen so I could talk to you again. We just never know when an accident like that can take our lives. I was ready to go—suppose it had happened to you? Are you ready to go?"

But he still wasn't ready. "It just isn't for me," he said.

I got on the plane thankful that God had spared my life but also sorrowful that, once again, this man had rejected the Lord Jesus Christ.

Failure. Fear of it can be one of the biggest cripplers of a faithful witness, for none of us likes to be "turned down." We tend to take it personally, regarding a rejection to our message as a rejection of our person. It hurts to be turned down.

It hurts even more when we've reached out in genuine love and we see the person refuse the greatest Gift ever offered to mankind, God's Son. Compassion for the lost does not come without tears.

But one of the liberating facts of the Christian life is that God does not ask anything of us which his Son has not already gone through himself. Jesus Christ, to whom crowds walked miles for teaching and healing, saw his message rejected by many. Unlike us, however, Jesus did not grieve because his ego had been hurt. He grieved because people rejected the Giver of life and the gift of eternal life.

Did Jesus "Fail" in His Witnessing?

Our Lord's ministry raises some interesting questions: Did he "fail" in his witness-ing? Did he fail when the rich young ruler walked away from him, refusing to give God first place in his life? Did he fail because Judas Iscariot never received him as his Messiah? Did he fail because one of the thieves crucified with him refused to acknowledge his lordship? Was he a failure because many in the throngs around him didn't receive him?

Our Lord himself answered these questions in his prayer to his heavenly Father at the end of his earthly ministry:

"I brought glory to you here on earth by doing everything you told me to" (John 17:4, TLB).

Despite rejection, or what we might call "failures," our Lord Jesus Christ knew his mission was near completion. He had obeyed his Father's commission. He had brought the message and was about to complete it with his death and resurrection.

While he grieved over those who had rejected him, he had not failed. He had done "everything" which God had given him to do.

All He Asks Is That We Obey

Our heavenly Father asks no more of us than this: that we obey his command to "Go, and preach the gospel to everyone." His command is not to "convert" everyone. Jesus did not, and neither can we. But we can obey; we can spread the message to all who will listen and trust God for the results.

The ministry of Jesus Christ modeled for us a liberating truth about our witnessing efforts: *Success in witnessing is simply taking the initiative to share Christ in the power of the Holy Spirit, and leaving the results to God.*

Jesus never failed in his ministry. He accomplished all his Father had commissioned him to do. Likewise, we do not fail if we obey what God wants us to do, motivated by genuine love and compassion. We fail in witnessing only if we disobey God's command to share his love in the power of the Holy Spirit: *Failure in witnessing = failing to witness.*

Had I not learned this truth, I would have been confused and defeated after that county commissioner rejected my message. Or I might have been discouraged one night in the parking lot in Washington, D.C., as I talked with the lot attendant about the Lord. I had just come from an exciting day on Capitol Hill, where I'd met with several national leaders for prayer and fellowship, and I sensed the Holy Spirit prompting me to ask the parking lot attendant if he was a Christian.

"My dad was a minister," he snapped, "and he didn't practice what he preached. So I had as much of that stuff as I could stand." He went on to tell how he had left the church and didn't want anything to do with God.

I couldn't help but get a lump in my throat as I thought of my own two sons: What if I had been inconsistent in my life and ministry? What if they had rejected God because of me?

We talked further. He had never received the Lord, and no matter what I said, he didn't want to do so now.

I went to my room in the hotel. But my soul wouldn't rest. Some may think, "He was just a parking lot attendant." But this man was important to the Lord, and to me—just as important as the senators and government officials I had shared with earlier, and my heart went out to him. He had come so close to a life with Christ but had never embraced him. I decided to go back downstairs, out into the parking lot, and talk further with him. But again he refused to receive Christ.

I hurt for him. His rejection of the Savior grieved me.

But had I failed?

If Christ's example is reliable, the task at hand was not to get results. That may or may not happen. The task to which God had called me at that moment was to obey him and share Christ as effectively and lovingly as I knew how.

No-Fail Witnessing

When you obey God, motivated by love, you cannot fail. Your message might be accepted or rejected, but when you share Christ in obedience to God's command and the Holy Spirit's leading, you "succeed" in witnessing, no matter what the immediate result.

Success in witnessing is simply taking the initiative to share Christ in the power of the Holy Spirit, and leaving the results to God.

Read that statement aloud. Memorize it. Whenever the fear of failure begins to immobilize you from obeying God in witnessing, repeat this statement to yourself. Success in witnessing is simply sharing Christ in the power of the Holy Spirit, and leaving the results to God.

This is not to be interpreted as advocating a "hit-and-run" approach to witnessing and ministry, without conscientious follow-up to help new believers get into God's Word and grow in their faith. We firmly believe in the importance of a new Christian getting involved in (1) a church where our Lord is honored and the Word of God is proclaimed; and (2) systematic training in assurance of salvation, prayer, Bible study, fellowship with others, and Christian growth.

Removing the Burden of "Results"

Rather, this definition is intended to remove from today's frustrated Christian the burden of "results." To the faithful witness, there will come many joyous experiences of leading others to Christ. In most countries and cultures, we find that between 25 and 50 percent of those who hear the gospel (when presented by properly trained, Spirit-filled believers) receive Christ as a result. But if these positive numbers are true, then between 50 and 75 percent will say "no," at least upon first hearing.

Do the "no's" constitute failure? Go back to the definitions of success and failure in witnessing. Repeat them aloud. Do these percentages justify our not sharing Christ, because we might hit a streak of "no's"?

Once I was at Wheaton College in Wheaton, Illinois, holding a lay institute where we gave training in how to share one's faith. Part of the institute consisted of an afternoon of actual witnessing, door-to-door.

A good friend of mine, a professor at the college, came up to me and said, "I want to go with you, Bill. You're the professional."

"Look," I replied, "there are no professionals. Unless God works in the hearts of men, nothing happens. He only asks us to be obedient and proclaim the message."

Well, my friend thought that since I had taught many Christians how to witness more effectively, perhaps some of the "magic" would rub off on him. And I don't know why the Lord allowed it, but that day was absolutely the worst witnessing experience I've ever had. We were almost bodily thrown out of one house. Another listener reacted very angrily. We didn't see one single person who was interested in even talking with us. We hit an incredible, unexplainable streak of "no's" all afternoon.

In almost forty years of sharing my faith, I can count on the fingers of one hand the number of hostile rejections that I remember. But a good portion of them seemed to hit all at once on that day!

But, if anything good came of it, the experience made my friend feel better. Maybe God wanted to encourage him by illustrating that even Bill Bright, the supposed "professional" at witnessing—didn't have any power to lead anyone to the Lord unless God himself did it.

What Christ Taught about Failure

For those who question whether we should even try, considering the chance that a number of listeners will say "no," there is assurance for us in the Parable of the Sower. Christ illustrated the varied effectiveness of his message:

> A farmer was sowing grain in his fields. As he scattered the seed across the ground, some fell beside a path, and the birds came and ate it. And some fell on rocky soil where there was little depth of earth; the plants sprang up quickly enough in the shallow soil, but the hot sun soon scorched them and they withered and died, for they had so little root. Other seeds fell among thorns, and the thorns choked out the tender blades.
>
> But some fell on good soil, and produced a crop that was thirty, sixty, and even a hundred times as much as he had planted (Matt. 13:3-8, TLB).

There are four types of listeners, Christ taught. And only one of the four will take the message (the seed) and put it to work in his or her life.

> The good ground represents the heart of a man who listens to the message and understands it and goes out and brings thirty, sixty, or even a hundred others into the Kingdom (Matt. 13:23, TLB).

The other three listeners (types of soil) will squander the message or reject it outright. Jesus Christ himself recognized that, and though his compassion drove him to love and long for every human soul, he knew that people would exercise his God-given power of free choice both for and against him. And people continue to do so today.

We Just Never Know . . .

So there will be "no's." We should pre-suppose a positive response, since the world is hungrier now for the gospel than ever before. Indeed, the fields are white unto harvest. But when the "no's" come, we shouldn't be surprised or discouraged.

And we just never know, really, where the "no's" will lead.

In 1976, Tom and Dorrine, a married couple from Washington, D.C., went witnessing from their church as part of the "I found it!" Here's Life, America Campaign. They visited a home where a man and woman living together unmarried were so loaded on drugs that they couldn't carry on a conversation.

So Tom and Dorrine left a gospel booklet on the coffee table, and suggested that when the couple felt like it they could read the booklet. Tom and Dorrine had received their "no," unspoken yet unmistakable.

Two weeks later, the woman came across the booklet and began to read. Its simple gospel presentation convicted her, and she knelt in her living room and received Jesus Christ into her life. Then she gave it to the man she'd been living with, and after several days he pulled out the booklet, read through it, and accepted the Lord.

Several weeks passed, and this couple listened to Christian programs on radio and TV. As they heard more of God's word, they wanted to attend church, and one Sunday they entered the church down the block. It was the same church from which my friends had gone witnessing.

When the pastor gave the invitation, the man and woman went forward to declare their new faith in God and to be baptized. They ceased living together as singles but soon were married. Five years later, they had grown so much in their walk with the Lord that he was asked to be a deacon in the church and she was active in several ministries.

When Tom and Dorrine left the haze of this couple's drug-filled living room that first day, they must have thought, "Boy, what a waste of time!"

But because of that initial contact, made out of obedience to a God who says, "Go, and preach the gospel," God turned this couple's "no" into a "yes" and brought two new dedicated believers into his kingdom.

There really is no wasted witness.

The Long Letter

Another "no" that stands out in my memory is a long letter I wrote to a nationally known sales consultant. I had met him at a conference where he was the featured speaker, and we struck up conversation and enjoyed a good visit together.

I did share Christ with him, and he seemed interested but was noncommittal. "Why don't you drop me a line with some more information?" he said to me as we parted company.

I went back to my office and thought and prayed hard about what I would write him. Over the next several days, I felt the Lord guiding me as I pulled together the key Scriptures and concepts of the plan of salvation into a letter to my new friend. I made a copy, mailed him the original, and prayed that God would use my effort in this man's life.

To my knowledge, this gentleman never did receive Christ into his life. He gave me an implied "no." But God was working in ways I never would have imagined.

As some trusted friends and I reviewed what I had written in the letter, they suggested that I print it in quantity, under a fictitious salutation, as a witnessing tool. I addressed the letter to a Dr. Van Dusen (I thought he sounded like an intriguing sort) and we printed several thousand copies. Over the years, the Van Dusen letter has been reprinted many times to meet the demand of our staff, Christian business persons, and other lay men and women who have used it to lead thousands of men and women to the Lord.

The Phone Call

One evening during our family dinner time, I received a long distance phone call. The woman on the other end of the line told me of a printed letter to a "Dr. Van Dusen" she had found in the seat of a commercial airliner.

"Are you the Bill Bright who wrote this letter?" she asked. She proceeded to ask me some questions, then said, "I would like to become a Christian. Can you help me?"

What a thrill it was to lead this sincere woman in prayer over the phone as she received Christ as her Savior and Lord. But it didn't stop there.

In the family room with her were five other family members and friends. Each of them had read the Van Dusen letter. One by one, each of them came to the phone and, after some questions and discussion, received Christ.

There really is no wasted witness.

We fail in witnessing only if we fail to witness.

Success in witnessing is simply sharing Christ in the power of the Holy Spirit, and leaving the results to God.

. . . It had been many years since my car accident in Oklahoma, and Vonette's father passed away. We returned to Oklahoma and were at the graveside service at the cemetery when the presiding pastor gave a challenge to the people standing there.

"Now, Roy Zachary was ready to meet the Lord," he said. "Are you? If you're not ready, Christ wants to come into your life."

I turned around, and behind me stood my county commissioner friend from years before. I could see tears forming in the corners of his eyes.

The last thing I wanted to do was disturb the sacredness of the moment. But I knew that, again, God was nudging me to speak with him.

"Are you ready, my friend? Don't you think it's about time?" And when the service ended, we moved to a private spot and he received Christ through a prayer that began:

"Lord Jesus, I need you . . ."

Isn't it great that we can leave the results to God?

Adapted with permission from *Witnessing without Fear,* (San Bernardino, CA: Here's Life Publishers, 1987)

16

MISSIONARY EVANGELISM
Franklin Graham

Franklin Graham is the president of Samaritan's Purse, a ministry with a primary purpose of meeting the emergency needs of people through existing church and missionary organizations, in order that the evangelistic task may not be hindered. Among Mr. Graham's writings is a book about the founder of Samaritan's Purse, Bob Pierce: This One Thing I Do.

Christ's own claims on the world of spiritually lost people (Luke 15:4-6) have been given by the Father. And, in turn, as the Father has sent his Son into the world (John 17:3), even so has Christ sent his followers out into the world of lost humanity with the message of the gospel (John 17:14,18) to save all people from the wages of sin, death, and hell! The purpose of the gospel has been defined by Christ for all of his followers until the end of time in Matthew 28:18-20. And the scope of its outreach he gave in Acts 1:8 just before his ascension into heaven— "... to the uttermost part [or end] of the earth."

This, then is *mission*—the first and foremost outreach of the church of Jesus Christ to a lost and dying world! It is the most important work of the church. In spreading the Good News of the gospel the church of Jesus Christ shares the burden of the "broken heart of God" who gave his most prized and valued possession—namely his only beloved, begotten Son to die for the world lost forever in separation from God because of sin.

Let's discuss some of the *Problems* involved, some of the methods of *Proclamation*, and look at some of the *Promises* that are related in obeying God's command in missionary evangelism.

Some Problems Involved in Missionary Evangelism

The gospel's impact on the world brings conflict. It cuts right across Satan's territory. The gospel also confronts the basic characteristics of human nature— pride, rebellion, greed, and selfishness. Because of these conflicts, the gospel produces crises demanding that men and women choose between the God of light and truth or the god of this world, Satan (Eph. 2:1-2), the god of darkness and error.

So, although the gospel is meant to be a unifying power, it may by its very divinely inspired message, separate. It is this separating power that forms the church of Jesus Christ as a community of obedient people who separate themselves from the dominion of Satan. They are united in Christ Jesus and *"in* the world, though not *of* the world" (John 17:11,18) as they pursue world missions for the glory of God.

1. Spiritual warfare is a major problem that has always confronted evangelism. This is true today as never before. One of Satan's most effective forms of opposition has been to cause confrontations between people against people and nations against nations. This is illustrated in several parts of the world in a very graphic manner.

The whole Muslim world is not only determined to drive the Jews out of Israel, but to evict all Christians from the Middle East areas of the world. The Ayatollah Khomeini accuses the United States of being the "Great Satan of the World." The rising tide of Muslim fundamentalism among the Arab nations will do anything within its power to oppose all those who claim the name of Christ. Harsh laws in those countries hinder persons coming to Christ. If a person in those lands changes his or her religion, he or she is subjected to the possibilities of long-term imprisonment. There have been incidents where converts' own family members have tried to kill them for making the change.

Staunch Hindu countries like India and Nepal continue to oppose the gospel vigorously. The government of India is no longer issuing visas to expatriate missionaries seeking to serve the Lord in that country. Within the next 10 to 15 years no missionaries will be left in that vast country with its teeming millions. The serious question facing the Christian church is: How can the people of such nations be reached with the gospel of the Lord Jesus Christ? With the doors to evangelizing closing to the 900 million in India and 15 million in the Hindu kingdom of Nepal, these people will be left in total spiritual darkness unless other effective ways of reaching them are planned.

2. Westerners' failures to understand and appreciate other cultures and ways of living and thinking is another problem. Well-meaning missionaries, perhaps not rightly trained, have not always recognized the nationals' way of thinking and their value systems. A lot of damage has been done through such experiences, and a hearing for the gospel has been hindered in those kind of unfortunate events.

Although Jesus certainly was referring to geographic distances in his famous and final instructions to his disciples in Acts 1:8, he seems also to have in mind the cultural differences and distances that can exist by two nations of people living side by side. Evidence of this is clear from his discourse with the woman at the well in John 4, and from the reaction of his disciples when they found him in conversation with her. The cultural differences between Judea and Samaria were far greater than the geographic ones.

Many differences exist between our Western culture and other cultures to which we are called to witness to the gospel of Jesus Christ. The evangelistic task is hindered as exemplified in the following illustrations.

In English we speak of the emotional center of our being as the heart. It is with the heart that we love and experience our deepest and most sincere feelings. Not so among the Chujs of Guatemala. They refer to their abdomens as the seat of the affections and emotions. And for the Marshallese Islanders it is from their throats that their feelings come; while the Totonacs from Mexico refer to their spleens as the emotional centers. To love someone from your heart would be totally incomprehensible to these people. This presents some very challenging problems, incidentally, to the Bible translators who have to grapple with the varying nuances of meaning and their implications.

When the missionaries first came to China, they were accused of worshiping their chairs. Their servants and friends saw them kneel in prayer to the Lord at their chairs. When the Chinese in that part of the country went to worship their idols, they knelt before them. They did not see any idols in the houses of the missionaries; so they assumed that the chairs were some form of their God and when kneeling they were worshiping that form.

For the Gaddang people of the Philippine Highlands in Luzon, when a rooster crows as visitors are preparing to leave, this brings bad luck unless the guests abort their plans and remain a while. The same is true for them if one of the little lizards that hang on the bamboo walls of their homes chirps as the company is getting ready to go. This can cause some interesting interruptions since there are many lizards, and they have a way of being very articulate. If a visitor-missionary laughs at such "taboos" or ignores them and continues on his way, fear may follow in the wake of his visit, and he may never be welcome there again.

We may laugh at the Asian tribal man who will go hungry so that he can buy a wrist watch which he cannot read but wants for a status symbol. But in our American culture we have people who will deprive themselves of proper nourishment, housing, and even education so that they can drive a Cadillac, which also is a status symbol for some. The importance of being objective when evaluating other peoples' customs cannot be overemphasized!

Some Methods for Proclaiming the Gospel

God, in his divine wisdom, nowhere in the Bible laid down one absolute method or pattern for evangelism. He has allowed a flexibility that provides ways and means of spreading the gospel which will fit the times and the cultures of the people.

However, the methods of evangelism should always have as their goals at least the following two purposes: (a) find the best way to overcome obstacles to the gospel for the sake of the ministry and the people the evangelist is trying to reach, and (b) find the best way to convey the gospel message to that particular people.

Having said that, it is also important to know that God's basic message never changes—and never will! Every generation brings with it new situations, new challenges, and new changes. With these come the new opportunities for the Holy Spirit to be innovative and creative through his chosen instruments for the sake of carrying the gospel to the ends of the earth.

The modern means of transportation and communications are God's gifts for sending the gospel to the farthest corners of the world. Jungles that are not passable and islands too remote for effective work have suddenly opened with the advent of the airplanes. With the jet age have come the possibilities of "short-term workers"—men and women who are now able to give vacation or extended vacation times to serving overseas in mission posts.

Missionary Aviation Fellowship and Jungle Aviation and Radio Services, the air and communications arm of Wycliffe Bible Translators, are two of the better known missionary flying services. Their services have unlocked many a tribal ministry that otherwise would have been impossible.

The Neal Kooyer family, working in Papua New Guinea, tell of such an experience. Maposi is a small, swampy village located in a remote spot of the Sepik River jungle. Up until the early 1980's no one from the outside world had ever been in that isolated hamlet. So the Kooyers made their way up to the area for a survey of needs. They taught the people, who were on a meager diet of starchy tago palm paste, to plant peanuts, sugar cane, and yams.

While there, they learned of yet another area much more remote and inaccessible called Yawa. Bill Cristobal, a Missionary Aviation Fellowship pilot, flew Neal in by helicopter, and plans began to take shape to help those deprived people in Yawa. Two months later the Lord provided funds and equipment to build a school there for the people and a few simple implements to upgrade their food production—all because of the modern flight facilities of a helicopter, a special gift from the Lord to reach the uttermost part of the earth!

The Bible teaches that God is conscious and concerned for all human needs—the physical as well as the spiritual. We must, however, recognize that meeting the physical and emotional needs of people must ultimately be a means to an end—namely, meeting the spiritual needs of humanity around the world. Jesus himself was the perfect model and example of this approach to evangelism in his earthly ministry and sojourn.

Samaritan's Purse and World Medical Mission are two sister organizations which God has raised up to minister to people's physical needs in order to give the gospel a hearing. Our mission is to strengthen the evangelistic efforts throughout the world by meeting the emergency needs of people through existing church and missionary organizations, with the primary purpose of seeing people come to faith in Jesus Christ.

Samaritan's Purse and World Medical Mission channel resources from the Western world to meet the needs of God's servants working abroad. This system does not operate its own programs overseas. Our mission is to work through local churches and evangelical missions to meet emergency needs so that the gospel can continue being shared on the various fields.

The following are some of the needs that have been met through our assistance because of this method of action:

Transportation has been provided for many national pastors in Borneo, godly men who care for congregations scattered along hundreds of miles of jungle trails. Lacking transportation, these faithful servants of the Lord have had to spend most of their time walking the many, many miles rather than having time with their families and ministering to their people.

In India many fresh water wells, which the nationals call "Jesus wells," have been dug on church properties. These provide safe drinking water for the people as well as an evangelizing opportunity for them to find the "Living Water" in Christ Jesus.

Sixty thousand people stream into Tenwek Hospital in Kenya, East Africa each year. Annually over 8,000 of the patients treated at this hospital come to faith in Jesus Christ through hearing the gospel preached in the compound. Because crowded conditions in this mission hospital limited the impact of the gospel (sometimes three to four people sharing one bed), funds were channeled into the construction of a new 110-bed wing to that hospital. Today hundreds more are hearing the message of salvation as they come for medical help.

Plans are being made to initiate "drip irrigation" projects in Kenya, Ethiopia, Zaire, Zambia, and Tanzania using this method to demonstrate to the nationals how to use better techniques to raise more and better food.

Dr. Bob Pierce, founder of Samaritan's Purse, often shared a kind of prayer that was behind the driving force of his dedicated life: "Let my heart be broken by the things that break the heart of God." This prayer lives on in the hearts of the Samaritan's Purse and World Medical Mission staff.

It is a ministry of compassion and concern, a ministry to match the gifts of God's people with the recognized needs of those across the world regardless of race or creed. God is using the unique opportunities of meeting people's physical needs to open the doors to their hearts and minister to their spiritual lives. This is just another in the long string of creative methods that the Lord has brought about for sharing the Good News of the gospel.

Jesus gathered his close followers around him a short time before facing Jerusalem and the cross. And in John 14:12 we have recorded one of the most astounding verses in all Scriptures: "Verily, verily, I say unto you, he that believeth on Me, the works that I do shall he do also; and greater works than these shall he do; because I go unto my father." This statement was not primarily referring to the performing of miracles, as some would have us believe. He was talking about the methods, the tools, and the resources that he was going to provide for his servants through the Holy Spirit as they faithfully obeyed the Great Commission to carry the gospel to every person until the Lord returns. When Jesus shared that truth with his apostles, he shared a truth that was to hold true right down through the ages until today.

Some Promises Given in Relation to Missionary Evangelism

Hope and assurance in the final triumph of the church of Jesus Christ and all her missions are integral parts of the Christian faith. That all of God's faithful servants everywhere are part of this triumph is reassuring. It provides great abundance of strength and courage from which to draw in times of stress, duress, and testings. Although immersed in spiritual struggles, the Lord's servants need to remember that Satan, in principle, was defeated at the Cross. And the battles are the Lord's— ultimately (1 Sam. 14:47). The Book of Revelation gives graphic illustrations of the culmination of the end of time—and of victory in Christ Jesus our Lord.

But there are more immediate promises for those engaged in evangelism. Not the least of these are promises in Scripture such as 1 Thessalonians 5:24; Psalm 1:3b; Psalm 36:5; and Psalm 84:11b, all of which speak of God's faithfulness in providing his supply of every need and blessing in the midst of great odds and opposition to the gospel.

In India an average of forty-five people die every minute, with approximately 100 new babies born in that same amount of time each day. Less than one percent of the population in India are evangelical Christians. Predictions by world population experts suggest that India's population will double within the next fifty years, projecting the numbers into more than a billion people. How are the promises of God related to these staggering figures?

God's boundless resources are promised to those who follow him in obedience to his directions. When the Lord gave the commission to make disciples over the whole world (including India), he promised: "You will receive the power of the Holy Spirit on you" (Acts 1:8). To see this power evident and demonstrated in the ministry of evangelists, to see people coming to faith in Christ, and to see evidences of dramatic changes in lives once given to debauchery or under bondage to guilt and enslaving habits, is fulfilling and rewarding, to say the least, for the missionary evangelist.

With help from Christians in North America, the Evangelical Church of India has planted many congregations over various parts of that land. Over 17 million people live in the state of Andhra Pradesh. Recently a Bible school was established in the city of Vijayawada, and already that school is filled to capacity. This is just one of the many evidences that the Holy Spirit is moving in special ways in

India today—in harmony with the promises of the Scriptures. By the teamwork of expatriates working with Indians, and Indians working with Indians, foundations are being laid that will enable the acceleration of God's work to move right on into the next century for his glory and the salvation of many souls. What a thrill this is to missionary evangelism!

Missionary evangelism is a mandate given to all of God's people everywhere and for all time. It is the proclamation of God's saving grace in Christ Jesus into a problem-ridden world. And the promise is given of blessings to those who serve in obedience to this mandate—and to those who believe and receive the good news of the gospel!

17

CRUSADE EVANGELISM
T. W. Wilson

T. W. Wilson is an executive assistant to Dr. Billy Graham, having served with Dr. Graham from the early years of his ministry. Dr. Wilson also serves as an associate evangelist for the Billy Graham Evangelistic Association.

Crusade Evangelism or Mass Evangelism?

Having served with Billy Graham and the Billy Graham Evangelistic Association for over forty years, I have often heard that our organization conducts mass evangelism. Most of us on the Graham team would prefer the term *crusade* evangelism because masses do not become Christians, individual persons do. Without prayerful one-on-one witnessing, a Billy Graham crusade would have little impact on the area in which the crusade is held. Most of the people who make decisions at Billy Graham crusades have already been evangelized individually, or have been invited to the services by someone using our "Operation Andrew" plan, which I will discuss later.

The Role of Prayer

History will verify the statement that every great evangelist has been an instrument used by God supported by the magnificent power of prayer. Yes, crusade evangelism does include the human elements of promotion, organization, and simple hard work, but it is so much more than a mere human enterprise. God-blessed crusades are saturated with prayer.

Look into the stories of Dwight L. Moody, Charles G. Finney, or George Whitefield. Each of these great evangelists, whose ministries span over two centuries, preached thousands of sermons that led tens of thousands to Christ. But each of these men acted with child-like dependence on the Holy Spirit to do the work of convicting and winning. And that dependence was epitomized in their prayer lives.

Billy Graham would be the first to admit that the "success" of his ministry is but a reflection of the power of prayer. Certainly he is a man of extraordinary gifts, one whose ministry has been touched by God. But the entire ministry of the Graham organization would be nothing without the infinite power of prayer.

Decisions or Disciples?

The Great Commission (Matt. 28:19-20) mandates that followers of Christ make disciples, rather than simply elicit decisions. Those who are involved in crusade evangelism must also be obedient to the command of our Savior.

It is therefore imperative that persons involved in crusade evangelism seek to make disciples. With the Graham organization, we have seen our ministry, sometimes through trial and error, place more and more emphasis on discipleship in the local church. We believe that no less effort should be placed in follow-up and preservation than in planning or in reaping. Too much of crusade evangelism has emphasized immediate decisions, only to ignore the future discipleship of the converts in local churches. Because of this "great omission," there is often little indication years later that a crusade had any impact on an area. The "converts" are not "disciples" in the context of the local church. If crusade evangelism continues to be a factor for the kingdom in the twenty-first century, it will be the result of disciple-making rather than decision-making.

Before the Crusade

Crusade evangelism is a "before," "during," and "after" process. Certainly the days of the crusade, where the proclamation and services take place, are vitally important. And certainly the days, months, and even years after a crusade are important, because this period involves disciple-making through the local church. But so much work and prayer must transpire before the crusade ever begins. Billy Graham believes that the most blessed crusades have been the result of the efforts of faithful Christians who have worked and prayed for months prior to the services.

One of the key factors to the future of crusade evangelism, as in the past, is the willingness of persons involved to work and pray, work and pray, work and pray before the proclamation takes place. I know something of the tremendous amount of preparation that precedes a Billy Graham crusade.

Who is to be involved in the pre-crusade work? If we in the Graham organization had to do all the work ourselves, the work would never get done. In fact we will not enter a city without the invitation of local churches. We must have local support for a crusade to "succeed." Literally thousands of volunteers are involved in witness training, music, ushering, counseling, and Operation Andrew. These volunteers come from local churches; their commitment and involvement are vital to our crusades.

We have learned, over many years of Graham crusades, that one of the most effective ways volunteers can be used prior to the crusade is to get people involved in "Operation Andrew." This program takes the name of Jesus' disciple, Andrew, who, immediately after becoming a follower of the Savior, told his brother about Jesus. The idea is that we are often able to lead those closest to us to a saving relationship with Jesus Christ. Here are the five steps of Operation Andrew:

1. *Look around*—because your mission field is right where you live, work, or go to school. List the names of seven individuals who need Christ.

2. *Look up*—for prayer changes people! Set aside time each day to pray for these seven, and for yourself—that God will give you natural opportunities to share his love with them.

3. *Look out*—for ways to cultivate their friendship and earn their confidence. Set a plan of action. An invitation to dinner or a ball game can do much to build bridges, opening the way for Christ.

4. *Look forward*—and several weeks before the Crusade, begin to talk to each one about coming to the Crusade with you (few will come alone). Have a definite date in mind, pray, and follow through.

5. *Look after*—those who respond to Christ; they need your encouragement more than ever. Those who do not come to him may be reached later on, so continue to love them and pray.

There are many ways in which crusades need local people to be involved. Perhaps the greatest need is for volunteers to establish relationships with the lost, pray for them, and invite them to the services. That relationship is so very important. It remains long after the crusade has left the city.

The Necessity of the Local Church

Local churches are an absolutely necessary ingredient for successful crusade evangelism. If crusade evangelism is to be a factor in winning people to Christ in the next century, local churches must be involved. Not only does Billy Graham require the invitation from local churches before he comes to a city, he also must be sure that the churches will be actively and integrally involved in the crusade.

The local church is not a tool for the use of the crusade; the crusade is an evangelistic tool for the local church. Too much of crusade evangelism comes into cities today, records decisions, and leaves without making disciples. I know of no other institution on earth that is better equipped to make disciples than the local church. Crusade evangelism should serve the church rather than the church serve the crusade.

Within the local church, the pastor is the key to church participation in a crusade. Most local churches will follow the leadership of its pastor. Crusade evangelism must have the enthusiastic support and participation of the local churches, and that support and participation can come only through pastoral leadership.

Perhaps the most effective participation of the local church is for every Christian to realize that he or she has been called to be an evangelist. Certainly some believers have the gift of the evangelist. That does not mean, however that other Christians are not to evangelize! One may have the gift of giving or serving, but all Christians should give and serve.

Effective personal evangelism is ultimately the key to effective crusade evangelism. One of the greatest benefits crusade evangelism can give a group of local churches is the clear communication of the command for all Christians to witness and evangelize. Every evangelist, Sunday school teacher, pastor, elder, deacon, and church member should be a personal "soul-winner."

Conclusion

The future of crusade evangelism is bright. And the reason for such optimism is that, in many crusade ministries, the crusade is emphasizing the making of disciples through the local church. And the making of disciples is precipitated by prayer and hard work.

Another reason for optimism is that increasing emphasis is being placed on personal evangelism. Crusade evangelism is only effective when individuals realize their personal mandate to spread the good news. Evangelists, pastors, Christian workers—indeed all Christians—must be active participants in the Great Commission.

What a joy and honor it is to contribute to this book in honor of Lewis A. Drummond! "Lewie" Drummond and his wife Betty are two of my dearest friends, and their work for God's kingdom has been inestimable.

I remember that special day in 1987 when Thom Rainer and I met together, as Thom shared with me his thoughts about honoring his mentor in the form of a book on evangelism. I passed the idea on to Billy Graham who enthusiastically endorsed the project and wrote the foreword to this book. Praise God for Lewis Drummond! May this book reflect some portion of the love and respect we have for him.

Lewis Drummond has been active in crusade evangelism both through the Graham organization and as an evangelist in his own right. What has impressed me about him is that he never neglects his responsibility as a personal evangelist just because he is a "preacher to the masses." It is indeed an honor to make a small contribution to a book in his honor. May we ever follow such an example as his.

18

EVANGELIZING YOUTH
Larry J. Michael

Larry J. Michael is pastor of the Switzerland Baptist Church in Vevay, Indiana. He recently completed the Ph.D. in evangelism under Lewis Drummond at the Southern Baptist Theological Seminary. Dr. Michael has served as a youth minister in churches in both the United States and England.

Young people ages thirteen to eighteen all have one thing in common: they need to be evangelized. Having served as a youth minister in three different churches in this country and in England, I have worked with many kinds of youth. Whether they were from broken homes, rebellious, drug abusers, immoral, abusive, athletic, intellectual, fun-loving, insecure, overly confident, serious-minded, spiritually keen, etc., I was convinced that they all shared the most basic need in life, whether they realized it or not. That need was to know Jesus Christ as personal Savior and Lord.

I remember one sixteen-year-old lad in Tonbridge, England, who made a decisive commitment to give his life to Jesus Christ. He first started coming to church because his parents did not want him to attend. They were fallouts from the post-war generation in England, disillusioned with traditional Christianity. Nigel was from a different generation. He was open to seeking and searching for truth in his life. After he heard the gospel proclaimed and noticed the change Christ had made in the lives of other young people, Nigel made his commitment. How amazing it was to baptize a young person whose parents tried to talk him out of it. They told him it would not last. They tried to make him believe it was nothing more than "emotional drivel." Nigel was convinced otherwise.

How different Nigel's experience was from Randy's experience "across the waters" in America. Randy grew up in a Christian home, deciding to follow Jesus when he was nine years old. Randy was an active part of the church youth group until he was fifteen, but then he dropped-out because it no longer seemed very important to him. His parents and church friends tried to convince him of his need for Christian fellowship, but Randy thought he knew better. He had gained new friends who spent many hours listening to rock music and experimenting with "recreational" drugs. Randy was drawn into that scene and did not return to his earlier Christian commitment until confronted with the need for drug rehabilitation at the age of nineteen. A loving family and congregation provided support, helping Randy make the difficult transition back into a regular pattern of Christian fellowship.

These two young men, while coming from different cultures and following divergent paths, ultimately experienced the same need—the saving knowledge of Jesus Christ. The English youth typifies a new generation of Christian youth in a post-Christian secular society where less than ten percent of the population attend church. The description of the American youth is not so atypical for many American Christian families where young people face the challenges of "owning their own faith."

Knowing the risk of over-generalizing, I suggest three words which may cover the bases of youth evangelism as we approach the twenty-first century. Those words are: *know* them, *show* them, and *grow* them.

Knowing Youth

There is a panorama of youth culture of which we must be aware. The writer of Ecclesiastes stated: "Know your Creator in the days of your youth" (Eccl. 12:2). While this Scripture verse is a good text for challenging youth, at the same time we may challenge those trying to reach youth: "*know your youth* in the days of your Creator." What are they like? What are they doing? Where can they be found? What is important to them?

Perception

Although there is a definite youth culture, young people within that phenomenon are as diverse as there are descriptions. They are concerned about many things. They feel that they have many problems. One concern universal among teenagers is their physical appearance. Puberty brings physical changes and subsequent anxiety among youth that they are developing in the right way at the right time. Pimples, awkwardness, voice changes among boys, shapeliness among girls, all contribute toward inadequacies youth feel during the teenage years. Physical changes often illustrate the disparities that exist in describing young people between the ages of thirteen and eighteen, yet both are considered teens.

There is much anxiety among young people over their acceptance among their peers. Although parents are important, friends and popular students at school become the focus of their attention. Knowing the right people and being accepted in a certain "clique" or group becomes paramount to them. Many are from single-parent families where the trauma of divorce and the break-up of families drive them to place greater importance on their peers. Depression often comes when young people feel the rejection of their peers and are left out of certain groups or activities.

Youth are passionate. Dating becomes a significant factor in the teen years. Boy-girl relationships consume much time and energy as they seek to discover more about their newfound sexuality. Christian families are concerned about promiscuity among their young people as well as those outside the church. Recent statistics seem to indicate that sexual activity and teenage pregnancy are increasing problems for Christian youth. Josh McDowell states in his "Why Wait" youth program that 43 percent of all Christian youth are sexually active. It is not surprising when one considers the sexual bombardment in the media, the increasing availability of pornographic literature and videos, and the general decline of moral standards today.

Young people today are overcome with pressure—pressure to succeed, pressure to perform up to their parents' expectations, pressure to conform to the "world" they find out there beyond the security and confinement of their homes. Some respond to the pressure by excelling and rising to the challenges before them. Others withdraw and become passive in their education and general approach to life, feeling little self-worth and purpose or direction.

Because they often appear impulsive, young people are not generally regarded as good planners. It is difficult for them to look beyond tomorrow or next week in plotting their course or direction. Their overarching concern with what is happening "today" makes it problematic for them to ponder the longterm, the future for which planning is needed. Thus, they sometimes make rash decisions or mistakes in their haste to get ahead in their current situations, not taking into consideration future consequences.

Most of all, when describing youth, it must be recognized in simple terms that they are "people." They are big and little, tall and short, skinny and fat, smart and not-so-smart, black and white, rich and poor, pretty and not-so-pretty, participants and observers, saved and unsaved. Regardless of their situation, good, bad, or otherwise, they need love. They need the presence of Jesus Christ in their lives. It is imperative that every young person be given individual attention to find out his or her make-up as one attempts to share the gospel.

Pastimes

An answer to the question "What are they doing?" also generates numerous responses concerning youth. Certainly they are pursuing pleasure. Living in a time in which spending leisure and finding entertainment are at an all-time high, young people seek to discover that which pleases them. It may take the form of parties— seeking the good times, going for "all the gusto." Getting the most out of the moment, living life to its fullest, often becomes the focus of many of their activities. When they are not in school, they are usually listening to music, involved in sports, wiling away the hours in front of the TV, or playing the latest video games. Some unfortunately get involved in recreational drugs, irreversibly harming their bodies and their minds with substance abuse. Others are imbibing increasing amounts of alcohol in their attempts to be "cool" and become the perfect "party animals." When it comes to pastimes, there is no shortage of activities, positive and negative, in which teenagers are involved.

Of course, some young people are spending much of their time at work. Outside of school, their financial situation may be such that jobs at fast-food restaurants, supermarkets, etc., occupy much of their free time. Family needs may necessitate the part-time work which provides extra income for their families. Some youth may be working to save for education beyond high school. Indeed, while they are working, at least they are involved in productive activity. At the same time, excessive hours at work over consecutive weeks and months may affect the degree to which certain young people are able to maintain their academic work at school. Adults and other youth trying to reach young people with the gospel message will need to investigate those activities which comprise the bulk of their time.

Presence

"Where are young people found?" What are their hangouts, the places in which they spend a lot of time? While already stating that some are at work, most often when they have free time, youth are with other youth. It may be at school, where many activities center around clubs, groups, sports, etc. It may be at a youth center, gymnasium, corner drugstore, church rec room, or the local shopping mall. Some may just be driving around, especially in small towns where "cruising" becomes a favorite pastime. For some, their cars become a way of proving to the world that they are coming "into their own" as independent persons. Rites of passage dictate that once you reach a certain age you hang-out with certain people and do certain things. Discovering where young people are found on a regular basis is one step toward reaching them with the gospel. But one must go further.

Priorities

"What is important to youth?" While we would like to believe that they are all concerned about their eternal destiny and seeking God's will, many youth are obsessed with other things. Yes, there may be fleeting moments of concern over where they will go when they die, especially when the death of a relative or friend occurs. But, by and large, most teens (especially outside the church) are more preoccupied with their present state of happiness than with thinking about the hereafter. Many of them are instilled with materialistic values from their parents.

Our affluent age reflects a great need among youth to acquire possessions, and their friends demonstrate the same priorities. So the latest clothes, records, hairstyles, video systems, or computers, are of utmost importance in maintaining their status with their peers. While nuclear annihilation is a continual threatening possibility in our technological age, many kids are more bothered with how to get the money for those stone-washed, acid-washed, tie-dyed jeans.

Relationships are paramount to young people whatever the age. How they are getting along with their parents, their friends, their boyfriends/girlfriends, etc. Their feeling of well-being is greatly dependent on their current status in various relationships. Their attitudes, insecurities, and needs for recognition and approval hinge on self-image, which often tends to fluctuate according to relationships. Depression among teenagers is a major problem today. Some cases even lead to suicide, the second leading cause of death among young people. When teenage suicide occurs, it is often the result of failed relationships. People who want to share the gospel with youth achieve a great inroad when they can touch that important element of "relationship" which is paramount to youth. A personal relationship with Jesus Christ can strike them at the center of their need.

Showing Youth

Knowing youth enables those who engage in evangelizing youth to be able to identify with their greatest needs and concerns. Showing youth allows adults and older youth an opportunity to demonstrate the life-changing force of the gospel of Jesus Christ. Who will be their Christian role models? Who will show them the parameters of responsible behavior? Who will exhibit the proper use of power and authority? Jesus said, "And ye shall know the truth, and the truth shall make you free" (John 8:32). Young people will recognize the reality of that truth and freedom as it is displayed in the lives of authentic Christians.

Pattern

Who are the role models for youth? Often young people look to rock stars, movie stars, and sports superstars for role models. They pattern their lives after a particular teen idol or macho image which appeals to their own desires and dreams. Often the person makes up for some specific inadequacy they feel in their own lives. Young people need Christian role models. They need adults and older youth at the local level who will portray authentic Christian lifestyles. There has been a lack of credibility and integrity demonstrated by prominent Christians at the national level. The recent revelations of certain televangelists involving sexual misconduct have eroded not only the trust of Christian leaders among adults, but young people are also inevitably affected by what they see and hear on TV and in the media. It is therefore imperative that Christian adults and older youth in the local setting become paradigms of Christian virtue and values. The need for consistent, committed Christian role models who will be a convincing witness of the gospel for youth in their town, community, or city, cannot be overemphasized.

Parameters

Young people need to know the limits of responsible behavior and activity. In a day and age when many people are living together outside of marriage, husbands and wives are being unfaithful to their spouses, pastors are running off with their secretaries, workers are quitting their jobs and deserting their families, politicians are being indicted for "white-collar" crimes—in spite of all these detractions, young people need to know what the boundaries are for those who profess to be Christians. We can tell them, but that may only go in one ear and out the other. They need to be shown.

How can young people be expected to be drawn to Christ and live out their Christian commitment when adults all across our nation are setting poor examples? There is a need for parameters, for discipline in our lives, for determination in defining the difference between right and wrong in our conduct. Can youth be told that curfews are a necessity, that sex is wrong before marriage, that money is not everything, that Jesus Christ can make a difference in their lives, when they see adult Christians and older youth who continually cross the boundaries of responsible Christian behavior? Jesus said that our righteousness must exceed that of the Scribes and Pharisees if we are to enter the Kingdom of Heaven. Young people need more than plastic performances. They need solid Christian role models who will exemplify what is good, pleasing and acceptable in the sight of the Lord.

Power

How do young people perceive the use of power and authority among Christian adults? Do they see those who are "lording over others" their influence and prestige? Rather than observing lifestyles of Christian service, youth often see adults who are pursuing power, selfish ambition, and personal pride in the way they live. Instead of seeing Christians who are outdoing one another in love and service, they often see people who are out for "number one" and willing to step on anyone in their path to the top. Church in-fighting, denominational power struggles, community squabbles, civil conflicts, and racial prejudice all give a nasty witness of the positive power of Jesus Christ.

If the gospel is Good News, it must be good for all people, regardless of their position or status. When young people see adults who properly exercise their use of power, and see themselves as true servants of Jesus Christ, then youth will be more convinced of the power of Christ in their own lives. Many young people are in a "holding pattern" with a "show-me" attitude, waiting for Christian leaders and other Christian youth to demonstrate growth, maturity, and a lifestyle of service to Christ and others. It is only in this way that adults and Christian youth will gain permission to share authentically the gospel with youth needing Christ.

Growing Youth

Knowing youth helps us to know where they are. Showing youth displays to them what direction they need to go. Growing youth marks a dedication to do everything possible to reach them with the gospel of Christ and a determination to support them in their journey toward Christian maturity.

Prepare

How important is our task of evangelizing the young people in our country? It is so important that we must be adequately prepared for the task. Our approach in reaching them cannot be "willy-nilly" or "half-baked" if we are serious about the salvation of their lives for Christ. There must be personal growth, strong devotional times, regular Bible study, consistency in worship, persistence in service, and a commitment to witness training. Any plan in witnessing is more effective than no plan for witnessing. Every Christian should be prepared to know how to lead a young person to Christ.

Utmost in our preparation is the practice of prayer. Prayer is the powerful force which unleashes the Holy Spirit in our efforts at sharing the gospel. Prayer prepares our hearts, it paves the way for the Spirit to act, and it creates an atmosphere of excitement and expectancy in communicating the good news of Christ! No significant revival has occurred in the history of the church without prayer. No breakthroughs in reaching youth will come without a commitment to ongoing, consistent prayer to our Lord for the effectiveness of his witness through our lives.

Permeating

Young people must be infiltrated, permeated with our personal presence if we are to reach them. One-on-one sharing of the gospel is most effective. In this manner, our care and concern for their deepest needs will be communicated. They will continue to be won in youth revivals and weekend retreats, but the best success will come from going where they are and communicating with them in their own setting. Too often we have employed the "come structures" of church and youth activities. There must be a commitment to "go structures" and reaching out to young people even to the peripheries if necessary. If it means being involved on the school campus, go! If it necessitates a pick-up game of basketball in the neighborhood, be there! If it requires going to the local video arcade, be present for the opportunities of interaction that will come!

Persuade

Proclaiming the gospel to youth mandates a need for persuasive proclamation. First, we must realize they are lost. As Paul wrote to the Romans, "For all have sinned, and come short of the glory of God" (Romans 3:23). Youth are in danger, their lives are in peril of eternal separation from Christ if we do not care enough to persuade them with every ounce of our being of the necessity for salvation. There is no compromise here. They need peace of heart and mind, they need the love of Christ, they need a change of purpose and direction, they need to repent of their sins. Christ is the answer! We must first be persuaded that he is the answer to life's problems, and then we must do all we can to persuade the youth we know that Jesus can make a difference in their lives.

Process

Evangelizing youth is not an overnight sensation. It is a process—a process of pre-evangelistic acquaintance, specific evangelistic encounters, and post-evan-gelism follow-up. We want to show them how Christ has changed our lives. We want to share the gospel with them personally. We want to make sure of their commitment once they have repented of their sin and received the forgiveness of Christ. We want to disciple them and involve them in ongoing opportunities for Christian growth and maturity. Once they have made a profession of their faith in Christ, followed him in obedience to the Lord's command to be baptized, become members of the local church, enrolled in a youth Sunday school class, and invited to youth fellowships, there still must be a determination to pursue them and make sure that they are included in the growth process. No one can be overlooked. No youth can afford to be forgotten. No teenager can be written off. Every young person is a prospect for the saving message of the gospel and "growing unto Christ." All communicators of the gospel must be knowledgeable of the process of evangelism and ongoing discipleship.

Perspective

Young people who become Christians will not automatically become perfect, just like their adult/youth sponsors are not perfect. There will be times of growth, times of stagnation, times of setback. Youth ministry is a periodic enterprise, and often cyclical in its effectiveness. Those who seek to evangelize and enable youth to grow in their faith must exercise patience. One's philosophy of youth ministry must include an overall perspective that allows for the "ebb and flow" of youth progress in the Christian faith. When we become impatient at the growth of our youth, let us remember that God must grow impatient at times with us. No one has arrived. But we are all on the journey to becoming the mature believers that Christ has called us to be. Perspective means a willingness to allow youth to develop according to their commitment and individual personalities.

Prognosis

A dedication to evangelizing young people indicates a positive prognosis. There is a wealth of potential available in the youth of our nation, and much of it is waiting to be discovered. The future of the twenty-first century in youth evangelism will be determined to the extent that adults and older youth who are presently engaged in youth ministry are able to have a positive vision and concerted plan for reaching youth. It will take positive, enthusiastic programs. It will take creativity. It will take persistence. It will take time, effort, and lots of energy. But the ongoing task of evangelizing youth is not just a probability. It is a possibility. Even more than that, it can be a reality for those who are willing to pay the price and count the cost of their involvement with today's youth. Nigel and Randy are just two examples of the numbers of youth in desperate need of the salvation provided through Jesus Christ. The success of reaching youth in the twenty-first century is pending the outcome of our perseverance in reaching their prospective parents today.

PART SIX:
Evangelism and the Local Church

As we move toward a new century, perhaps the most important means for reaching people for Christ will be through the local church. The final three chapters examine the task of evangelism in the local church from three perspectives. Jim Wilson looks at the pastor's role in evangelism, especially in the context of the message that must be proclaimed. Stephen Drake offers a pastoral perspective on the need for a high view of the Bible in order to do evangelism in the local church. And Kenneth S. Hemphill provides a case study of his church as one model for doing evangelism in the local church today.

19

THE PASTOR AND EVANGELISM: PREACHING THE GOSPEL
Jim Wilson

Jim Wilson is the pastor of the First Baptist Church of Beaumont, Texas, where many people have been reached for Christ during his ministry. Dr. Wilson studied under Lewis A. Drummond at the Southern Baptist Theological Seminary.

The band of believers of Jesus Christ often called "the early church" held evangelism as their priority. Personal soul winning was never an option for New Testament Christians. It flowed from intimacy with the Lord Jesus Christ which each individual New Testament Christian daily maintained. It was their reason for existence! Because they believed that God was worthy of every person's devotion and because they believed that men and women outside of faith in Jesus Christ were eternally lost, those early church members "turned the world upside down" (Acts 17:6).

It was unfathomable for the writers of the New Testament to think that a person could be a "believer"—one brought from death unto life through Jesus Christ—and not share his faith with others. For those who had been redeemed, no excuses would satisfy the Savior who had shed his blood for their sins. For a Christian not to evangelize would be comparable to an athlete who would not compete, a soldier who would not fight, or a farmer who would not farm (2 Tim. 2:1-6). Evangelism was the "heartbeat" of the New Testament church.

The Motivation for Evangelism in the Local Church

As modern believers in Christ as Lord, we must remember that we, as his church, are the visible expression of the living Lord. We will be the "only Jesus" some people are ever going to see. The statement has been made that "witnessing is the whole work of the whole church for the whole age." The truth is that every Christian is a witness. If we claim to be followers of Jesus Christ, the way we walk and talk is either a "good" or "bad" witness. Either way we are witnesses. We give testimony to the fact that Jesus Christ has radically and supernaturally invaded our lives, or we communicate the fact that this Christian experience does not mean very much, because there is nothing supernatural about our lives.

As pastor-evangelist, I have attempted to lead my congregation to see people as Jesus sees people. The Lord Jesus, speaking to a little sinner by the name of Zacchaeus, said, "The Son of Man is come to seek and to save that which was lost" (Luke 19:10). Our Lord and Master has a passion for the souls of men and women. We must see people as "sheep having no shepherd" (Matt. 9:36). A lost person is not simply riding "second class" while believers are riding "first class." The awesome fact is that a person outside of Jesus Christ as Savior is headed in a totally different direction. They are not going to the "slums of Heaven." Rather, they are lost and standing "condemned already" (John 3). If there is ever going to be a passion for souls, the church must develop a renewed belief in the lostness of persons outside of Christ.

We live in a day of creeping universalism. More and more evangelical Christians, perhaps unconsciously, are accepting a false belief that "God loves the world, therefore, the world will be saved." The Lord Jesus spoke pointedly in Mark's gospel, "He that believeth and is baptized shall be saved; but he that believeth not shall be damned" (Mark 16:16). He clearly says that there is not salvation without faith. The writer of Hebrews says, "Without faith it is impossible to please God" (Heb. 11:6). And Luke, in Acts 4:12, said: "Salvation is found in no one else, for there is no other name under heaven given to men by which we must be saved." What is the saving faith that pleases God? Is it believing in "the god of your choice?" Is it sort of a nebulous, vague, "no-cost" type of evangelism? It must be an attitude whereby a person abandons all reliance on his or her own efforts to obtain salvation. It must also be an attitude of complete trust in Christ, of reliance on him alone for all that salvation means.

The motivation for a new passion for evangelism is rooted in the fact that men and women cannot save themselves. They are lost sinners incapable of understanding spiritual truth on their own (1 Cor. 2:14). Because of the totally depraved state of humanity, men and women cannot obtain salvation through their own deeds of righteousness. Saving faith, therefore, is abandonment of all human effort to save ourselves, and a total reliance upon the finished work of Jesus Christ. To maintain the passion for evangelism, which will be generated by the recognition of humanity's lostness, a daily intimacy must be maintained with Christ through his Word. It is out of the "abundance of the heart" that the mouth will consistently and constantly tell others of the majesty and mercy of our God and Savior, Jesus Christ.

The Message of Evangelism in the Local Church

Simon Peter delivered one of the most powerful and penetrating sermons immediately after Pentecost in Acts 2. He, along with the rest of that small band of believers, had just been so empowered, so totally captivated, so completely possessed by the person of the Holy Spirit of God, that this weak-kneed, impulsive, undisciplined apostle, stood boldly in the face of the enemies of Christ to deliver a model message for any and every church to hear, comprehend and emulate. This was the same Peter who had three times denied his Lord and who left Christ on the cross to return to his fishing nets with no thought of victory.

If there is any message that would appear to be our example to follow, our pattern for teaching and preaching, it ought to be the Spirit-anointed message delivered immediately after Pentecost. The need for urgency in our preaching is a burden on my soul.

The work of the preacher today is being rethought, revamped, and re-examined! Some think the preacher is just to be an organizer and church visitor. Some think the preacher is to be a community and political leader or an entertainer. A priority question to be asked is, "What kind of preacher or preaching do we need today?" A simple answer is, "We need the same kind we have always needed, because nothing has changed." Just because we've split the atom and sent men to walk on the moon does not mean we need a new brand of Christianity.

There is a need for the passion and the urgency for evangelism in the local church. If there were ever a need in the church into the twenty-first century, it is the need to have an all-consuming passion to communicate the message of the gospel of Christ.

The pattern of Simon Peter's message in Acts 2 identifies six characteristics of biblical, evangelical, "soul-winning" preaching. The story is told about the seminary student who asked the homiletics professor, "How many points should a good sermon have?" The abrupt reply came back, "Young man, at least one!" Acts 2 gives us six points, six principles, that should be included in a good sermon.

A Courageous Word Should Be Preached

We do not automatically have a burden and a concern for evangelism. We do not automatically preach with power. The story is told about the little weak-kneed preacher, motivated to be popular, who wanted not to offend the "church pillars." On Sunday morning, he said, "Now, dear friends, if we don't repent—as it were—and believe—at least in a measure, we might accidentally go to hell—that is, to some extent." That kind of preaching has never done anyone any good! Our "soft soap" evangelism is so anxious not to disturb anyone. We want to philosophize rather than evangelize! We want to change the offense of the cross into an offer for fire insurance.

Modern philosophy may be described as "a blind man in a dark room searching for a black cat that is not there." What a far cry that is from the apostle Paul who said, "Woe is me, if I preach not the gospel," and to the anguish in the soul of Jesus who wept over a doomed city, saying, "Oh, Jerusalem, how oft would I have gathered thee unto myself."

Observe Peter in Acts 2:14: "But Peter, standing up with the eleven, lifted up his voice, and said unto them, 'Ye men of Judea, and all ye that dwell at Jerusalem, be this known unto you, and hearken to my words. . . .'" Where did he get this courage, this boldness? Most of us preachers would just as soon not be too bold—or speak too pointedly. We are not interested in creating enemies—especially within our churches!

The key to courage in preaching lies in two facts: (1) the fullness of the Holy Spirit; and (2) the realization that the message is not mine, but his.

The power, the unction, the anointing oil, is not sold over any counter in a store. Dr. Vance Havner has said,

> A preacher may be wrapped in the robes of learning, and his study walls may be decked with diplomas. His home may be filled with travel souvenirs from many lands, and he may wear all the trappings of ecclesiastical prestige and pageantry. But he cannot function without unction.[1]

Our great need is to be filled with the Person of the Holy Spirit, very God himself, and to function in the power of his Presence.

John Wesley began his ministry with great theological qualifications. No man was better qualified but less prepared to preach than Wesley. Prior to his Aldersgate experience with God, Wesley had no courage and no message. Many a young, "pre-Aldersgate-type-of-Wesley" will today start out to convert the heathen without ever being converted himself!

This fullness of the Holy Spirit does not necessarily imply strange hallucinations and odd behavior. What did the Holy Spirit primarily come to do? The business of the Holy Spirit is to magnify Jesus Christ! Our preaching takes on his power to proclaim his message only when we are filled with him.

One of our problems today is that pastors have led their churches to become "old-Adam-improvement societies." They have preached in such a way to produce lay leaders with unsanctified flesh who have never died to sin and risen to walk in newness of life. These carnal Christians and sometimes lost laypersons are leading the church! They are, "blind leaders of the blind" and "bland leaders of the bland." If pastors will function in the fullness of the Spirit of God, and recognize that the message to be preached is not human-made, but Christ-directed, it will give us courage![2]

A Comprehensive Word Should Be Preached

That simply means that we are to preach the Scriptures, the Word of God. Evangelistic preaching is not to be opinions and stories, however emotionally stimulating they may be. We are to give "meat" to those bones!

Some of the criticisms of evangelists and evangelistic pastors are unfounded and unjustified. But, to be honest, some of it is true, because of the lifestyle and shallowness that have brought the gospel into disrepute! In 2 Corinthians 6 Paul said, "We give no offense in anything, that our ministry may not be blamed." The pastor must live and preach a comprehensive gospel—a whole gospel! You do not simply preach cheap evangelism without a call to commitment.

The Bible says we are to proclaim "the whole counsel of God." Notice how Peter preached a comprehensive message in Acts 2:16-21. He quoted from the Old Testament, which was the authority to the Jews. Then, in verses 22-24,32-33,36, he spoke of: (1) the life of Jesus; (2) the cross; (3) the resurrection; (4) the Holy Spirit; and (5) lordship! But we will not preach it if we do not believe it. A preacher who does not believe that the Scriptures are God-breathed, that Jesus was born of a virgin, that he died on a cross for our sins, that he rose bodily from the grave, and that he is coming again will not preach with any power.

One preacher put it this way, "You cannot preach Jesus Christ the same today and tomorrow, if you do not believe what he was yesterday!" What he was then, he is now!

Much of the preaching today is shallow. People need sound doctrine; they need solid theology. My dear uncle, Grady Wilson, tells the story of the Texas Christian Rancher's Round-up, where he spoke three years in a row. One tall, lanky rancher slapped Grady on the back and said, "Brother Grady, I shore do like yo preachin'; you don't give us no theology, ner nothin'." I told Uncle Grady, "It is the 'ner nothin' part I'd be worried about."

We must preach God's Word! Expound the Scriptures! Evangelistic preaching can be, and most of the time should be, expository preaching. There are great evangelistic texts that should be expounded such as John 3:16; Romans 3:23 and 6:23; Romans 10:9-20; 1 John 5:11-13; and Luke 19:1-10. "Exposition" means "revealing the truth of God's Word." The task of the pastor is to unfold the truth within the context of the particular passage.

A pastor can preach through a book of the Bible and end every sermon with an evangelistic appeal. Contrary to much popular belief, evangelistic preaching is not just so much froth with little substance. There ought to be both exposition and emotion. The preacher should practice preaching the truth with a sound doctrine and also preaching it with emotion and power. Something is wrong when emotion becomes legitimate in everything except Christianity! There needs to be a balance between fundamentals and feeling! God wants a response from the whole person: "Thou shalt love the Lord thy God with all thy heart, and with all thy soul and with all thy mind, and with all thy strength."

Some of our evangelistic rallies are rather cheap. It is an insult to the intelligence of young people today to cheapen the gospel to make it "understandable." Medical schools don't cheapen their curriculum to appeal to the student. The legal profession doesn't change its terminology to make it acceptable. Too many Christians, including those leaving for universities of "higher learning," do not have the foggiest idea what they believe about the great doctrines of our faith! We stamp our feet, clap our hands, and yell "hallelujah" about religion. They "jump on every band wagon that comes by without asking who's leading the parade and where they are going." A great task in evangelistic preaching is to be biblical, Scriptural, and comprehensive.

A Convictive Word Should Be Preached

Communicating the gospel of Christ means that we keep in mind two things: (1) what is said—the message itself; and (2) to whom it is said—the listeners. Again, remember Peter's historic sermon at Pentecost, its context and its content:

Acts 2:23: ". . . You nailed him to a cross by the hands of godless men and put him to death."

Acts 2:36: ". . . this Jesus whom you crucified."

Acts 2:37: "Now when they heard this, they were pierced to the heart, and said to Peter and the rest of the apostles, 'Brethren, what shall we do?'"

Simon Peter confronted sin. His was a convicting message! They were "pricked and pierced in their hearts."

The message is an absolute message; it is a dogmatic message. "Absolutes" are not popular today, but the Scripture describes the way of the cross as a narrow way. I remember being in Puerto Rico, flying a one-engine plane with one pilot. I did not want the pilot to be broadminded. I think of what Dr. Vance Havner used to say, "Some folks don't like the fact that the gospel is narrow. They are so broadminded that they become flatheads."[2] The Lord Jesus Christ was and is absolute! He said, "He that is not with me is against me, and he that gathereth not with me scattereth abroad" (Matt. 12:30). That's an absolute statement! Sin is dogmatic, death is dogmatic, hell is dogmatic, and our message better be convictive!

Every time a pastor stands to preach the Good News of the gospel, there should be conviction in the hearts of the listeners! The natural response to anointed preaching should be that found in the book of Acts: "They were pricked in their hearts and said, 'Men and brethren, what shall we do?'"

A Corrective Word Should Be Preached

Convictive, comprehensive, and courageous preaching should always have the goal of spiritual correction. Our purpose is not complete without the preaching of a comprehensive, theological, and biblical exposition. Neither is it complete without the stirring of the soul and spiritual conviction! Many men, women, and young people under deep, spiritual conviction will still walk out of a service and say "no" to the Spirit of God.

A corrective message—a message of repentance and changed lives is our goal! In the New Testament, the concept of "correction" (2 Tim. 3:16) is the restoration of God's original design in a person's life. Such must be the goal of our preaching.

Hear Peter at Pentecost: "Repent and be baptized in the name of Jesus Christ . . ." (Acts 2:38).

Listen to Paul: "Therefore if any man be in Christ, he is a new creature: old things are passed away; behold, all things are become new" (2 Cor. 5:17).

Several years ago, in an evangelistic crusade in California, during the invitation, a young couple came forward to receive Christ as Savior. God saved them and changed them completely. After the counseling session, the young man immediately said, "We've been living together. I know that is wrong, but where am I going to sleep tonight?" I was thrilled when one of the deacons offered his couch for the young man. He stayed at the deacon's house for several weeks.

The couple gave their public testimonies and were baptized. After a few weeks of premarital counseling by the pastor, this young couple, born again in Jesus Christ, were married in the church. That is Holy Spirit correction. God's design for their lives was miraculously re-established.

I think of another young couple who were living together. The young man had been raised in the church. However, his life took the course of rebellion into alcohol and drugs. He began living with a young girl who was working in a nightclub as a dancer. During a church outreach program, my wife and I were asked to go by to visit this particular couple.

When we arrived at their apartment, the atmosphere was obviously uncomfortable. Remembering that Jesus was a "friend of sinners," my wife and I made a conscious effort to love this young couple. We asked them if we could share the most transforming experiences of our lives. They responded in the affirmative.

What a joy it was for my wife to lead the girl to faith in Christ. Then the young man was gloriously converted. In fact, after a few weeks of his living at home with his parents, he not only shared his testimony with the entire church body, but he helped reclaim his parents, who had drifted away from God. Following several months of discipleship and counseling, I had the privilege of performing the Christian marriage ceremony for this "new" couple. I'm thrilled that they are continuing to "walk in the truth." There is no greater joy for a pastor than this kind of spiritual correction.

Evangelistic preaching means preaching for a decision. Jesus came into Galilee preaching, "The time is fulfilled, and the Kingdom of God is at hand; repent and believe the gospel." He preached an urgency to choose and to decide!

The truth is, no person can call himself or herself "a Christian" until he or she has come to terms with Christ. An evangelistic pastor is to make a person confront the person of Christ until that person asks, "What shall I do with Jesus?"

A call to repentance is mandated in presenting the gospel. It is not a call for "self help," not a challenge to "turn self around." Repentance means a "change of mind" about who God is and who I am and an acknowledgment of my desperate need for God to change me—for his holy correction. That must be a part of evangelistic preaching.

A Compassionate Word Should Be Preached

I don't believe that spiritual compassion means that the preacher paints a word picture of the man from Galilee who went about doing good and setting an example of love and compassion. All that is true, but that alone cannot be called the gospel.

Notice the pattern in Acts 2. Peter had confronted the sin of his Jewish listeners, accusing them of putting the Lord Jesus to death. In the midst of convictive, corrective, and courageous preaching, he offered the grace and mercy of GOd. That is the element of compassion—true forgiveness of a personal God! It is by mercy and truth that iniquity is purged.

Some great evangelistic communicators preach the truth boldly, but they communicate no love! Ephesians 4:15 says, "speaking the truth in love." We need to get the mixture right! If you put one foot in boiling water and one foot in ice water you would be quite uncomfortable. But when you mix the two you are much better!

The truth we preach will keep us from melting into sentimentality; and love will keep us from hardening into severity! Someone said, "Truth will keep you from turning into syrup, and love will keep you from turning into vinegar." Evangelistic preachers need to remember that the same Lord Jesus who drove the money-changers from the temple also wept over Jerusalem with a broken heart. He saw the people "as sheep having no shepherd." He was "moved with compassion." He knew their names, natures, and needs!

It was said of D.L. Moody that he could hardly wait until he had finished his sermon, so that he could go to the inquiry room and share in the needs of people. There was consuming love and compassion in the heart of the great evangelist! Today's spirit-impelled, soul-seeking, compassionate pastors will do much to lead their congregations to become soul-winners.

There ought to be a "humanness" about our preaching and ministry. Sometimes a gulf exists between the pulpit and the pew. The very nature of preaching tends to separate the speaker from the listener.

One of the comments sometimes made of pastors is "our pastor is a wonderful preacher, but he seems distant and unloving." We ought to make every effort to come down out of the pulpit and listen, touch, and love the people. There is no substitute for compassion!

A Compelling Word Should Be Preached

Every sermon we preach ought to be with the goal of leading men, women, and children to eternal decisions. An invitation should follow proclamation!

Having been raised in the Billy-Graham-team family, I have come to realize the power of the invitation. Dr. Graham begins his invitation prior to his message or with his opening prayer. He uses words and phrases like this: "Some of you are here out of curiosity, some of you have family problems, some of you have deep, spiritual questions and are searching for answers. Tonight you can find the answer. . . ." Dr. Graham encouraged me, as a pastor, when he also said, "The greatest evangelistic opportunity in America is for evangelistic pastors in the pulpits of local churches."

Sometimes evangelistic preaching is associated with high-pressure appeals, motivational tricks, or the misuse of mass psychology. Some evangelistic preachers feel pressure to "get results"—more members and baptisms, better programs and bigger attendance. Often this leads to trusting techniques and manipulation. It brings the danger of premature, abortive decisions before people have really faced the demands of the gospel! Nevertheless, in spite of these very real dangers and legitimate warnings, it is a tragedy for a preacher to fail to give an invitation. Jesus gave public invitations. As Billy Graham often says, "Every person Jesus called in the New Testament, he called to follow him publicly." Such examples are found in Mark 3:3-5; Luke 8:47-48; and Luke 19:1-10. The idea of secret discipleship was unknown to the New Testament writers.

Look at the pattern in Acts 2 again. When Peter came to the end of his great message, it was only natural to compel the hearers to respond, to receive Christ!

Acts 2:40: "And with many words did he testify and exhort, saying, Save yourselves from this untoward generation."

Acts 2:41: "Then they that gladly received his word were baptized; and the same day there were added unto them about three thousand souls."

Some pastors are afraid to give a strong invitation because of the fear of failing to generate a response. Other pastors feel no confidence in their messages. They may feel ineffective or inadequate as to just how to develop a sound, spiritual, evangelistic thrust in their services and messages.

Here are a few suggestions:

First, do your best and leave the results with the Lord. The invitation belongs to the Holy Spirit. Don't be timid about giving a strong, expectant invitation. Don't rely on the "come today in any way in which this church receives members." People need a strong, urgent appeal! They need a real opportunity to make a valid decision for Christ.

Second, plan some whole services around evangelism with dynamic music, few or no announcements, short prayers, and thorough preparation.

Third, personally enlist and train some counselors who know how to present the gospel personally and lead a person to the point of decision. Send the inquirers to a designated counseling room.

Do not fear the results. You are not a "success" or "failure" according to the response. We have no reputation to keep or to build. We are simply ambassadors for Christ!

Someone said, "There is only one thing that will ever take the place of great preaching and that is greater preaching." Evangelistic preaching is a priority! May God help us to hear the challenge to young Timothy, "Do the work of an evangelist . . . make full proof of your ministry. . . ."

Without question, one of the great crying needs of the hour is to return to the apostolic injunction to "preach the Word" (2 Tim. 4:2).

The Methods for Evangelism in the Local Church

Let me share some practical methods for doing the work of evangelism in the local church.

Every Bible-believing pastor must know that methods may vary and change from year to year, but principles never change. The principle of evangelism, which is "sharing Jesus Christ in the power of the Holy Spirit and leaving the results to God," never changes. One preacher has defined evangelism as "simply, one beggar telling another beggar where to find bread." That principle of "giving away your faith" must not change. There is no substitute for it. No program, church work, study course, prayer meeting or fellowship activity can ever take the place of one person verbalizing to another person the Good News that God was in Christ reconciling the world unto himself.

As it relates to methods of evangelism, these scriptural principles must be considered. The Apostle Paul, in Colossians 1:27-29, tells fellow believers to communicate the gospel in such a way that they are informed, involved, and initiated. The Phillips translation is wonderfully descriptive for this particular passage.

Be Informed. Colossians 1:27 (PHILLIPS): "And the secret is simply this: Christ in you! Yes, Christ in you bringing with him the hope of all the glorious things to come." Evangelism involves the proper transmission of truth. People need to hear and understand the facts! To be saved, a person must experience transformation, but transformation starts with information. The witness for Christ needs to be informed and trained in a clear method of evangelism. For several years, I have trained my church in a simplified, direct method of personal evangelism. Then, we go out in teams to share our faith in the community. A weekly evangelistic outreach program for any and every local church is an absolute necessity. Our laity "possess" the faith in a great way when they regularly "give it away." The pastor and staff must lead the way in a program and pattern of personal soul-winning.

Be Involved. Colossians 1:28 (PHILLIPS): "So, naturally, we proclaim Christ! We warn everyone we meet, and we teach everyone we can, all that we know about him, so that we may bring every man up to his full maturity in Christ." Every believer needs to use all his or her resources to do all in his or her power to reach all the people that he or she possibly can.

Whether it be door-to-door visitation, neighborhood Bible studies, surveys, or developing friendships for soul-winning purposes, the point is to "do the work of an evangelist . . . making full proof of your ministry." I remember conducting a single church evangelistic crusade several years ago when the pastor complained that his people were not evangelizing. He said, "we've not baptized one soul in a year!" I rebuked the brother lovingly and challenged him to set an example. I urged him, "My brother, it seems to me that you, all by yourself, could have won and baptized somebody in the course of a year. I believe that your people will follow your leadership and example." Thankfully, he received my words with love and appreciation.

Be Initiated. Colossians 1:29 (PHILLIPS): "This is what I am working and struggling at, with all the strength that God puts into me." Soul-winners need to go to work! I have found that it is good for the life of the church to have a periodic public "commitment time" for our people to declare their intention to begin the work of personal evangelism.

Throughout the years, I have tried to utilize the services of a Church Evangelism Committee to help me as pastor to plan an annual evangelistic crusade. I believe every church should schedule at least one week of special evangelistic harvest. Youth evangelism events, one-day "revivals," and special guest testimonies can be incorporated in the morning services. Gospel tract distribution, community events and productions (i.e., evangelistic musical events for Christmas and Easter, an annual "Wild Game Dinner" for the whole community, etc.), and radio and television outreach can be planned. Depending on the budget of the church, these are all workable methods for evangelism in the local church.

As pastors, we must urgently do the work of evangelism, setting a lifestyle example for our people, and urging their own initiation into the work of winning souls for Christ. Remember, the Word of God tells a pastor and the people ". . . we proclaim Christ! We warn everyone we met, and we reach everyone we can, all that we know about him, so that we may bring every man up to his full maturity in Christ" (Col. 1:28, PHILLIPS). There are multitudes, multitudes in the valley of decision. They await for the message we have to give them.

Endnotes

1. Havner, Vance, *Upon This Rock* (Grand Rapids: Baker Book House, 1983), p. 110.
2. Ibid., p. 113.

20

A PASTORAL VIEW OF THE BIBLE AND EVANGELISM
Stephen D. Drake

Stephen D. Drake is the pastor of Newton Baptist Church in Newton, Alabama. He studied under Lewis Drummond during the years 1983 to 1986 at the Southern Baptist Theological Seminary. Rev. Drake has done doctoral studies at the University of Tennessee at Chattanooga.

The professor of my first college class in New Testament made the remark one day, "All men believe in God. The question is not 'Do you believe in God?' but 'What do you call the name of your God?' God is that to which one gives himself."

The ability to believe is essential to human existence. Who would rise from bed in the morning if he or she did not believe his or her legs would hold up? Who would drink a glass of water without believing it was free from harmful toxins? Who would ever board a carrier which would move at five hundred miles per hour six miles above the earth without believing that the carrier would also provide safe delivery back to solid ground?

The basis of our belief may be false. Airplanes do sometimes fail to deliver passengers safely. People do inadvertently consume harmful drinks. People do die in "unbelief," but their unbelief is the exercise of a belief that they did not need God in their lives. Indeed, we exercise belief in just about every situation we encounter throughout any given day.

Belief and the Bible

To be sure, one's belief in the Bible is somewhat removed from belief in the everyday matters of life, but they are related. Yet the way we believe in particulars is rooted in the larger framework of how we believe in universals.

Down through the ages, philosophers and scientists, poets and writers have tried to offer a system of belief which would correspond with reality, i.e., with the way things really are in the universe. They have tried to answer the deep questions about our existence and our destiny.

From the original thinkers in the pre-Socratic era to those in our present day, the mountain of ideas, theories, speculations, and conjectures continues to grow. What is the truth about our existence? Is there a God or are we the result of chance? Can we speak accurately about what or who is "out there?" Why are we here? How did we get here? What is our ultimate destiny?

Evangelical Christianity has answered these questions in its appeal to divine revelation. We believe that God does exist and that he has chosen to reveal himself to mankind by means of the Bible in propositional truth. The Bible refers to this appeal in 1 Corinthians 2:9-10 as the Apostle Paul writes: "But as it is written, 'Eye hath not seen, nor ear heard, nor have entered into the heart of man, the things which God hath prepared for them that love him. But God hath revealed them unto us by his Spirit. . . .'"

Think of it: Here is a book that claims to have been the handiwork of God himself. If this is true (and conservative evangelicals along with many other ecclesiastical groups believe that it is), then God has revealed the "deep things" of himself to us by his Spirit who guided the minds and hands of the biblical writers.

When the Apostle Peter wrote his second epistle, he related his experience of the glorified Christ at the Mount of Transfiguration and hearing the audible voice of God. He followed this account in the next verse by referring to Scripture as something to be relied upon with more certainty than even his eyewitness experience of Christ, Moses and Elijah, and the audible voice of God:

> We have also a more sure word of prophecy; whereunto ye do well that ye take heed, as unto a light that shineth in a dark place, until the day star arises in our hearts: knowing this that no prophecy or Scripture is of any private interpretation. For the prophecy came not in old time by the will of man, but holy men of God spake as they were moved by the Holy Spirit (2 Peter 1:19-21).

Our belief that God has provided for us a perfect treasure of himself and his will for us is the basis for our commitment to that treasure as our authority in all matters. We may choose to believe anything, but every belief must have a basis. Our basis for biblical authority is that the Bible is not the product of religious minds, but the product of a real, objective, transcendent reality which we recognize to be our loving heavenly Father.

In recent years, those who have pressed for the highest degree of authority for the sacred text have been labeled with various disparaging titles. But throughout the history of Christianity any stand worth taking was a stand met with harsh resistance.

A strong view of biblical authority often fosters the criticism that one is simply trying to force others to accept his or her interpretation of the Bible. In contrast I have observed that these men and women have an estimate of the Bible which urges them to say with the great Christian leaders down through time, "What the Bible says, God says." This belief engenders within them an urgency to share its message. It gives rise within their hearts to a desire that this view of the Holy Scriptures be set forth in the classrooms of the colleges and seminaries where their children and grandchildren will be educated.

Interpretation and Authority

Those who feel this way about the Bible are sometimes called "bibliolators" by others who question the veracity of the Scriptures. They complain ". . . there is room among us for many interpretations of the Bible. We will not be boxed into this narrow interpretation."

I fully agree that there is indeed room for other interpretations. Here is where a critical and seldom-mentioned distinction must be made. The evangelical who holds the Bible to be verbally accurate and without error in the autographs[1] will also say, "There is room among us for many interpretations of the Bible." This matter of interpretation has to do with what some text of the Bible means. The issue is not the interpretation of the Bible, but the status or estimation of the Bible.

It is not nearly as important how one interprets Scripture as it is how one esteems it. Interpretation has to do with what the Bible means. Estimation has to do with what the Bible is. So our critical issue is not "What does the Bible mean?" but "What is the Bible?"

The conservative evangelical derives his concept of biblical authority from an estimate of the Bible which maintains that these canonical Scriptures are the actual words of God through human instrumentality. This is not to say God dictated words to his writers, but that he protected their accounts by the Holy Spirit. The Bible becomes authoritative practically only in the heart of one who accepts it as the "words" of God, i.e., divine propositional truth.

No doubt it grieves the heart of God that there should be among his children a difference of opinion that causes divisions among us, but such differences will not likely come to compromise for they are matters of conscience. They are based upon presuppositions which form the way we think about reality.

There is one certain thing which can be said to all who esteem the Bible as the words of God and hold it to be their sole authority for faith and practice. God has told us that we are to love him with all our substance and that we should love our neighbor as ourselves. On these two commandments hang all the law and the prophets. There is therefore no place in the heart of any Christian for unloving thoughts. "Beloved let us love one another: for love is of God and every one that loveth is born of God, and knoweth God. He that loveth not knoweth not God for God is love" (1 John 4:7-8).

Thus our search has come to a conclusion. Some of us have traveled far in our quest for truth. Some of us have searched throughout much of our lives for answers to the issues of life. It seems we have passed this way before. Perhaps we have looked squarely into the face of God as we stumbled by in our search. No doubt at times we have thumbed through the little Bible with the zipper on it which grandmother gave us one Christmas, but for some strange reason now, the truths we encounter sandwiched between the timeless pages of God's book are precious and self-evident. One articulate thinker put it this way:

> We search the world for truth
> We cull the good, the true, the beautiful
> From graven stone and written scroll
> And old flower fields of the soul.
> But weary seekers of the best,
> We come back laden from our quest
> To find that all the sages said,
> "It's in the Bible our mothers read."[2]

"In the Bible our mothers read." What a beautiful little phrase this statement is to so many evangelical Christians. What is it that inspires in the heart of the conservative evangelical so great a commitment to a book? It is such an old book. Could it possibly be relevant to a society married to the empirical sciences, high technology, and an overwhelming desire for personal peace and prosperity?

The Bible and Evangelism in the Church

While the Bible is a book, it is not just any book. It is instead, a collection of propositions inspired by God. God so acted upon the human authors of the Bible that they wrote down words which show us about God and his plan for all humanity. From it proceeds answers to the issues of life and more importantly eternal life. In providing humanity with this revelation, God not only wanted to show us about himself, but also to show us how to come to him in the next life, eternal life.

Eternal life is the fruit in the baskets of the laborers who serve in the fields which are white unto harvest. The process of collecting that fruit is evangelism. Evangelism and biblical authority are closely related. Evangelism is dependent upon biblical authority in that faith requires an object and the object of saving faith is Jesus Christ, the Jesus Christ of the Bible. This is why the Bible says, "Faith cometh by hearing and hearing by the word of God" (Rom. 10:17).

Biblical authority gives the laborer a reason for service in the field, not by demanding that every Christian "get out there and knock on doors," but by providing every child of God with the knowledge that the test of love is obedience. Jesus said, "If you love me keep my commandments" (John 14:15). Notice he did not say, "If you are afraid of the chastisement I will give you, then you better get out there and evangelize." He is not looking for servants who serve because they are afraid not to. He said, "If you love me . . ." Evangelism ought to be an expression of love. We show God our love for him as we obey his command to ". . . be fishers of men" and to "go out into the highways and the hedges and compel them to come in." Until Christians begin to view evangelism as a privilege, an act of obedience to show God how much we love him, there will be little results in our efforts.

Before I could read or write I knew the good news of God's love for me. Before I could quote the "ABC's," I could quote John 3:16. I learned these wonderful things in the Sunday school of a Southern Baptist church in Fayetteville, Arkansas. I also learned to trust the Bible in that little church. Often we would sing, "The B.I.B.L.E. yes, that's the book for me. I stand alone on the Word of God, the B.I.B.L.E." We would also sing, "Jesus loves me. This I know, for the Bible tells me so . . ." I was taught to ". . . stand alone on the Word of God . . ." regardless of what the world had to say about it. They taught me that I could believe Jesus loves me, because the Bible says he does. I am grateful today for the confidence in the Word of God my church instilled in my heart.

Moving into the Next Century

But what does all this talk have to do with evangelism in the twenty-first century? Much. If the Bible is authoritative, it exercises authority over the area of evangelism.

Thousands of songs have been written which testify to the change that has come about as a result of the "good message," the gospel. Millions of individuals have given testimonies of their personal salvation after hearing of the Savior's love and forgiveness freely offered to them. It is this mountain of testimonies that gives evidence to the power of God's plan of salvation. And while these testimonies thrill the hearts of Christians who remember the accounts of their own conversions, in themselves they are not enough. They are old. What has happened in the past, as glorious as it is, will not meet the spiritual needs of our successors in the twenty-first century. Their faith must be based upon something more than the experience of another. Their belief must be infused with something living and eternal.

"Heaven and earth shall pass away but my words shall not pass away" (Matt. 24:35). If our children are not taught to love the Bible and to esteem it as the Word of God, they will not carry into the next century the foundation upon which to build the dynamic body of Christ.

"So why the lecture on the veracity of the Bible?" you may ask. If any guidebook is to exercise authority, the degree and permanence of its authority will be related to its source. A book of baseball rules will be updated and amended from time to time as the game evolves. Even the American Constitution is constantly facing some new amendment.

If, like these kinds of documents, the Bible were written by men apart from divine inspiration, then it surely is in no less need for amendments than the book of baseball rules or our own constitution. On the other hand, if the Bible was penned by men guided by the omniscient eternal God who is the ultimate source of its contents, then we have a sure word from heaven, an authoritative guide for life in time and eternity.

With this kind of Bible in hand, a Christian is armed with the effective weapon against every kind of sin which would hinder us from a godly life. With this kind of Bible, we find in our possession a tool which unlocks the problems of depression, addiction to various vices, family problems, and a myriad of other difficulties humans of all ages, classes, and races face daily. With this kind of Bible we have a shield to protect us from the fiery darts of Satan. And with this kind of Bible we have the wonderful and mysterious message which is able to bring to life the inner person and transform the outer person.

Our message is not a logical message. Neither is it illogical. It is *super* logical. It is not a message of reformation, but a message of regeneration. The message of the Bible is not one which seeks to make the "bad person" a "good person" but the "dead person" a "live person."

If the fountainhead of our guidebook were people of like passions as us, what have we to say to the lost person that is in any way better than what a secular psychologist might offer? What claim to ultimate truth could we make were we not able to say, "Thus saith the Lord"? And how can we make that statement apart from the written Word of God?

Let me say outright that I recognize the circularity of the argument that "the Bible is the Word of God because the Bible says it is the Word of God". This a fallacy of logic. But remember the Bible is not liable to humanity's rules for logical consistency. Humanity requires an objective point of reference for logical consistency, but for God there is no object of verification greater than himself. When God says something is so; it is so simply because he has declared it to be so.

The greatest gift we could leave to future generations is a strong stand for the veracity of the Word of God. It alone contains the hope to challenge another generation to attempt great things for God and expect great things from God. Nothing but the Word of God is alive and powerful and sharper than any two-edged sword. Nothing in the whole world can serve to guide another era of Christians better than the Bible.

Christians desperately need to take a fresh look at their roots. We need to rekindle the love for God's Word we had before humanism began to seduce us. Many Christians today do not realize the debt they owe to Martin Luther, John Calvin, Charles Spurgeon, and many others, for the great love of the Bible they passed down to us.

In only a few years we will be entering the twenty-first century. If the Lord tarries, a good number of our children who are now in the sixth and seventh grades will be graduating from seminary in May 2000 A.D. Will they have confidence in the Bible? Will they be able to hold up the Scriptures and say, "Thus saith the Lord?"

These children are now under our tutelage. Be faithful to them, dear parent. Sunday school teacher, do not fail to teach them to "stand alone on the Word of God, the B.I.B.L.E."

Endnotes

1. The "autographa" are not copies of biblical text, i.e., one of the many manuscripts used to translate our current Bibles, but the actual Scripture penned by the author himself.

2. Author unknown.

21

EVANGELISM IN
OLD FIRST CHURCH
Kenneth S. Hemphill

Kenneth S. Hemphill is the pastor of the fast-growing First Baptist Church of Norfolk, Virginia. He was the first Garrett Fellow (teaching assistant) to Lewis Drummond at the Southern Baptist Theological Seminary. Dr. Hemphill's latest book is Spiritual Gifts: Empowering the New Testament Church.

I consider it a privilege to offer this small essay in honor of Lewis Drummond, my former professor and continuing friend. I first met Dr. Drummond while a student at the Southern Baptist Theological Seminary in Louisville, Kentucky. Not only did I take all his courses that I could manage to schedule, I also had the opportunity to serve as his first Garrett Fellow. This relationship gave me ample opportunity to talk about evangelism and the local church. Not infrequently my appointments, originally established to talk about some technical matter concerning the class, would soon wind its way around to the practical application of evangelism in the local church.

On some occasions we literally took to the air as we discussed evangelism methods. Dr. Drummond was finishing his qualifications for an instructor's permit and often needed a flying companion. Our trips provided interesting hours of dialogue as our attention and conversation moved from the technicalities of flying, headings, and instruments panel readouts to the logistics of evangelism. On one occasion, while flying to St. Louis, we became so engrossed in discussing evangelism that we strayed well off course. None of our ground sightings corresponded with the map before us, and then suddenly St. Louis loomed several miles to our left. It's a good thing somebody stuck that big arch in the middle of the city, or we might still be looking for St. Louis!

Dr. Drummond not only helped me develop a strong focus on personal evangelism in the pastoral ministry, but he also encouraged me to consider graduate work in England. I shall forever be grateful for these specific contributions and for my continuing friendship with "Lewie" and his wife Betty.

My Personal Pilgrimage

I was born of good evangelical stock. My dad is a Baptist pastor and a personal soul winner. I recall occasions as a youth listening as he led persons to a saving knowledge of Christ. I accepted Christ when I was just nine years of age and soon turned my attention to leading my friends to Christ. I was long on zeal but short on know-how. The best I could do was get them to church and trust my dad's preaching and the Holy Spirit to do the rest. The strategy worked well. I can still recall the joy I felt as I walked the aisle with my boyhood friends. There is little to compare with the feeling of being used by God in leading someone to a personal knowledge of Christ.

I headed off to college with a football scholarship. I became active in Fellowship of Christian Athletes and had numerous opportunities to share my testimony. Occasionally I was asked to speak at a youth banquet or church service. I was simply overwhelmed when I would give the invitation and people would walk the aisle and accept Christ as Savior. It was a miracle beyond my comprehension. During my college years I became active at Calvary Baptist in Winston-Salem, where I served as youth minister. It was here that I received my first formal evangelism training. It was a personal breakthrough. For the first time I combined my know-how with zeal. Now I had a tool that would help me to share my faith in a natural and conversational way. My effectiveness as a witness grew overnight with a practical and usable tool. I am still convinced that most Christians don't share their faith because they're not given a tool that makes them confident and comfortable.

The moving van was packed, and my wife, Paula, and I left on a pilgrimage to the Southern Baptist Theological Seminary. Our passion to see lost persons won to Jesus Christ still glowed within. We joined with several couples in witnessing in the parks nearby the seminary campus. Dr. Drummond's teaching and personal encouragement added biblical and theological roots to both zeal and knowledge. My seminary days were enhanced by opportunities to serve both as a youth minister and a pastor. To see evangelism work on the field in a rural Kentucky setting was further encouragement. In a small country church we sharpened our skills and the Lord blessed as fifty-three persons accepted Christ and were baptized during an eighteen month ministry.

From Wolf Creek, Kentucky to Cambridge University is quite a leap, but such was the leading of God's Spirit. My graduate studies with Professor C.F.D. Moule led me into an intensive look at the life of the great apostle Paul. I was simply amazed at Paul's tenacity. In spite of all the insurmountable difficulties that he faced, he continued to fight the good fight, to continue the race. I found my answer in 2 Corinthians 5:14-21, a passage I consider to be a personal testimony of the great apostle. Paul's personal knowledge of the love of Christ was that which literally controlled his life. Once Paul had come to a saving knowledge of Christ his life was no longer his own; he was compelled to live for him who died on his behalf. Paul further stated that the truth of the Cross is experienced not only in our personal reconciliation but in the very ministry of reconciliation. There was the key. I realized that no matter what ministry I was called to perform, be it in the pastoral role or staff role or professional role, I have been given the ministry of reconciliation by God himself. Whatever else I do, I must do this! The calling to be an ambassador must have precedence in my life, in every Christian's life. It must be such a passion that we beg persons to be reconciled to God.

With this biblical priority clearly in focus, I returned to the States for service. Now I had it together. Zeal was firmly linked to biblical and practical knowledge. Yet to my personal shame in those early years of ministry, I lost this focus. The day-to-day demands of the pastoral ministry took their toll, and I soon lost my zeal for evangelism. I found convenient excuses. I reasoned that I was doing the work of an evangelist through my preaching and didn't need to share the gospel. Training others was sufficient to fulfill my responsibility.

God used a most unusual event to refocus my ministry. One evening I was putting my six-year-old daughter to bed. That evening we were memorizing John 3:16. I'll never forget that moment. For the first time she said the verse correctly. She was thrilled, her crystal blue eyes leaped with joy. Then she looked straight into my eyes and repeated a single phrase, "Do not perish, daddy, *do not perish.*" I had read and studied that verse time after time, and I had never underlined that phrase. But in that moment the Holy Spirit underlined it for me. The truth is that people without the gospel are perishing. I cannot neglect my calling as ambassador to beg persons to be reconciled to God. That event joined with so many others to shape my personal ministry.

It was not long after that evening that the Lord brought me to First Baptist of Norfolk. I am convinced that my heart first had to be broken for the plight of the lost before I was ready to be entrusted with such a fertile mission field. I do not believe that a church will ever give evangelism a priority until it is a priority in the heart of the pastor. The pastor must first experience and then visibly express a passion for lost persons.

An Historical Retrospect

First Baptist Church of Norfolk was organized and admitted to the Portsmouth Association in 1805, reporting a membership of 150. The church continued in a normal pattern of growth and development. Membership peaked at 2,246 in 1947. The decades of the fifties and sixties were ones of decline for First Baptist. After the war effort church leaders discovered church rolls filled with names of persons who no longer lived in the Norfolk area. A purging of the roll produced a figure of 1,057 active members. This period also saw the decline of the church's immediate neighborhood and the increase of juvenile delinquency and racial tensions. The vicinity of the church was witness to numerous commotions, and the church began seriously to consider relocation. The decline of the neighborhood accompanied by the development of suburban Norfolk and the expanding Virginia Beach community drew an increasing number of families from the downtown church location, which had little off-site parking.

Nevertheless, the church leadership had made a commitment to maintain a vital witness to the downtown area. This strategy continued unabated until October 2, 1970. The church building, which had been the home of First Baptist Church of Norfolk for sixty years, went up in flames. On the first Sunday after the fire, 350 persons gathered in Lakewood Elementary School and there was, according to Paul Mims, the pastor, a "rebirth of the church." Numerous plans were considered, but the church soon decided to relocate and purchase a seven-acre site at the junction of the major highways linking Norfolk, Virginia Beach, and Chesapeake. The church would still be located in Norfolk, but clearly accessible to other Tidewater communities.

The church began to grow and soon moved from Lakewood School to Lake Taylor High School. A bus ministry provided the means to reach a community for Jesus Christ. It was during this time that Paul Mims led the church to establish ministry priorities that listed evangelism first. Soon a minister of evangelism was called on staff and the training of outreach workers began in earnest. The new building was occupied in October of 1974 with a total membership of 1,173. The church had actually grown during this four year hiatus. In fact, its phoenix-like emergence from the ashes of defeat produced results that won attention from the Home Mission Board of our denomination as being the 119th fastest growing church during the period of study. Sunday school attendance reached its highest point in 1976 when the average for the year was 575.[1]

From that high point the church experienced four years of decline. Sunday school attendance settled back to an average of 460 in 1981. Baptism went from a high of fifty-five in 1976 to twenty-eight in 1980. The building was saturated and the church failed to produce additional space to continue to reach the community. The church had reached a plateau and needed to renew its vision and commitment to evangelism.

Role of Prayer

I began my ministry with First Baptist, Norfolk in February, 1981. I sensed from the beginning that this was a special church with a unique opportunity to reach its community for Christ. The church had the benefit of strong leadership and had developed a focus on evangelism and expository preaching. Yet even more basic to the character of First Baptist was its emphasis on prayer. I experienced this first hand with the pulpit committee. I was still struggling with the decision to accept the call of the church to become its thirty-second pastor. One evening after dinner we began our discussion period with prayer. That prayer period seemed like only moments, but actually stretched into the evening. It was during the period of concentrated prayer that I was assured of God's direction in my move to First Baptist.

I soon discovered that there were great prayer warriors in First Church who had long been praying for revival. They had laid the prayer foundation necessary for the explosive growth that was to follow. Some of these great prayer warriors have now gone on to be with the Lord, but I know without question that their prayer ministry was the launching pad for all that God has done here. Prayer is the very breath of the evangelistic church. The truth of the hymn "Bringing in the Sheaves" has often been neglected in the modern day church. "Going forth with weeping, sowing for the Master, Tho' the loss sustained our spirit often grieves; When our weeping's over, He will bid us welcome, We shall come rejoicing, bringing in the sheaves."

Beginning Strategy

I began my ministry with a clear emphasis on the Great Commission as the marching orders for the church. I believe that the Commission gives to the church a three-fold task which must be clearly reflected in all that we do. Our programs must therefore reflect our priorities. The command of the Commission is "to make disciples." The raw material for making disciples is persons who have not previously been numbered among the followers of Christ (i.e., the unsaved).

Often I will hear a pastor or layperson respond to the story of our church's growth by saying, "Your church emphasizes evangelism, but our church is primarily a discipling church." They treat discipling as if it were the process of "apple polishing." We'll polish the fruit that has already been harvested. Remember, the Great Commission commands us to "make disciples." Making disciples is fleshed out in Matthew 28:19-20 by the three participles which are translated "go," "baptize," and "teach." Church leaders must bring evangelism and discipleship together in their thinking. They are not separate and distinct actions, but they simply describe the ongoing process involved in leading persons to faith in Christ. The initial step must be to go out into the highways and byways and seek the lost. We cannot fulfill the Great Commission until we break free of the four walls that confine the church. We must train and mobilize our laity if evangelism is ever to become reality at "Old First Church."

Our responsibility to the "newborn" believer does not cease when the verbal confession has been secured. We must lead new converts to follow through with baptism. I see this public profession and obedience as the critical juncture in the new believer's public stand for Christ and with Christ's body, the church. The public confession of baptism not only fulfills the responsibility of Romans 10:9-10, but it also incorporates the individual into the ongoing life of the body of Christ. God has so designed physical birth and spiritual birth so that both occur in the context of the family. New believers must be nurtured in the ongoing life of a New Testament church. In Acts 2:41 we are told that about 3,000 persons were baptized on the day of Pentecost. The next verse stated that "they were continually devoting themselves to the apostle's teaching and to fellowship, to the breaking of bread and to prayer." Baptism has both an individual and a corporate significance for the believer. It marks the disciple's personal identification with the death and resurrection of Christ and further it denotes his or her identity with the body of Christ. The end result is to "teach them to observe all that I commanded you." The evangelistic church has a mandate not only to impart biblical knowledge but to teach people to obey the Word of God. Teaching is the full scope of the commission and of evangelism.

I felt such a burden to communicate these truths to our church that I preached a series of expository sermons on the church with clear, practical application to our own situation. We planned a deacon's retreat and a church council meeting to discuss the implications of "being the church." In order to illustrate the commission of the church to our entire congregation, I designed a visual representation of our task.

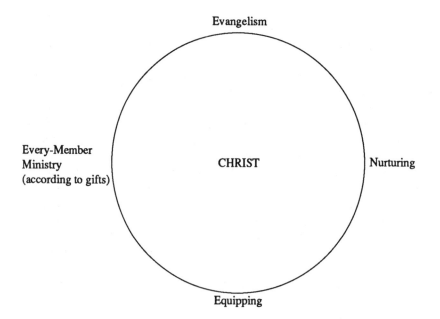

Every-Member Stewardship

We used the terms evangelism, nurturing and equipping to represent *"go," "baptize"* and *"teach."* The ministry circle is completed when disciples begin to minister to others according to their own gifts in the life of the body. This does not suggest that the growth process for the individual believer ceases at this point. The circle is actually more of a spiral in a three-dimensional sense. Christ must, of course, be at the center of the church's life. Every-member stewardship, in the full sense of that word, must be the base of our operation. This diagram was developed in the first year of ministry and remains in use today. We have found it necessary to communicate continually these priorities as the church grows and new people are added to the life of the fellowship. One of the keys to growth at First Baptist has been the clear communication of the task of the church to the full membership. Many laypersons have never been given a job description for church membership and therefore fail to participate fully in the life of the church.

I found it necessary to communicate these truths through my own ministry. When I arrived, our deacons had been divided into four ministry groups. One of these groups had been given the responsibility of prospect visitation. I met with the deacons in this group, we located the prospect cards, and we began to plot a strategy. Many of the prospect cards had become dated because the outreach visitation had been spotty during the eighteen-month interim period. I made an arrangement with the deacons: "You drive and pray, and I'll do most of the talking." This helped with two areas of fear—my fear of getting lost, and their fear of not knowing what to say.

I soon discovered that the area was so large we could waste large chunks of time driving to empty houses. I started calling persons whose names were on file in our existing prospect files and new visitors cards and setting up appointments for visits. The telephone calls paid rich dividends, and we began to see immediate results. Families started joining the church. Beyond that growth, the Lord gave us numerous opportunities to share our testimony and the gospel. I'll never forget one evening when a deacon and I visited a Norfolk policeman and his family. The Lord provided a completely natural opportunity to share the gospel in a conversational manner and the husband and wife prayed to receive Christ. I was thrilled but the deacon visiting with me was ecstatic. I didn't know if I would ever get him back on terra firma. He went back to church and told everybody about his experience. I had people lining up to visit with me. Events like this led to our first witnessing training program. The people literally demanded it. "Can you teach me to do that?" In 1982, we started training our people through Evangelism Explosion materials. I have heard people criticize the various "canned" approaches to evangelism, but unless we give our people some basic outline or method they will continue to be reluctant to share their faith.

Dr. Drummond, in one of our personal evangelism classes, once made a statement that has helped me in the use of "canned evangelism" training programs. He acknowledged that all of us can find elements of any program that we dislike. Nevertheless, while some people are sitting around waiting for the "perfect" evangelism training program to be written, people are dying and going to hell. The bottom line is to find the best one you can and use it or design one of your own, but by all means, train your laypersons to witness.

Developing Strategy

We have refined our evangelism strategy since those early months, but the original concept of training laypersons and penetrating the community remains intact. Our present system works as follows. Our Evangelism Explosion training occurs on Sunday evening from 5:00 - 6:15 p.m. during our regularly scheduled Church Training hour (Church Training is a Southern Baptist discipleship training program). The teams visit from 6:30 - 7:30 during our evening worship hour. We have discovered that most non-Christians (and many Christians) are at home on Sunday evening. The teams do door-to-door survey work and follow-up on names received from events such as concerts, youth camp, vacation Bible school, and the like. We do not use this visitation as our primary means of follow-up on visitors to the church, but as a ministry designed to penetrate the non-Christian community. Evangelism teams do visit inactive church members. We find that some folks who have become inactive have an inadequate understanding of the gospel and need to accept Christ as Savior. We instruct the evangelism teams that have a testimony concerning their team's visit to come back to the sanctuary as soon as they return. We allow them time to share their visitation results with the entire church. This allows the church family to share in the results of the evangelism ministry.

Our outreach to those who have visited the church is organized through the Sunday school. Every Sunday school class should have an outreach leader, trained in evangelism, who leads the class in outreach visitation. The training in evangelism is essential because we qualify everyone we visit to be sure that they know Christ as personal Savior. We have found that many folks have been members of various churches over the years but have never heard and responded to the gospel. Visits are assigned to Sunday school classes according to the age, enabling persons making the visits to answer specific questions concerning ministries available for that age group.

We have several steps for outreach to the Sunday visitor. Visitor cards are removed from the offering plates and copied on a map page while the worship service is still in progress. A deacon stops by the visitor's home on his way home from church. The deacon does not go inside the house. He simply expresses our joy at having them visit our church and explains that someone from the staff will be calling them to see if we can set up a personal visit. This visit prepares the visitor for the call from our staff. Originally I made the phone calls on Sunday afternoon. Presently, the visitor cards are divided among staff members according to ministry responsibility. All visitors are called and an appointment for a visit is made. These visits are then assigned to the appropriate Sunday school class and the visit is made on Wednesday evening after our mid-week service. While many of these visitors are folks who have just moved into the community and are thus transferring from other churches, we still want the outreach team to share their testimony and qualify the individual to be sure they know Christ. We have found that Christians are not offended by this evangelistic approach. In fact, most are delighted to know that we care enough to seek to determine their spiritual condition.

We encourage our people to invite and bring unsaved friends to church events and to Sunday school. We actively enroll unsaved persons in Sunday school. In Sunday school growth conferences we are often told that two out of three unsaved persons enrolled in a Bible study group will accept Christ within twelve months. We continually make folks aware of this fundamental opportunity and responsibility for evangelism through the simple invitation to attend Sunday school.

We use the big events such as concerts and musical productions to reach out to unsaved persons. Our music ministry has a major event at Christmas and Easter, and we attempt to register everyone who attends. We always give an invitation to respond to the gospel at the event itself and then we send our evangelism-trained visitation team by the home soon after the event. We continue to see results from big events throughout the year as we cultivate the seed that was sown during the performance. The spirit of evangelism literally permeates all that we do. Our church believes that we must actively be ambassadors for Christ! The need of the lost demands that "we beg them to be reconciled to God."

We continually work to improve our ability to integrate new believers into the life of the church and thus nurture and teach them. We attempt to facilitate this in several distinct ways. We have an initial class for all new Christians. We are planning to switch to the *Survival Kit* (a Southern Baptist discipleship manual for new Christians) for this initial discipling stage. We are also making the deacons and care leaders in Sunday school responsible for follow-up and immediate integration into the appropriate age-graded Sunday school class. We believe the small group context is essential to the nurturing of believers. We are also developing a ministry team called "First Impressions" which will follow-up on all new members. Once the new Christian completes the New Member orientation, he or she will be enlisted in our Sunday night small groups (through Church Training). Here the courses are specialized and include such basics as: Introduction to the Bible, Baptist Faith and Message, and Every Christian's Job. We continually modify the plan to patch up the cracks that people can slip through. We struggle with the reality that we are not accounting for every person we lead to Christ. We are presently looking at the possibility of encouraging the person who leads someone to Christ to commit themselves to a full year of one-on-one responsibility for the new Christian. It seems that the person responsible for facilitating the new birth has a more natural spiritual bonding than just an assigned discipler. We do feel a heavy responsibility to nurture and mature those we lead to Christ.

I would not want to suggest that all or any of these programs work faultlessly or that we have found the answer to evangelism through the local church. We are committed to incorporating the Great Commission in all that we do.

Endnotes

1. William Lumpkin, *First Baptist Church of Norfolk 1805-1980,* Eastern Printing Company, Norfolk, VA (available through the church office).

2. Our ministry of gifted membership is based on the interpretation of gifts covered in my book *Spiritual Gifts: Empowering the New Testament Church,* Broadman: Nashville, TN: 1988.

ANNOTATED BIBLIOGRAPHY

Books by Lewis A. Drummond (Listed chronologically)

Drummond, Lewis A. *Evangelism: The Counter Revolution*. London: Marshall, Morgan & Scott, 1972. Drummond's first book. Published in the United States under the title *Leading Your Church in Evangelism* (see comments below). This book was translated into Polish, Romanian, Spanish, and Korean.

————. *Life Can Be Real*. London: Lakeland, 1973. Straightforward biblical discussion on personal revival and the work of the Holy Spirit in individuals.

————. *Leading Your Church in Evangelism*. Nashville, TN: Broadman, 1975. Primarily written for pastors, this excellent book on evangelism in the local church is still in print today.

————, ed. *What the Bible Says*. Nashville, TN: Abingdon, 1975. *Christianity Today* rated this book the best on systematic theology in 1976.

————, ed. *Here They Stand: Sermons from Eastern Europe*. Valley Forge, PA: Judson, 1976. Also published in England the previous year by Marshall, Morgan & Scott.

————. *The Awakening That Must Come*. Nashville, TN: Broadman, 1978. One of the best books in print about the need for a spiritual awakening in our world today.

————. *Witnessing for God to Men*. Nashville, TN: Convention, 1980. On personal witnessing.

————. *The Revived Life*. Nashville, TN: Broadman, 1982. American publication of *Life Can Be Real* (see above).

————. *Charles G. Finney: The Birth of Modern Evangelism*. London: Hodder & Stoughton, 1982. An account of the amazing life and conversion of the lawyer turned evangelist.

————. *The Life and Ministry of Charles G. Finney*. Minneapolis, MN: Bethany, 1984. American publication of the biography of Finney (see above).

————. *The People of God in Ministry*. Washington, D.C.: Baptist World Alliance, 1985. Produced by the Commission on the Ministry of the Laity of the Baptist World Alliance. A good, biblical overview of the role of the laity.

————. *Spiritual Awakening: God's Divine Work*. Atlanta, GA: Home Mission Board, 1985. An insightful monograph dealing with five revivals in the Bible.

————— and Paul R. Baxter. *How to Respond to a Skeptic*. Chicago, IL: Moody, 1986. Excellent presentation on witnessing to nine types of skeptics, including the scientific skeptic, the suffering skeptic, and the humanist skeptic.

————. *The Word of the Cross: A Contemporary Theology of Evangelism*. Nashville, TN: Broadman, 1989. The written culmination of years of teaching about the necessity to wed theology and evangelism.

General Evangelism

Barrett, David B. *Evangelize! A Historical Survey of the Concept*. Birmingham, AL: New Hope, 1987. The best monograph on the various meanings assigned to the word "evangelize." Very broad in scope and thorough in its research.

Coleman, Robert. *Master Plan of Evangelism*. Westwood, NJ: Revell, 1964. A classic. Examines Jesus' ministry and strategy for evangelism. Book has been through many printings.

Miles, Delos. *Introduction to Evangelism*. Nashville, TN: Broadman, 1983. Good introductory text covering a broad range of topics in evangelism.

Packer, J. I. *Evangelism and the Sovereignty of God*. Downers Grove, IL: Inter-Varsity, 1961. A classic study demonstrating that a sovereign God is not a barrier to evangelism, but an incentive for greater evangelistic efforts.

Sweazy, George E. *Effective Evangelism*. Rev. ed. New York: Harper & Row, 1976. First published in 1953, this book is a good general introduction to evangelism.

Watson, David. *I Believe in Evangelism*. Grand Rapids, MI: Eerdmans, 1976. Introduction text to evangelism. Well written by Anglican pastor in Eerdmans' "*I Believe . . .* " series.

Wirt, Sherwood Eliot, ed. *Evangelism in the Next Ten Years*. Waco, TX: Word, 1978. Thirteen essays written in honor of Billy Graham. Deals with several pertinent topics in evangelism.

History of Evangelism

Green, Michael. *Evangelism in the Early Church*. Grand Rapids: Eerdmans, 1970. The best book of its kind. Already a classic. Scholarly, with numerous primary and secondary sources.

Rudnick, Milton L. *Speaking the Gospel through the Ages*. St. Louis, MO: Concordia, 1984. History of evangelism from the New Testament period to the present. Good survey, but nature of book does not permit in-depth discussions on any topics.

Theology of Evangelism

Kolb, Robert. *Speaking the Gospel Today.* St. Louis, MO: Concordia, 1984. One of the few theology of evangelism texts available today (also note Drummond's book). Good survey of the essential theological tenets relating to evangelism.

Personal (Confrontational) Evangelism

Bright, Bill. *Witnessing without Fear.* San Bernardino, CA: Here's Life, 1987. An outstanding work by an author whose name is synonymous with personal evangelism. He addresses the great fears of personal witnessing in an easily-understood format.

Little, Paul. *How to Give Away Your Faith.* Downers Grove, IL: InterVarsity, 1962. Probably the best book in print today on "how-to" personal evangelism. Combines the best on incarnational/relational evangelism with confrontational evangelism.

McCloskey, Mark. *Tell It Often, Tell It Well.* San Bernardino, CA: Here's Life, 1985. An excellent discussion on personal/confrontational evangelism with good interaction with those of the lifestyle (relational/incarnational) school.

Lifestyle (Relational/Incarnational) Evangelism

Aldrich, Joseph C. *Lifestyle Evangelism.* Portland, OR: Multnomah, 1981. Thorough presentation of witnessing from the lifestyle evangelism perspective.

Brestin, Dee. *Finders Keepers.* Wheaton, IL: Harold Shaw, 1983. A lifestyle evangelism perspective that focuses on small groups as a means to evangelize. Good suggestions for friendship evangelism.

McPhee, Arthur G. *Friendship Evangelism.* Grand Rapids, MI: Zondervan, 1978. A good contribution to the lifestyle perspective. McPhee is the radio speaker for "The Mennonite Hour."

Petersen, Jim. *Evangelism as a Lifestyle.* Colorado Springs, CO: NavPress, 1980. One of the leading spokespersons for lifestyle evangelism, Petersen writes from years of experience in a cross-cultural setting. The author is a divisional director for The Navigators.

Pippert, Rebecca Manley. *Out of the Saltshaker and into the World.* Downers Grove, IL: InterVarsity, 1979. A major contribution to the lifestyle evangelism perspective.

Thompson, Jr., W. Oscar, with Carolyn Thompson. *Concentric Circles of Concern.* Nashville, TN: Broadman, 1981. A very readable book on building relationships for lifestyle evangelism. The book was completed by Thompson's wife after he died of cancer.

Spiritual Awakenings/Revivalism

Cairns, Earle E. *An Endless Life of Splendor.* Wheaton, IL: Tyndale House, 1986.
    An outstanding historical survey of revivals and awakenings from the Great
    Awakening to the present. The annotated bibliography is second to none in this
    field.

Coleman, Robert C., ed. *One Divine Moment.* Old Tappan, NJ: Revell, 1970. A
    brief but dynamic description of the Asbury College Revival of 1970. The
    principles of spiritual awakenings are very evident in this great revival.

McLoughlin, William O. *Modern Revivalism.* New York: Ronald, 1959. Though
    the author writes from a "secular" perspective, he has made invaluable con-
    tributions to our knowledge of revivals and awakenings. This book and the one
    below are two of his best.

—————. *Revivals, Awakenings, and Reform.* Chicago, IL: University of
    Chicago, 1979.

Orr, J. Edwin. *The Eager Feet.* Chicago, IL: Moody, 1975. The late Dr. Orr's
    writings are the single best source for historical studies of spiritual awakenings.
    The four books shown are representative of some of his best works.

—————. *The Fervent Prayer.* Chicago, IL: Moody, 1974.

—————. *The Flaming Tongue.* 2nd rev. ed. Chicago, IL: Moody, 1973.

—————. *The Ready Tongue.* London: J. E. Orr, 1968.

Evangelism in Theological Education

McGavran, Donald A. *Effective Evangelism: A Theological Mandate.* Phil-
    lipsburg, NJ: Presbyterian and Reformed, 1988. A cogent argument for heavy
    concentrations of evangelism in theological education. McGavran has lost
    none of his zeal in his eighties.

Evangelism and Social Ministries

Miles, Delos. *Evangelism and Social Involvement.* Nashville, TN: Broadman,
    1986. A balanced treatment about the two areas that are often set in opposition
    to each other.

Evangelism and Prayer

Cho, Paul Y. *Prayer: Key to Revival.* Waco, TX: Word, 1984. The pastor of the
    largest church in the world tells of the real power behind church growth and
    revival.

Evangelism and the Local Church

Armstrong, Richard Stoll. *The Pastor-Evangelist in Worship*. Philadelphia, PA: Westminster, 1986. The author misses few opportunities for evangelism in the worship service. He discusses such areas as church bulletins, preaching, and different types of worship services.

Greenway, Roger S., ed. *The Pastor-Evangelist*. Phillipsburg, NJ: Presbyterian and Reformed, 1987. Fourteen essays discuss different ways the pastor can evangelize and revitalize the local church.

Streett, R. Alan. *The Effective Invitation*. Old Tappan, NJ: Revell, 1984. Excellent theological, historical, and practical guide to "public invitations" after evangelistic sermons.

Crusade Evangelism

Huston, Sterling W. *Crusade Evangelism and the Local Church*. Minneapolis, MN: World Wide, 1984. An excellent discussion of the relationship between crusade evangelism and the local church. The author has been with the Billy Graham crusades for many years; his comments describe the behind-the-scene events of the crusades.

Youth Evangelism

Finley, Dean, ed. *Handbook for Youth Evangelism*. Nashville, TN: Broadman, 1988. Several good contributions to the area of youth evangelism.

Smith, Glen C., ed. *Evangelizing Youth*. Wheaton, IL: Tyndale House, 1985. Another good series of essays on youth evangelism.

Televangelism

Hadden, Jeffrey K. and Charles E. Swain. *Prime Time Preachers: The Rising Power of Televangelism*. Reading, MA: Addison-Wesley, 1981. Fairly objective insight into the often controversial ministry of evangelism by television.

"Signs and Wonders" Evangelism

Wagner, C. Peter. *How to Have a Healing Ministry without Making Your Church Sick*. Ventura, CA: Regal, 1988. The leader of the American Church Growth Movement offers insight on "signs and wonders" evangelism in the local church.

————. *Spiritual Power and Church Growth*. Altamonte Springs, FL: Creation House, 1986. A study of Pentecostal churches' rapid growth in Latin America. Wagner's openness to "signs and wonders" evangelism began with his research on this book.

Wimber, John, with Kevin Springer. *Power Evangelism*. San Francisco, CA: Harper & Row, 1987. A fascinating look into Wimber's experience with "signs and wonders" evangelism. Written from Wimber's own testimonies with theological apologia in other chapters.

Biographies of Evangelists

Dallimore, Arnold A. *George Whitefield: The Life and Times of the Great Evangelist of the Eighteenth Century Revival*. London: Banner of Truth, 1970, 2 vols. The definitive biography of the great British evangelist.

————. *Spurgeon*. Chicago, IL: Moody, 1984. A less thorough treatment than the Whitefield biography, but nevertheless an interesting reading on London's finest.

Gundry, Stanley. *Love Them In: The Proclamation Theology of D. L. Moody*. Grand Rapids, MI: Baker, 1982. A scholarly treatment of Moody's theology.

Thomas, Lee. *The Billy Sunday Story*. Grand Rapids, MI: Zondervan, 1961. Popular account of the controversial evangelist.

McGaw, Francis. *John Hyde*. Minneapolis, MN: Bethany, 1970. Small monograph provides insight into the power of prayer in evangelism through the life of this humble prayer warrior.

Findlay, Jr., James F. *Dwight L. Moody: American Evangelist 1837-1899*. Chicago, IL: University of Chicago, 1969. Good biography of the famous American evangelist.

Pollock, John. *Billy Graham: An Authorized Biography*. New York: McGraw-Hill, 1966. The best biography on the famous evangelist. Though authorized, it is still an objective account of Graham's first fifty years.

Church Growth

Conn, Harvie M., ed. *Theological Perspectives on Church Growth*. Phillipsburg, NJ: Presbyterian and Reformed. A candid assessment of some of the major theological tenets of the Church Growth Movement.

Gibbs, Eddie. *I Believe in Church Growth*. Grand Rapids, MI: Eerdmans, 1981. A good contribution to Eerdmans' *I Believe* . . . series. One of the better theological discussions of church growth.

Hunter III, George G. *The Contagious Congregation*. Nashville, TN: Abingdon, 1979. Presents an inductive model for evangelism based on Maslow's hierarchy of human needs. Both a church growth and an evangelism work.

McGavran, Donald A. *Understanding Church Growth*. Rev. ed. Grand Rapids, MI: Eerdmans, 1980. The magna charta of the Church Growth Movement written by the father of the movement. C. Peter Wagner is updating this book for a 1990 publication.

Miles, Delos. *Church Growth: A Mighty River.* Nashville, TN: Broadman, 1981. A good introduction to the Church Growth Movement, especially its historical perspective.

Peters, George W. *A Theology of Church Growth.* Grand Rapids, MI: Zondervan, 1981. Not exactly a theological rationale for the Church Growth Movement, but a theology for church growth focusing on the Book of Acts.

Wagner, C. Peter. *Church Growth and the Whole Gospel: A Biblical Mandate.* San Francisco, CA: Harper & Row, 1981. A landmark church growth book that brought the movement into greater acceptance into the theological community.

————. *Leading Your Church to Growth.* Ventura, CA: Regal, 1984. The best "how-to" book on church growth for the local church.

————. *Strategies for Church Growth.* Ventura, CA: Regal, 1987. A good theological survey on church growth methods and strategies.

————. *Your Church Can Grow.* Glendale, CA: Regal, 1979. One of Wagner's many good church growth books dealing with specific application to the local church.

———— with Win Arn and Elmer Towns. *Church Growth: State of the Art.* Wheaton, IL: Tyndale House, 1986. An excellent reference book on the Church Growth Movement. Features include an annotated bibliography and a "who's who" in church growth.

INDEX